LINKS GOLF

LINKS
GOLF

THE INSIDE STORY

PAUL DALEY

AURUM PRESS

*For Penne – a great partner in life, whose patience,
love and understanding is a constant source of strength*

First published in Great Britain
2000 by Aurum Press Ltd
25 Bedford Avenue, London WC1B 3AT

Copyright © Paul Daley, 2000

First published in Australia 2000
by Hardie Grant Books
12 Claremont Street
South Yarra Victoria 3141

A catalogue record for this book is available from the British Library.

ISBN 1 85410 738 0

10 9 8 7 6 5 4 3 2 1
2004 2003 2002 2001 2000

Cover and text design by Andrew Cunningham – Studio Pazzo
Typeset by Andrew Cunningham and Pauline Haas – Studio Pazzo
Printed by Tien Wah Press
Printed and bound in Singapore

PREVIOUS PAGE: Relatively few
golfers have played the Scottish
links at Machrie. If uncrowded
golf is your aim, coupled with
an enjoyable links experience,
look no further than this
destination

Contents

Acknowledgements

Firstly, my sincerest thanks to Peter Thomson for his thought-provoking and delightful foreword. His beautiful image of golfers and woolly sheep sharing territory at Brora links will live forever in the minds of the readers and myself. To have the support of a five time Open Champion, one who remains passionate about the health of links golf, is indeed fortunate.

Michael Wolveridge, one of Peter's partners in golf course architecture, was always on hand in the early days to give valuable 'critical' feedback to the project. I discovered that Michael's love of links golf is rivalled only by his love of pasta. With fondness, I recall our lunchtime meetings of golf chat and great Italian cooking. I'm honoured that he chose to donate both the 'Good Walk' essay and his sketch of the 11th hole at St Andrews Old – which reveals a deft hand.

Donald Steel's all-round knowledge of golf, acquired through an international amateur playing career, quality golf writing and empathetic golf architecture is well accepted. His book, *Classic Golf Links of Great Britain and Ireland* fired my imagination and caused me to redouble my own efforts to discover more about those fabulous links, far away in cooler climes. Thank you Donald for crafting an excellent afterword which gives insight into how golf professionals feel about playing seaside links. His piece, which incorporates modern pitfalls and misconceptions, should be read by all aspiring architects and students of the game.

It is a pleasure to acknowledge the assistance of designer Pat Ruddy, who is carrying on the links tradition in Ireland, while at the same time redefining a few traditional links aspects he deems to be outdated. To have such an individual in our midst is important, for he challenges us to rethink our own links philosophies and question whether they are held sacred purely by convention, or on merit. You will enjoy reading his commentary as it surfaces in several sections of this book.

When playing Carnoustie last June, it was timely to meet links superintendent John Philp at the 10th green hut while contemplating the brutal stretch of golfing ahead. During the informal discussion he queried us on our general impression of his links and we noted pride of the genuine variety. Due to this chance meeting and the ensuing correspondence, a friendship was established. Despite a chaotic work schedule, befitting the lead-up period to an Open Championship, John has found time to deliver a masterful chapter on 'Preparing for the Open Championship' – in Carnoustie's case, after an absence of twenty-five years from the rota.

Alistaire Gilchrist is one of the quiet champions of the links scene. His headlines are not for a succession of birdies and eagles — no, Alistaire's work is far more pressing. Sadly, links are an endangered species and the largest threat is from nature itself. By devising ingenious methods of coastal fortification, Alistaire and his team of engineers help many clubs wage a fair fight with their main adversary. His chapter on 'Dune formation and management' makes compelling but sobering reading.

For any author, it is impossible not to speculate and worry over the approval of their book. Thank you to Ian Baker-Finch and Michael Clayton for your reassurance and ongoing interest, the support and kind words.

To Barry King, congratulations on the attractive collection of faithful pastels — 'Images of Links land'. His depiction of some of golfers' favourite links land terrain is all the more impressive given it was his first attempt at golfscape artwork.

OPPOSITE: The par three 15th hole at Seapoint Golf Club, Termonfeckin, County Lough, Ireland. Designed in 1993 by Des Smyth & Associates, this challenging championship course has been fashioned out of 260 acres. The closing holes which border the ocean are many golfers' favourites

A collective thank you to the many managers, secretaries, links superintendents, starters and club officials who 'answered the call' by giving freely of their time and research material. Their support also confirms what we've known all along – golf people are great people.

Without the contribution of Joe Dora as my guest editor, this project would not be before you today. The countless hours that he poured into the project, along with a keen sense of humour, have been most appreciated. I'm also grateful to his wife, Linda, for being so understanding of his time away from family duties. Thank you to all at Hardie Grant, in particular Amanda Finnis and Kirsten Abbott, for your hard work and support.

A special big thank you to three golfing friends – Jan Kautsky, Ken McNamara and Sean Murray – who accompanied me on a links pilgrimage to Great Britain and Ireland in May 1998. Your tolerance level was noteworthy and allowed this effort to proceed in good conscience. Who of us will ever forget the first tee scene at Ballybunion Old?

Specifically, thank you to the following:

A. Anderson – Manager, Machrihanish Golf Club

H. 'Hootie' Baillie – Historian, Brora Golf Club

M. Barrett – Lahinch Golf Club

E. Bowman – Operations Manager, Turnberry Hotel, Golf Courses and Spa

G. Brown – Golf Course Manager, Turnberry Hotel, Golf Courses and Spa

I. Bunch – Manager, Prestwick Golf Club

S. Burns – Sales Executive, Portmarnock Hotel and Golf Links

J.W. Chandler – Manager, Royal Troon Golf Club

S. Craig – Starter, Prestwick Golf Club

N.T. Crewe – Secretary, The Royal Birkdale Golf Club

Cecil Doherty – Ballyliffin Golf Club

J.S. Duncan – Secretary/Manager – Royal Dornoch Golf Club

R.G. Dunne – Secretary, County Sligo Golf Club

Leslie Edwards who, at age 92, is in a nursing home and wrote the marvellous story about (caddie) Alexander Campbell – Royal Liverpool Golf Club

W. Erskine – Manager, Royal Portrush Golf Club

I. Forbes – Links Manager, St Andrews Links Management Trust

R.K. Fowler – Secretary, Royal North Devon Golf Club

N. Gallagher – Assistant Manager, Royal Portrush Golf Club

J.R. Griffiths – Secretary, Aberdovey Golf Club

H.J. Harvey – Secretary, Great Yarmouth & Caister Golf Club

S. Henney – The Machrie Hotel & Golf Links

W.M. Howie – Secretary, Princes Golf Club

S. & I. Knight – Proprietors, 'Hopefield House' bed and breakfast, Gullane

J. McKenna – Manager, Ballybunion Golf Club

W. McLachlan – Green Superintendent, Royal Troon Golf Club

N. McLean – Captain, Lundin Links

M. Mills – Office, Carne Golf Club

E. Mangan – Director, Carne Golf Club

C. Moore – Secretary, Royal Liverpool Golf Club

D. Nicoll – Course Superintendent, Montrose Golf Club

M. O'Connor – Assistant Manager, Tralee Golf Club

R. Pittendrigh – Manager, Cruden Bay Golf Club

F. Prescott – Secretary, Royal Porthcawl Golf Club

W.D. Ramage – Secretary, Southerness Golf Club

T.C. Reynolds – Secretary/Manager, Saunton Golf Club

P.E. Rolph – Manager, Royal County Down Golf Club

D. Scaletti – Photographer, Bentleigh

M. Sims – c/- Pinewood Camera Supplies

M. Stewart – Manager, Montrose Golf Club

A. Sneddon – Secretary, Elie Golf Club

M. Shanahan – the late Secretary/Manager, Dooks Golf Club

D.R. Thomson – Secretary, Lundin Links

G. Walker – Scottish Natural Heritage

D. Walsh – *The Kerryman* Newspaper, Tralee

G.E. Watt – Secretary, Royal St George's Golf Club

M.T. Whybrow – Secretary, Hunstanton Golf Club

The units of measurement given in this book in relation to hole lengths and fairway distances are those which appear on the official score card of each club and therefore vary from imperial to metric depending on the club.

Hole **1**
Par **4**
Stroke **15**

Old Course
BURN

1st tee, St Andrews Old — this
revered piece of links land has set
more nerves aflutter than any
other opening tee–shot in golf

Foreword

by Peter Thomson, CBE
Open Champion 1954, 1955, 1956, 1958, 1965

Links are not everyone's notion of an ideal golf course. Most have nothing in the way of exotic furnishings that might decorate a box of chocolates. But then, beauty is in the eye of the beholder. To some who might be termed 'golf's faithful', *links* is the *real* golf, and all other forms are imitations.

To explain this is not simple: the easiest way out is to put forth the point that links golf is the highest of golf's many exhilarating experiences. Lying, perhaps lurking, in a links is the most demanding golf challenge of all. Pushing out into a stiff wind on an arena with no protection, needs a strong resolve and stout heart. It takes a deal of energy too.

Newcomers to links golf often find that many normalities are missing. For one thing, there are no high corridors of trees to frame a fairway. It is common enough to be driving over a ridge with nothing but a white post on the skyline to give a clue to what is beyond. Hazards, in the form of bunkers, are hidden from sight, which makes them more daunting than normal.

Another aspect of links golf that remains unappreciated is the meanness of turf grass. The ball never sits up. For the most part, lies are tight and therefore unhelpful when there are problems ahead. Links turf is far different to park grasses. It is usually hard and bare, which gives the ball bounce – something that has to be imagined and allowed for.

These items plus many more make links golf different and precious to the game. It is therefore worth celebrating links golf in text and picture images, and this is done fairly and fully in Paul Daley's book. The subject, of course, is as unfathomable as the deepest ocean, but even a bit of snorkelling is important, because we can peer through the medium and enjoy the coral.

Also by emphasis, *Links Golf – The Inside Story* focuses world attention on what is absolutely vital to the preservation of the game, in the face of commercial and professional pressures, which would have us end up with artificial turf and endless senseless smoothness.

The links were formed by nature and are best left undisturbed. Indeed one only has to cast an eye over the fascinating photographs to appreciate that no mere mortal can design anything as intricate and faultless as a true links.

One of my favourite links is Brora on the Moray Firth, where the golfers share a precious piece of territory with a hundred or so woolly sheep. What could epitomise nature better than such a communion? I pray it will continue and last as long as the world.

The golfing showpiece on
Scotland's west coast is the
455-yard 9th hole at Turnberry.
Known as Bruce's Castle, the
championship teeing ground sets
golfers amid an isolated rocky
outcrop. The Turnberry lighthouse
is a constant talking point and
this prominent stone represents
the ideal aiming spot when
driving. A well-trained draw shot
is an added bonus (for the right-
handed golfer) to avoid running
through the fairway

Introduction

The purpose of this book is fourfold: to investigate the unique features of links land and to celebrate them, to examine the enduring traditions associated with links golf, and lastly, to defuse any complacency that may exist on their collective welfare. With only one hundred and sixty true links in existence, they are precious in the extreme. To highlight the tenuous struggle for survival to which many links can relate, and to spotlight the co-conspirators is, I am told, long overdue. This account of links golf is most definitely not a stroke by stroke instruction manual or an exposé of the fast-running game through rose-coloured glasses.

In yet another regard, this book is timely. Other than the oldest of links which appear along the eastern Scottish coastline, the grand majority of links golf clubs have recently celebrated their centenary or are approaching the milestone.

While links golf is my favourite style of golf, the aim of this book is not to denigrate the valuable contribution of the inland variety to the world of golf. Indeed, the reputation of links has only grown through the opportunity of being able to make comparisons.

Just what is a links? The commonly held belief that links golf is seaside golf is simplistic enough but leaves too much unsaid. After all, if courses are sprinkled liberally with rows of firs, Norfolk pines, tea-trees or palm trees (as are some seaside courses), they are not authentic links. Some of these radiate the appearance of a links, but the presence of thick, matted kikuyu and other luxuriant grass species, exclude them. Because of these determinants, many seaside courses are stamped 'inland' in style and cannot hope to re-create the links challenge or their playing conditions. There is much conjecture as to what really constitutes a links. Reduced to the bare essentials, any layout purporting to be a links should look like one. But more importantly, it must play like a links. What some people fail to acknowledge, is that these two elements do not automatically coexist.

Others may propose that a links 'links land and sea'. This advances the argument somewhat and usually they are hard by the sea; aesthetically, it is a major part of the attraction. However, to fully accept this concept is to deliver a tremendous slight to Royal Lytham and St Anne's Golf Club. This marvellous links lies several kilometres from the sea and is surrounded by suburbia on all sides. But it regularly hosts the Open Championship – and as we know the world's premier tournament can only be played on a links. As anyone who has played Lytham can attest to, its terrain is classical links. Clearly, the definitive answer is not straightforward.

Greater accuracy is found in an old Oxford Dictionary definition: 'level or undulating sandy ground near a seashore, with turf and coarse grass'. It refers to links as 'rising ground' and introduces the Old English derivation of *hlinc*.[1] Expanding further, *hlinc* means lean and it is this very element of leanness that sets links apart from the lush inland variety of course. Uninviting, in the sense of offering little hope for agricultural prosperity, links land has that unmistakable desolate appearance throughout the terrain. St Andrews, for example, is just one of many links centres to have tried and failed at agricultural practices. Thinking in terms of a barren landscape is apt and addressing how the land evolved into magnificent golfing country will assist our knowledge base.

GOLFING LITERATURE is full of references as to how these sandy wastelands evolved. Invariably though, most accounts written after 1952 are variations on the essay postulated by legendary orator, writer and golf course architect, Sir Guy Campbell. I like its descriptive power and have encountered nothing to rival it. The essay goes as follows:

Nature was their architect, and beast and man her contractors. In the formation and overall stabilisation of our island coastlines, the sea at intervals of time and distance gradually receded from the higher ground of cliff, bluff and escarpment – to and from which the tides once flowed and ebbed. And as during the ages, by stages, the sea withdrew, it left a series of sandy wastes in bold ridge and significant furrow, broken and divided by numerous channels up and down which the tides advanced and retired, and down certain of which the burns, streams and rivers found their way to the sea.

As time went on, these channels, other than those down which the burns, streams and rivers ran, dried out and by the action of the winds were formed into dunes, ridges, and knolls, and denes, gullies and hollows, of various height, width and depth.

In the course of nature, these channel-threaded wastes became the resting, nesting and breeding places for birds. This meant bird droppings and so guano or manure, which, with the silt brought down by the burns, streams and rivers, formed tilth in which the seeds blown inland and regurgitated from the crops of the birds germinated and established vegetation. Thus eventually, the whole of these areas became grass covered, from the coarse marram on the exposed dunes, ridges and hillocks, and the finer bents and fescues in the sheltered dunes, gullies and hollows, to the meadow grasses round and about the river estuaries and the mouths of the streams and burns. Out of the spreading and intermingling of all these grasses, which followed, was established the thick, close-growing, hard-wearing sward that is such a feature of true links turf wherever it is found.

On these areas in due course and where the soil was suitable, heather, whins, broom and trees took root and flourished in drifts, clumps, and coverts; terrain essentially adapted to attract and sustain animal life. Nature saw to this. First came the rabbits, or 'Cunninggis' as an ancient St Andrews charter describes them; and after the 'Cunninggis' as naturally came the beasts of prey, followed inevitably by man.

This sequence had a definite effect on these wastes or warrens. In them, the rabbits bred and multiplied. They linked-up by runs their burrows in the dunes and ridges with their feeding and frolicking grounds in the straths and sheltered oases, flanked and backed by whins and broom. The runs were then gradually worn into tracks by foxes, and man the hunter in his turn, widened the tracks into paths and rides. Generations later when man, the sportsman, having adopted golf as a past-time, went in search of ground suitable for its pursuit, he found it waiting for him, in these warrens, almost ready to hand. In form it was certainly primitive, but it supplied lavishly what today are regarded as the fundamental and traditional characteristics of golfing terrain. The rides, leading from one assembly place to another, made the basis of each fairway; the wild and broken country over which the rides threaded their way provided the rough and hazards — rough and hazards that would now bring a blanch to the faces of the most accurate and phlegmatic of our 'Professors'. The sheltered enclaves, used by the 'Cunninggis' for their feeding halls and dancing floors, presented the obvious sites for greens.[2]

This then is how links came about — often imitated but never bettered. In light of the above, you may appreciate why many blush when the term 'links' is applied to inland courses, 250 km (155 miles) from the coastline. Granted in many parts of the world, freakish climatic and geomorphologic events can bestow on a course a 'links-like' appearance, but rest assured it is not a links.

GOLF COURSE MANAGEMENT is a fine art today, but there was a time when the collaboration between sheep, rabbits and horses regarding links housekeeping was real. Prior to modern maintenance methods, all had a role to play in the regulation of fairway grass height.

Rabbits have never been salaried employees, yet their gratis work has been appreciated by some, despised by others. The unspoilt condition of many of the finest links at the turn of the century owed a great deal to these toothy creatures. It really was a question of balance: too many rabbits could wreak havoc, too few would see the fairways (prior to mowers) deteriorate. But when rabbits bred in balanced numbers, their role in nature's upkeep was ingenious.

As part of their regular duties, keepers of the green removed droppings from the greens, and attended to the rabbit scrapes. But this was little hardship to endure, when considering the gifts in return. Nibbling away gave rise to a playing condition seldom seen today — rabbity turf. Along with those of sheep, the droppings of rabbits were perfectly suited to fertilising the links. Over time, a direct correlation between rabbit populations and links condition became apparent. But, in an effort to keep rabbits under control, they were systematically wiped out at many golfing centres. As they diminished in number, some links reported an increase in the spread of plantains and other weeds.

The influence of rabbits was clearly evident at the Gullane links, Gullane Hill as it is known, east of Edinburgh. This area was prone to hawthorn and buckthorn, which happened to rank high on the diet of rabbits. With each new shoot, the rabbits nibbled away, keeping the links free from shrubs and bushes, as was desired by committee and members, but after a myxomatosis virus in 1956, which all but sealed the fate of the rabbits, hawthorn and buckthorn threatened to overrun the course.[3] Other less intense viruses have struck since, but equilibrium among rabbits and low lying shrubbery has been restored today.

Horse-drawn mowers finished off the work being done by rabbits and systematically tidied up what they missed. The result of mowing was considerably more predictable. Many clubs counted their horse, invariably a Clydesdale, among their priceless assets. One such asset, and a greatly loved one at that, was Dobbin at Brora links. Up until the mid-1920s Dobbin keep the fairways in order. To prevent damage to the links by his equine feet, he was fitted with a set of booties with thick padded leather soles, the size of an elephant's foot. By necessity, Dobbin had a sack arrangement fitted, which served to catch his manure before it reached the grass and became entangled in the gang mower. At the end of the day's work, Dobbin was free to graze and he usually did so around the home end of the links.

CHAPTER ONE

The lure of the links

Links land is sacred and ancient. While this book is not meant as a geological tutorial, it is worth mentioning that Ireland, home to some of the best links land, was formed between 200 and 400 million years ago. The magnificent County Kerry, that hosts such giants as Ballybunion, Tralee and Waterville links, is considered to be one of the oldest parts of Europe. The earliest evidence of human occupation in Kerry is Ferriter's Cove dating from circa 5000 BC.[4] The settlers were hunters and gatherers who fished and used rhyolite for their hunting and household utensils. An area of ground on Ballybunion's Old 18th fairway (Sahara Beach) is thought to be a burial site from this Mesolithic Age and best steered clear of.

Scottish links land was primarily formed by the Ice Age meltdown from melt-water carrying and depositing enormous amounts of sand into the bays and estuaries along the eastern Scottish seaboard. Shifting sands, moved by the wind and tides, formed dunes and, with naturally sown grasses, a links land strip evolved.

Just why do links stir up such special emotion? Can it be the wildlife alone? I doubt it but even so, our visitation rights to their territory are most appreciated. The Tralee Golf Club environs, for instance, are home to a plethora of bird life which has the power to distract even the most single-minded golfer. Herons, whooper swans, brent geese, curlews, oyster catchers, widgeons, lapwings, herring gulls, black hooded gulls, great black-back gulls, black-tailed godwits, mallard and teal all visit at various times throughout the year.

The emotional appeal of Tralee and nearby Fenit Island and Barrow Strand, was not lost on Hollywood director, David Lean. Some of his most memorable shots from the film, *Ryan's Daughter* were taken here.

Sea birds are a real feature at Brora links – the colony of Arctic terns which nest annually have inspired the club's distinctive logo. Oyster catchers nest on the links and, once famously so in the gents tee-box at the 9th hole. They competed with gulls and ringed plover.

At Machrihanish Golf Club, Kintyre, an interesting story is told about why the oyster catcher is the official club symbol. They are prolific along the shoreline of Machrihanish and both the club's

OPPOSITE: A picture paints a thousand words – Glashedy Links, Ballyliffin, Ireland

1

tie and flag prominently display the bird. Legend has it that St Bridget, an Irish saint of the fifth century AD, came as a Christian missionary to Scotland, where she was known as St Bride. On one occasion, while in retreat on an uninhabited Hebridean islet, she became so seriously ill, it became impossible for her to look after herself. But the oyster catchers on the shore discovered her plight and brought food and drink to her until her health was fully restored. Ever afterwards, the oyster catchers have been called in Gaelic 'Gille Bride' – the servants of Bride.

The Turnberry region on the Ayrshire Coast, is classified as an SOSS (Site of Special Scientific Interest) area by the Scottish Natural Heritage. It remains an entomologist's and birdwatcher's dream with several beetles, weevils and spiders considered to be national rarities along with a great variety of butterflies and moths. As for birds: cuckoos, skylarks, short-eared owls, sand-pipers, golden plovers, lapwings, oyster catchers, Manx shearwaters, gannets, kittiwakes, fulmars and gulls, ducks, dunlin, redshank and many others reside or visit Turnberry at intervals.

Looming large off the Turnberry coast, is the famous granite craggy island of 'Ailsa' Craig, a haven for much bird life, especially during the annual breeding season when thousands of pairs of gannets come to nest. Among these coastal environs, it does no harm to realise that golfers are not the sole thrill-seekers.

LOCATED IN WHAT OFTEN AMOUNT TO BE SLEEPY HAMLETS, links courses allow the golfer to escape pollution-ridden cities and take in a little fresh air. The way this world is heading, such a modest aim is becoming increasingly difficult to achieve. Like nothing else, the sea air coupled with a purposeful stride will help relieve your catarrh and the nagging worries associated with modern life. Links golf contains the right ingredients to stir any real golfer's blood and make each round an invigorating adventure.

Ballybunion is typical of the fact that some of the tiniest villages house some of the world's greatest courses – links or otherwise. Take the villages of Gullane, Aberdovey, Carnoustie, Lahinch, Sandwich, Dornoch, Portrush or Porthcawl, for example. If you have visited them, you will readily agree they are hardly thriving metropolises. To the casual observer they appear nothing more than sleepy little hollows, the type that may inspire a motorist to pass them by unaware. But oh, don't still waters run deep. Their industry is essentially golf and annually it draws links enthusiasts from all over the globe with a common purpose.

Primarily because of the association with golf's origins, links golf is, for its loyal band of supporters, the real McCoy. You must walk briskly on the links, not only to ward off a *slow play* slur but also to prevent your blood from icing up. When the coastal squalls start to kick in, links are no place to dawdle. Put any notions about booking an electric cart right out of your mind. They, like many other golfing modernisms are scoffed at and considered out of place. Be warned about your pace, for strategically placed signs on first tees suggest in no uncertain terms how long your journey should take. The one at North Berwick is plastered across the starter's hut and cannot be misconstrued: 'a round of golf should be no longer than three hours'.

For some, the beauty of links golf is slow to register with the aesthetic senses, at least not triggering the regular meaning of beautiful as one may associate with the heathland belt near London. Three clubs that spring to mind – Sunningdale, St George's Hill and Swinley Forest golf clubs – are among the prettiest from which you will ever draw a divot. The visually myopic, fixated with these examples as the ideal of beauty, will fail to see the attraction of a rugged links or appreciate its enduring qualities.

As a teenager, I noted the effects of coastal salt and its rust producing qualities on cars. The wonder of golfing links land is that its turf cannot only survive the constant salt spray but positively thrive on the assault. If you seek a particularly unbending links, visit the remote Connemara Golf Club on the west coast of Ireland. A tough and high quality links, Eddie Hackett's layout is generally unsympathetic to poor golf.

Apart from its predisposition to golf, links land has over the years served other purposes. Turnberry has twice been utilised for wartime service, its fairways decimated and converted into concrete runways and hangers. In 1932 Irish athletes were quick to praise the springy texture of Ballybunion's links turf when training for the Los Angeles Olympics. Setting up camp there proved to be a successful ploy — Bob Tisdall won the medium distance hurdles and Dr Pat O'Callaghan collected his second gold medal. During preparation Tisdall placed his hurdles down the 5th fairway, which was originally the 18th.

Infiltration is all part of the deal, but many clubs are less than enthusiastic about non-golfers trudging through their links in search of the beach. Hunstanton overcomes the dilemma by installing right-of-way systems to assist safe passage, the first of which operates on the sandy roadway at the 1st and 18th holes. Another right-of-way, and busier at that, is found at the far end of the links on the 8th–9th hole crossing. Summer weekends are sufficiently hectic to require the employment of a white-coated attendant. With the modern mentality of litigation, any attitude towards prevention makes good sense, ensuring people's safety while play is in progress. Despite this, one E.J. Readwin attained instant fame by driving off the 8th tee and landing his ball outright in a baby's pram being pushed to the beach. The baby, untouched, was as cool as a cucumber — the mother, badly shaken and a nervous wreck.

THE VILLAGE OF LAHINCH, fondly known and promoted as the 'St Andrews of Ireland' has completely surrendered itself to the game. Young local caddies were always granted the week off school for the important September meeting, an indication of how golf has woven itself into the fabric of everyday life. The club derives much fame through its resident goats whose weather predicting abilities are legendary. If the sun is out but the goats are inside their convenient 1st tee shelter, the message is clear — expect rain at any moment.

Lahinch owes much, if not all, of its current prosperity to golf. Prior to the laying out of their links in 1892 by placing feathers to mark the positions of greens, tees and fairway lines, the township was poor — although a pleasant destination for sea bathing. The golf course heightened the need for improved hotels and lodges for travellers and, with the advent of the West Clare railway line, things were on the move at Lahinch.

Over the years, Lahinch has suffered untold pummelling from the advancing Atlantic (Alister MacKenzie's 1928 links lost two holes in this manner). But the threat to the township's survival had been a pressing matter for much longer. An old Irish prophecy was constantly reflected upon: 'Cill Ruis mar a bhi, Cill Stiafinn mar ata agus Leacht Ui Chonchubair a bheidh fe tonntaibh na mara' (As Kilrush

Dawdlers beware at North Berwick

was, Cill Stiafinn is, Lahinch will be under the waves of the ocean). Much of this threat was averted by the construction of a massive promenade in 1893. The credit for its construction went to a local government official, Mr William Edward Ellis, who had survived the horrific storms of 1883. Casualties of those lashings included the leading hotel, many of Lahinch's most distinguished buildings, the sea promenade and its sea-wall. Today, Lahinch is an esteemed links centre and a must for those embarking on a links scholarship.

Any such learning must draw reference to the role of the architect. The art of golf course architecture, relatively speaking, is in its infancy. It is believed that when Alan Robertson effected his revolutionary changes to the Old Course in 1848, he became the first 'designer'. However, it was some time before the industry got organised and this occurred primarily with 'Old' Tom Morris and Willie Park in the latter half of the nineteenth century.

As the seas retreated, one legacy was the abundance of naturally occurring green and tee sites, troughs and valleys — all fashioned by nature's decree. However, with the exception of the miracle at St Andrew's Old and a few other links, what was missing was the co-ordinated structure, where routing would make the most of these natural features. This is where the early links architects came to the fore, doing, as it were, a touch-up job on what nature had provided.

ARCHITECTS VISITING THE ANCIENT SANDY wastelands of Great Britain and Ireland understood the practicality of merely following the lines through the sand hills and general topographical inclinations; in essence, being guided by nature. (At these early stages they did not have access to heavy earth-moving equipment — this invention was let loose on inland courses much later). Pioneering architects such as Willie Park, Tom Morris Snr, Harry Vardon, James Braid, J.H. Taylor and the Dunn brothers did just that. Indeed it was Tom Morris Snr who, standing on 'yonder hillock' with club founder, Commander Stuart, spoke of Machrihanish in complete awe, 'Eh Mon. The Almichty had gowf in his e'e when he made this place'.[5] Prior to the advent of any formal training for budding golf architects, Open champions, as part of the honour, were commissioned to lay out new links. Tournaments were mainly confined to the British Isles and most workings and redesigns of golf courses were done by these men.

Better than any other form of golf today, the links game maintains the connection with ancient golfing terminology and its principles. The majority of rules we play under today have been directly adapted from the unruly beginnings of the game. Each prominent golf club had its own isolated code of golf rules, by which its golfers competed. For instance: The Honourable Company of Edinburgh Golfers introduced the first code in 1744, a fact that surprises many who were reared on the thought that the Society of St Andrews Golfers was responsible for all early golfing developments. In 1754, the Society of St Andrews Golfers devised its own code. In 1773, Edinburgh Burgess (Royal Burgess) Golfing Society framed another code although only two years later, its rules were reframed by adopting the recent update of The Honourable Company's code. Over the next sixty years, golf clubs such as Montrose, Crail, Aberdeen and Musselburgh devised their own code of rules. It was not until 1899 that a unified set was adopted throughout the golfing world and this honour was accorded to the Society of St Andrews Golfers.

The rules have been studiously cleaned up as golf progressed, or rather golf progressed because the rules were refined. Bearing out this point, there was a time when many of the codes referred to vegetation, such as whins and rushes, as hazards. Today, they remain hazardous to your score but are not officially referred to in this manner. The modern code, as we know it, limits its definition of

One of the views that inspired 'Old' Tom at Machrihanish

hazards to two different varieties of water hazards and bunkers. As a service to club golfers, perhaps the club bore could be added as an additional hazard.

Over time, golfing 'style' evolved. Styles were weird and wonderful and as varied as the links themselves. Depending on the particular qualities, peculiarities and requirements of the individual links, the players adapted their styles to suit. Leading players were constantly refining their knowledge of each course and intricacies of hickory shafts, in particular, issues relating to 'torque'. For instance, the 'St Andrews Swing' was a slashing motion, long and loose, making it a near certainty that a 'crossing of the line' at the top of the swing would occur. It is only an idle thought mind you, but perhaps this crossing of the line encouraged a hooking style which diverted the ball away from the pernicious right-hand gorse? Today, a good deal of this has been cut back by the Royal and Ancient Golf Club or trampled and hacked away through overuse.

At Montrose nature's impact is
progressively being noticed at
this fine Scottish links

CHAPTER TWO

Precious coastlines

Images of Mark O'Meara striding serenely down Royal Birkdale's fairways suggest a clean bill of health for the state of links golf. Any doctor will tell you, however, that basing a diagnosis on superficial appearances can result in a incorrect test result. When this happens, treatment goes down the wrong path and improvement in the patient is stalled. Sometimes the patient may never recover. Looking at the links game in isolation can lead to the same predicament. Failing to appreciate the peripheral but integral issues involved with links preservation could threaten their survival. A links has its own ecosystem which is inter-related to that coastal region. Coastal regions put in place strategies that are related to regional plans, and in turn their plans are monitored by national policies on preservation. Increasingly, national policies must reflect the ongoing international co-ordination programme of good practices.

Coasts are among the most dynamic, complex and diverse of all environments. Physical processes alter their shape and character over a relatively short time, and the flora and fauna for whom this is a natural habitat must respond to these changes. Moreover, the impact of changes in climate, including those arising from global warming, will be most deleteriously felt in coastal regions.

The coastlines of Britain have extensive coastal zones containing many resources of economic, recreational, aesthetic and conservation value. They are, however, finite and have evolved over a long period, but are now under increasing pressure and competition for further development. Golfers are not the only lobby group in this regard; others would have the shores populated by marinas, restaurants and amusement parks.

The requirements of nature conservation have led, or are leading to the designation of substantial parts of coastlines as natural heritage area and special areas of conservation, special protection areas. These designations therefore restrict potential future development, which in turn increases pressure on adjacent non-designated areas. Vulnerability to coastal erosion and flooding also limits the areas available for commercial development.

OPPOSITE: A linking of land and sea is highly evident with this aerial shot of West Lancashire Golf Club

The coastal zone

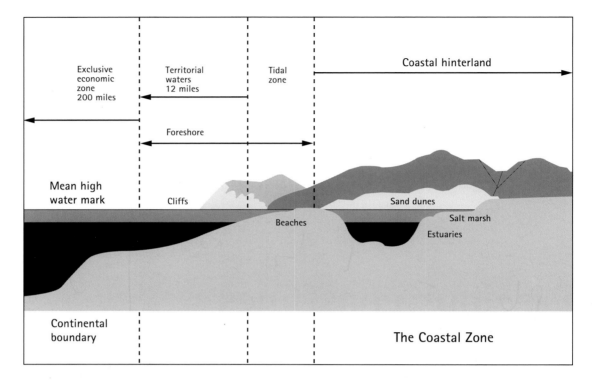

British coasts are internationally important for nature conservation, especially where they include sand dunes, lagoons, estuaries, cliffs, islands, shingle bars and shallow marine inlets and reefs. Some areas, which are in a semi-natural state, require protection. Others require appropriate strategic management to ensure their conservation.

The coastal areas are highly dynamic and erosion is a natural and widespread process around much of our favoured golfing countryside. Some areas are in need of continual or improved protection to avoid substantial loss. Responsible authorities need to quickly establish priority affected areas and decide upon the best methods of protection, taking into consideration environmental impact, public access and safety. It must be stated that the level of finances currently set aside by governments and golf clubs alike for the purpose of minimising erosion is inadequate.

Present erosion problems may worsen as a result of anticipated climatic change: increased sea levels will increase the number of storms and, in turn, increased wave heights will have detrimental effects on the flooding of low-lying coastal areas. At a recent scientific forum, it was postulated that sea levels will rise by over 50 cm (2 ft) in the next one hundred years.

The links featured in this book lie on areas referred to as links land. Broadly speaking, links land is subordinate to a much larger area, described as the coastal zone and, as such, is under threat.

Seapoint's majestic par three
17th hole. From this green, the
mountains of Mourne can be seen
in the far distance, where
thoughts instantly stray to Royal
County Down

CHAPTER THREE

Essential links golfing skills

The principal skills required to get you around a links remain the same, regardless of whether you are playing in Wales, Scotland, Ireland or England. In appearance, no two links will look the same, however, similarities abound. While parochial club interests will push the claim, 'The windiest links in all UK', let's face it, wind is wind, humps and hollows are precisely that elsewhere and the penalties for straying off the fairway are usually consistent. So if you can adapt to the demands of links golf you will embrace one links after another without having to re-invent your game. This goes some way to explaining the high occurrence of multiple winners on the Open Championship honour roll and why some such as Messrs Thomson, Watson and Faldo prefer the style.

Whereas target golf is demanded of the archetypal inland course, and best played through the air (in relatively windless conditions), a good deal of links golf is best played as near to the ground as possible to escape the airborne hazard of wind. The links challenge demands that the open-minded golfer roll the ball into the greens — both from nearby and long range. (This usually produces a chortle from Americans when playing links for the first time.) In keeping with architectural soundness, being summoned to fly your ball over bunkers guarding the front of greens is the exception rather than the rule. As links golf is typically fast running and bouncy, architects have tempered their styles, knowing that bunkering the entrances would surely present mayhem.

Some golfers with a shallow grounding in the relationship between architecture and shot making, assess links golf as terribly over-rated. Many links are deceptively strategic, so those waiting to be bludgeoned with confrontation — well they have misjudged the challenge. In this instant gratification society, all too often a formula for a definite way

Lahinch 2nd hole — open entrance to the green with township in background

17th hole at Muirfield – a pivotal hole in many championships

to play the hole is required for some golfers to be satisfied. I do wonder, whether these golfers realise they are unwittingly advocating the 'penal' school of golf course architecture? St Andrews Old is perhaps the best example of a links where the limitation of your imagination can put you at a distinct disadvantage.

No red-blooded golfer can be expected to embrace a bad bounce, but a degree of acceptance of the inevitability of such an event will do no harm. While his competitors had firmly made up their minds prior to the 1962 Open Championship that Royal Troon was a fit of too many bad bounces, Arnold Palmer thrived on the links ravaged by summer drought, feeling this aspect relieved the pressure. Getting the odd bad bounce did not detract from what he later called 'the four greatest consecutive rounds of my life'. At the peak of his game, Palmer won by the huge margin of six shots and with seven holes to go was actually ten to the good.

Bad bounces are less prevalent at Muirfield. Today, this links remains the preferred Open Championship venue for many USA professionals: flattish terrain, relatively few blind shots and an overwhelming aura of fairness.

To the credit of Nicklaus and Palmer, their continued presence in this oldest of Championships eventually rubbed off on other tour players and today, the majority of leading Americans thrive on the challenge of links golf. When Palmer was captivated by the traditional Open atmosphere,

Byron Nelson was quick to applaud his actions and said, 'I think it's wonderful that Palmer is going to England. The one regret I have is that I never made an effort to win the British Open when I was playing so well'.[6] Unlike many of his era, Palmer saw golf as needing to be played on an international scale and, seeking to be a global star, he was better placed to cope with adversity — such as a bad bounce — when encountering it.

6th hole at Cruden Bay is a prime example of how prevailing winds can hammer links vegetation

PLAYING THE BALL AS IT LIES is integral to links golf. The next time you view the Open Championship, the relative absence of rules queries among the competitors may strike you as odd. Are the professionals suddenly going soft by refusing to exploit loop-holes in the rules? More likely, due to the lack of artificial trimmings, opportunities to gain benefit by massaging the rules dry up. When a controversial incident occurs, and it did during the recent Carnoustie Open, it does make news. For the rank and file links member, the coastal philosophy has always been — 'find your ball, give it a thump and then go hit it again'.

Links land evolved as narrow, finger-like tracts of land, and starkly demarcated from the less exciting, neighbouring pasture land. Commissioned architects generally routed their outward nine along the shoreline and dunes, with the inward nine returning adjacent and inland to them. Whether their intuition tapped into golfers' urgency to get among the dunal countryside first, or some divine instruction from Nature, is unsure. Not uncommonly, the oldest of traditional Scottish links have their holes arranged in straight-line formation out to a distant point, before rounding the turn and heading for home. Under these circumstances, you can expect to play one of the nines downwind and the other, with feet anchored to counter the into-the-wind challenge.

At most seaside links, the prevailing wind can usually be relied upon, and initially, this information assisted architects with decision making about hole configuration and length. The same knowledge then allowed match committees to establish the stroke index of the holes. But how does the newcomer to links golf come to grips with its direction? Other than your caddie, look no further than the rough or the marram-covered dunes — the near permanent hammering of the vegetation reveals all. Whichever way it falls, this direction is the prevailing one.

An interesting phenomenon exists whereby you may be 'king hit' by encountering, thanks to a sudden wind shift, two nines into the wind. Don't expect to set your watch by it, but should the change occur on the 7th, 8th or 9th — you have had prior notice. Less common, is the dream round where both your nines are played downwind, and seldom has the golfer complained about this shabby treatment. While this only adds to the lottery and excitement of links golf, a professional endeavouring to win the Open Championship will disagree. Indeed, some tragic king hits have been played out in final rounds of the Open.

IN ANY LINKS EXPERIENCE, wind is an integral force. Golfers learn to accept that occasional unplayable gales are part of the attraction. Should it be excessively calm, one intuitively senses an anticlimax among group members. Unlike inland golf, where your morning tee time can shield you, gale force conditions on links are non-discriminatory and can greet you at first light. The truth of the matter is that links players bemoan windless days as 'impostors'.

The 1st hole at Lahinch demands an exacting uphill approach to an exposed green

A Lahinch member told me of one freezing day when the wind wrenched the flag stick clear out of the cup on the exposed first green. As he graphically described it — 'the pin was racing back down the first fairway hill' — his pride in being out in these conditions was hard to mistake. Another day, he saw the flagstick posing almost horizontal, before a late afternoon wind change was its saviour. Golfers without links experience may not fully appreciate the buffeting effects of wind on body, mind and soul. Horror stories are commonplace, but until you have struggled to put the tee in the ground, as many recount when the elements are at full blast on the exposed 2nd tee at Tralee — you haven't played in wind. This wind factor is vital, and apart from making the greatest of links courses decidedly difficult, it bolsters the integrity of the weaker ones by providing the main line of defence against ridiculously low scoring. With most links bereft of trees, wind is a must. In what other form of golf can the golfer strain to hit a two iron 120 m (132 yd) and then from another direction, caress an easy wedge 150 m (165 yd)? Under these conditions, golfers reared on the security of yardage markers must quickly dispense with this umbilical cord and try relying on feel.

Local Brora identity, Hughie 'Hootie' Baillie, told me of the effects of wind at his home links — 'When the sea wind blows from the Russian steppes, even the children stop growing'. Anytime the Open Championship is won with unusually low scores of 13 under par (1989: Mark Calcavecchia) or 18 below par (1990: Nick Faldo) it raises the index of suspicion towards benign weather conditions. The modern maestro's skill level is wondrous, but today, few play with the grace and poise of Sam Snead. And yet, in 1946 on the Old Course amid poor weather, the great man took 290 shots (2 over par) to win the Open.

After Nick Faldo humiliated the Old Course in 1990, there were fears that after 500 years of great service, its reputation was on the wane. Rumour mongers gave fuel to the idea of extending many holes and making the professionals pay for his arrogant feat. Indeed, a couple of tees have been extended. However, admirers of the links game breathed easily again upon her comeback in 1995 when John Daly, in a victory over his personal problems, and a defiant Constantino Rocca, went only five strokes below the once forbidden mark of par. If you play enough links golf, you will invariably run into somebody who is all too happy to condemn the Old Course for being too short, too easy and way out of date. I have heard this said so often, I am almost deaf to the sentiment. To put the issue in proper context, it is worth recalling that Daly's winning score was among the highest of the last twenty years. High winds played a huge part.

A GOOD DOSE OF WIND rescued the 1998 Open Championship at Royal Birkdale. The month of June was among the wettest on record, which made the links alarmingly green and thus vulnerable to being humiliated. The potential for embarrassing low scores was great, and in practice rounds the target golf skill of backspin was being used to great effect. Professionals were relaxed in the knowledge that the fairways were holding and this was a huge psychological boost — particularly to the large American contingent. Despite two par fours of nearly 500 yards, a winning score of 6–10 under par would not have surprised. But thankfully by the opening round, wind had dried the links out and presented a fearsome challenge, one befitting an Open Championship. For competitors, any thoughts of the greens allowing inland style backspin became distant memories. As a result, the scoring was uniformly horrendous and level par won the event. The third round at Royal Birkdale tells the tale: those who survived the half-way cut averaged a score of 78 (8 over) on this day. Notable casualties included Tiger Woods 77, Larry Mize 79, Nick Price 82, Justin Leonard 82 and Phil Mickelson 85.

When it comes to the skill of playing golf in a wind, the words of Open Champion, James Braid, are worth heeding: 'Most players fail in a wind, not because they have not often played in one, but because they have never practised in one'.[7]

Nevertheless, gifted or a damn good punter is the golfer with a finely tuned sense for weather forecasting. At Royal Porthcawl, that fine links in South Wales, they had a long-serving professional by the name of Wally Gould who was renowned for the art. Upon rising each morning, he was inundated by phone calls from members seeking his advice — true homage to his skill. He was sufficiently confident to record his maxims for posterity. Stopping short of calling them rules, he acted on 'signs' — what you feel and see at the same time. They were as follows:

1)   **Tide:**

Tide: coming in or tide going out does not have any effect on conditions, tide at the turn however, has an effect, with that at low water having the most effect. If the weather is unsettled, this is the time when the wind may change; *veering* is for good weather, *backing* is for bad weather.

(2)   **Wind:**

Use the wind direction. A prevailing west to north-west wind allows an accurate forecast of 2-3 hours to be made at any time.

West-north-west — good, maybe showery, but with a fair amount of sun.

South-south-west — doubtful, could be windy with heavy showers. Not as much sunshine as west-north-west.

East-south-east — usually long periods of rain and wind.

North-north-east — awful, very drying in summer, very cold in winter, mostly dry, could be sunny but not much good.

(3)   **Local signs:**

Early morning — very clear visibility off foreland light and Coch y Bryn in the Gower is a sign of rain during the day. A light covering mist, however, is a good sign. If the beach sand appears 'ribbed', there is a big wind about.

Note: Veering = changing direction. Backing = having changed direction, going back towards its original direction.[8]

When playing links golf, it is not unreasonable to hope for fairness but even Jack Nicklaus has lapsed into the misguided belief of expecting it. By the time the 1968 Open Championship rolled around, his links experience was extensive, and one assumes, he would have come to grips with the vagaries of British golf. During this Carnoustie event, Nicklaus was particularly annoyed at a small mound down the 9th fairway some 250 yards away. Repeatedly, it halted the progress of his rifled one irons from the tee. Being reared on American principles, he suggested to the links management committee that it was unfair and needed levelling. He got his wish. Upon returning to Carnoustie in 1975 for the Open he discovered it was completely shaved off, so much so, the groundsmen, after first levelling it, converted it into a 2-m (6-ft)-deep bunker. Suffice to say, Nicklaus was not impressed.

At many links, one must acknowledge that to drive perfectly, even on the right line, will not in itself guarantee an easy approach to the pin. Your ball need only take one extra roll to finish alarmingly downhill, sidehill or a combination of the two. Invariably, your stance will not be level; starting out with this knowledge is wise. Should your ball kick at right angles into the scrub, that hardly constitutes news either. It happens and it is part and parcel of links golf, as is the poor drive of your opponent that manages to find a flattering lie.

Close-cropped lies are typical of links turf, and around the greens, cutting up with your wedge, as favoured on your own course, can be a highly provocative act. Take the low route whenever possible and if on vacation, you may as well perfect the art. The 'bump and run' shot was first contrived on the east coast of Scotland and will do much to preserve a respectable score.

In 1953 at Carnoustie, Ben Hogan played in his one and only Open Championship. To experience the rigours of links golf, he came over ten days prior to the tournament, primarily for two reasons. Firstly, the business of acclimatising to the smaller 1.62 in. British ball needed attending to. He was surprised but pleased to see the vast distance it travelled in comparison to the US 1.68 in. size — particularly with the long irons. The second reason was to get used to the marked change of fairway

Traversing the 'Valley of Sin' at St Andrews Old 18th poses the same dilemma for all golfers — a traditional Scottish run-up shot or a lofted approach?

lie — as the US tour was played on lush courses. A good deal of his practice time was devoted to a slight swing modification that enabled him to pick the ball clean with irons as opposed to his normal habit of divot taking. Hogan left nothing to chance in becoming acquainted with the characteristics of links turf.

The putting greens at many links clubs are slow and require adjustment. Slow at least, in comparison to the famous Melbourne 'Sand-Belt' greens or the slick collection at Augusta National. But it wasn't always so. Many old-timers attest to the lightning nature of links greens before World War II — especially during droughts. During the 1953 Open though, Hogan conceded that his hardest opponents were the slow greens. This also coincided with a low period in links golf, when those involved with links management engaged in some wild ideas as to links welfare. And yet, links greens are inherently capable of producing firm, fast conditions, for they are made up of the poverty grass species of fescues and bents. But in winter, you should expect some modification of speed. Since the war, there have been unacceptably high levels of meadow grass, in the form of *Poa annua* taking root in the greens. The causes are many, but the primary ones are: unsound green-keeping practices, too much fertiliser and water, lack of adequate aeration and insufficient funds to address the issue.

Nairn Golf Club in the highlands of Scotland is yet another of James Braid's great works. Whisper only about slow greens while there, otherwise you will be lynched for blasphemy. They are relatively fast all year round and as true as a billiards table. Many who play here rate Nairn's greens, along with Luffness New, as the finest in all Scotland.

One must quickly come to terms with Scotch mist, a loosely applied term to golfing conditions where your visibility is impaired to the point of gloominess. Scottish golfers became protective of their beloved mist and with pride even slapped on a nationalistic patent. I found this to my amusement when first playing Ballybunion Old. Winter had just passed and on a bleak, grey morning I made the visitor's faux pas, 'Looks like we are in for a little Scotch mist'. Not before curling his lip, my Irish caddie replied, 'Excuse me, that's Irish mist I think you'll find'. I discussed this phenomenon with architect Michael Wolveridge, of Thomson, Wolveridge and Perret Co., and he related his own experience with what he assumed was thick mist at Ballyliffin. He spoke of his round as being 'punctuated by darts', as he endured a stinging sensation on the face and neck. As it turned out, it was not mist but fine sand granules, whipped up and hurled by the gale force wind.

JUDGEMENT IS EVERYTHING WHILE PLAYING A LINKS. With judgement comes feel and with feel comes improvisation. And who could improvise and bump the ball around better than five times Open Champion, Peter Thomson? It has been no coincidence that this brilliant manipulator of the small 1.62 in. British ball reigned supreme on the links. If it was fast running and especially dry, all the better were his chances. And what about yardage markers? He did not need them, rarely used them, rarely had them at his disposal. He employed great caddies who knew their business, but regardless, Thomson walked over his rivals with his skilful eye and advanced judgement.

More commonly today, many insist upon being spoilt. If your preference is inland golf, you may fail to see why yardage markers are not part of the links scene. Administrators argue that golf reliant on this armchair ride is alien to the tradition of true links golf. Besides, they are practically useless in the advent of a strong wind, when judgement is of paramount importance. Inevitably though, some links have succumbed to the pressure. Thankfully the grand links have stood firm on principle and limited themselves to only occasional markings. Missing are the inland style tap covers which normally appear every 35 m (38 yd) or so. This built-in protectionism preserves the local caddie industry, an industry inexorably associated with much links folklore. These intriguing characters are celebrated more fully later in the book.

The requirement for sound judgement is omnipresent. Allowing for the roll into the greens will cause much confusion and embarrassment, as it cannot be taught, and books will not help. As this skill is now rarely called upon on most inland golf courses, regular links golfing is the only way to acclimatise. You will call on dormant senses in trying to figure out the riddle. The internal dialogue and assessment of landing spots is another necessary skill, but alas, amounts to little without quality shot execution.

In essence, links golf showcases what the ancient sport was initially designed to be — a battle between man and the elements. Any flaws in your mental capacity to handle adversity quickly become public knowledge. It is just you, your clubs and the elements.

Having a caddie of repute will even the odds, and I have encountered many excellent and cheery ones; nevertheless, a whisky-stained one can certainly reduce them. To ignore the accumulated knowledge of your caddie is madness. A good one performs right from the start and if experienced, will select your club after just two or three hits, engage in a bare minimum of caddie chat and then issue a firm command. This is especially important when reaching blind holes. For golfers who are new to this experience, taking aim over a rock perched on a cliff-top or a distant hillock requires a good deal of trust.

The skill of ball finding must not be taken for granted and this is never so true as when playing links golf. What do you line your ball up against as a reference point? Most links are bereft of trees and clouds are unreliable. Gorse-strewn links present clarity problems — from a distance there is a confusing similarity with each thorny projection. There are advantages in having an agreement among group members whereby each commits to following the ball's path all the way — from club head impact to endpoint. This is invaluable on the tee, when the premium upon accuracy is highest. A not uncommon sight on the links is four players walking in a straight line, systematically combing the rough with feet and eyes. A march in this manner covers a lot of territory very quickly.

The art of escaping from rough, back onto the fairway, is one seldom practised and certainly never discussed. Newcomers to links golf are often shocked at the difficulty of this task. From low lying vegetation and sandhills, even skilled players can fail to move the ball a bare metre. In many instances, the one stroke penalty for an unplayable lie will save you plenty of angst. Plain old rough — the long grassy variety — is trouble enough. At impact, the club is severely retarded, leading to its nasty habit of prematurely closing down and all too often this activity sends the ball into deeper trouble.

With the Carnoustie Open (1999) still fresh in our minds, we saw untold examples of this, but one of the most tragic episodes was that of Craig Parry. Being three under par after eleven holes on the final round, Parry was carving out one of the great final rounds in a major championship. Starting out five shots behind Jean Van De Velde, he had closed the gap with a marvellous display of accurate shotmaking, and on the 12th tee, was leading the tournament by one stroke. But here, all his good work unravelled. The drive, hardly a poor one, was pushed only slightly and found the rough. His recovery was tugged badly away to the left finding residence in knee-high grass, from where he moved the ball only a few paces. Still in the rough, Parry's fourth shot careered out with little backspin and whisked through the green. Badly shaken, his normally reliable short game broke down and ruefully, he marked down a triple-bogey seven. Surprisingly, he also took four shots to get down from just off the 17th green. Despite all this misadventure, the gallant Australian golfer missed a play-off by just a single shot.

You are reminded of these facts for two reasons: first to show how deep rough on links can destroy a round in progress, and second, to dispel a myth that will surely take hold over time. It has become a popular view, is certainly easy, and requires little thought to buy into the argument that the Frenchman 'blew' the tournament. At the very least, I agree that Van De Velde's playing on the final hole was disastrous. But I also firmly believe it was Parry's tournament to win, and we tap into Van De Velde's 18th hole 'Greek Tragedy' only because Parry failed to fully grasp his chance.

Long grass was the ruination of Van De Velde on the 18th hole, not his untimely visit into Barry burn as was commonly portrayed. While it may have appeared a simple matter to put his 40-m (44-yd) third shot on the green and two-putt for a comfortable two shot victory, his efforts were sabotaged by the strangling nature of the rough. The rest is history. Either way, both he and Parry must have endured their share of sleepless nights over proceedings.

Graduations of rough at Montrose — 1st and 2nd cut. The 2nd cut promises little hope of recovery

It is human nature to be ambitious from poor lies in the rough, but when it goes wrong, the cause is simple enough. Usually, the cause is attacking the ball with too straight-faced an iron. When receiving anything other than a fluke lie in the rough, take your medicine and get your ball back on the fairway. A wise old Scottish pro advised me, 'Aim a wee bit to the right laddie, hold on tight, pick the club up abruptly and belt your wedge hard'. If you are sufficiently wild from the tee to be considered part of the habitat, you will get your share of good lies, but more likely, this will encourage misguided and insane complacency. Yet the optimists will go to their graves muttering, 'If I can see it, I can blast it on'.

Most of the great links are sufficiently narrow to put you on notice — as for the cabbage off the fairways, it will beat you most times. This thought was uppermost in the mind of Jack Nicklaus, as he outsmarted the field at Muirfield in 1966. His inclination towards reducing the links to pulp with customary firepower was put on hold. Rather, the tactical ploy of one iron from the tee, kept

It is unwise to miss the fairways at Ballybunion New

Nicklaus' ball in play more than his rivals, and that was the difference. Remarkably, his driver was unsheathed only seventeen times during the whole tournament.

The point may be laboured but straight hitting is a must. At Prestwick, the 15th is not known as The Narrows for nothing and many recall it as the narrowest of any hole they have played. But if so, they will not have played a fine links known as The Island on the outskirts of Dublin — here the claustrophobic 14th hole is skinnier yet again.

At Ballybunion New, in part due to the severity of the sandhills and a golfer's insatiable desire for distance from trouble, it is common to view the ball heading backwards after being hacked at. How to keep from falling about in laughter? Equally humorous, is when the golfer among the steeply inclined sandhills, buries the ball in front of his nose with an ambitious attempt — the quintessential golficide.

CHAPTER FOUR

Styles of links and the great clusters

Some critics of links golf suggest that, 'having seen one links, you have seen them all'. But this is clearly fallacious. The more you delve into the links game, the more aware you become of the richness of its diversity. With this realisation, it becomes a dangerous thing to generalise about a typical links description; you are bound to offend the champion of one style or another.

One could say, however, that championship links in Ireland, such as Ballybunion Old, Royal County Down, Royal Portrush, Tralee, The European Club, Portstewart, Carne and Waterville have generous portions of sandhills, while Open Championship links in Scotland such as St Andrews, Carnoustie, Muirfield and Royal Troon tend to be flatter with less dunal territory to negotiate. Montrose, one of the oldest of all links, is relatively flat, as are Nairn and Southerness.

There are no absolutes in this game, only trends and an intermingling of genres and one can name numerous Scottish links that are mountainous enough, such as Cruden Bay (in places). Similarly, there is no shortage of flatter Irish links courses: Portmarnock and Royal Dublin to name but two.

As for English championship links, Royal St George's and Royal Birkdale are abundantly dunal, while Royal Liverpool (Hoylake) and Royal Lytham and St Anne's are less noted for this feature. By comparison to Scotland, England was slow to get actively involved with links golf. Royal North Devon in 1864 was its initial foray into the fast-running seaside game and it was five years before a second, Royal Liverpool

OPPOSITE: North Berwick's 13th hole – Pit. An old-fashioned dinky links hole

BELOW: Easy enough to see why golfers enthuse over the links at Cruden Bay

(Hoylake), sprang forth. In 1875 Seaton-Carew was instituted. In England's case, the great clusters of links were still some years away.

Many links are laid out upon common land and one in particular, Royal North Devon, has special provision for animals. The grazing scene is deeply soothing for golfers and is a long-standing tradition; currently, club regulations allow twelve hundred sheep and one hundred horses to roam peacefully. Each green is surrounded by white tapes designed to avert the threat of equine stampeding. It works well and protects the greens from damage.

Actually, the horses at Royal North Devon are the least of their worries — natural forces pose a far greater danger. Northam Burrows, on which their links is laid out, is protected by a pebble ridge which has been progressively shifting. The movement (not so gradual at times) has caused a worrying amount of land to be devoured by the sea. Born of necessity, a new 8th hole was built in 1998 — the original hole was prone to flooding during times of high tide when the elements were whipped into a frenzy.

Apart from its fine golfing, there is a unique aspect surrounding Royal Lytham and St Anne's Golf Club. The links is fenced off and suburbia runs rampant on all side and the sea is a few kilometres away. In fact, the biggest shock during the round is that you never spot the sea. On first sighting, it hardly resembles a links, with an opening par three through an avenue of trees. 'Strange

The 18th hole at Royal Lytham and St Anne's with stately club house in background

A peaceful grazing scene at Brora

goings on here', you mutter to yourself. But once into the round, you quickly see how it lives up to its tag as a links, complete with links feel. As each Open Championship rolls around, it never fails to test the professionals and the inward nine is among the hardest individual nine on the rota.

Despite their wild and woolly reputations, not all links have rough. Brora is an example of this type, where grazing cows and sheep keep the rough well under control and balls visible. Only twenty-five minutes north of Royal Dornoch, this fine links with tremendous vistas is surprisingly overlooked by many golfing tourists. But what a haven for those who enjoy finishing the round with the same ball — and this is possible if the 'wee' burns are successfully negotiated. While the golfing world struggles with the curse of slow play, a brisk pace can be anticipated on this Northern Scottish links.

The view from Brora's club house

Notwithstanding the relative absence of rough, Brora presents a well-balanced golfing challenge. Master architect, James Braid, devised an inspired routing, where the four par threes each dissect a different point on the compass — this fact alone makes the links intriguing and his fee of £25 plus expenses in 1924, can only be viewed as a bargain. Brora's links is laden with beguiling contours and the need for fine judgement soon becomes apparent. Due to its interesting features, Brora can be held up as an example of a traditional Scottish links: predominantly open entrances to their greens, burns that torment, proximity to the sea, guide markers to assist blind approaches and more or less, an out and in routing configuration. The roaming cattle are dissuaded from invading the lovely putting surfaces by electric fences which surround the greens.

On all links, the presence of rough, its upkeep and overall virulence have long been issues of great importance to golfers and their psyche. Hunstanton Golf Club, considered one of the finest links on England's east coast, had confirmation of this in 1972. Their rough had been toughened up in preparation for the British Ladies Open Amateur Championship — an honour that was returning for the fifth time. Keen to present a thought-provoking challenge, the administration took to growing the rough, in the opinion of its playing members, excessively. They were up in arms and one, L.N. Roddis, vented his spleen in the suggestion book:

> As the present state of the rough is such as to deprive the majority of members of much of their enjoyment, which they are entitled to enjoy on the course, these conditions cannot but have an adverse effect on the number of visitors. The majority of people playing, including the visitors have long handicaps and it is the majority upon whom the very existence of the club depends.[9]

Within a short time, the strangling rough was cut back to its normal height.

Nature has never operated under a strict code of slide-rules, and thus, links land terrain varies from the gently undulating to the heaving magnitude. Not far from St Andrews in the kingdom of Fife, a relatively flat links is found at Elie. Completely windswept and generously open, this links which has little rough to speak of, lies along the bank of the firth of Forth. Among other things, it is famous for producing three very well known golfers in days gone by — James Braid, Douglas Rolland and Jack Simpson. A good example of a natural barren links, not one of the green sites was built by man. Elie is a little unusual in that it has no par fives, but one hole in particular, the 13th, which James Braid reputedly called 'the best in all Scotland', will long stay in your memory.

Trees flanking the left hand side of Carnoustie's 9th hole

Like Elie, another links close to St Andrews is bereft of low-lying vegetation. It goes by the name of Crail Golfing Society and is situated on the most easterly golfing strip of Fife. A terrific antidote to the back-breaking play of other links, the play at Crail is very relaxing and a magnet for historically minded golfers. Instituted in 1786, it is the seventh oldest club in existence. The 19th-hole views from the club house across the North Sea will hold you spellbound.

Treed links are in short supply, but one of the finest is Carnoustie, on the eastern Scottish seaboard. Evolutionary processes have made it quite possible for mix-ups to occur, and thus, sporadic clumps of trees on true links do exist. Nevertheless, any course purporting to be a links with (hole-after-hole) negotiation through trees, clearly is not a links — despite invariably being seaside in location and style.

An example of nature gone wrong is Carnoustie's 9th hole which supports a massive tree colony along the out of bounds fence (right-handed hookers beware). As far as driving width goes, it is rather narrow. At the following hole, when approaching the 10th green, four towering trees will catch a long iron shot that leaks to the right — the hole is known as 'South America'.

The 10th hole at Carnoustie presents a difficult start to the inward nine. Bunkers, trees and a burn complicate matters with your long iron approach

Carnoustie's double green — 4th and 14th holes

Predominantly featuring natural links land, Carnoustie presents a formidable examination. A real feature of Carnoustie is the ever-present burns that cut an insidious swathe and the uncompromising rough. Played from the Medal tees, it is highly demanding — approach shots being an endless array of long irons and woods. Carnoustie is not pretty, but it does not pretend to be. By way of gifts or soft holes, Carnoustie offers the golfer no respite. Among what often seems to be a bleak environment, the links has a certain 'chestiness' about it, making it foreboding and unforgiving to all, including the top rank.

To illustrate this point, consider the treatment it doled out to Rod Pampling during the 1999 Open Championship. The Australian golfer capitulated from first round leader, to missing the half-way cut and being an unlikely weekend spectator. As an aside, dismiss all thoughts of St Andrews Old being unique for its double greens. Many newcomers to links golf are surprised to see the shared arrangement of Carnoustie's ample 4th and 14th hole greens.

Royal Birkdale has its share of trees and shrubbery. Recently though, they took to removing 8 ha (20 a) of white poplars (Lancashire weed) in the interests of promoting an enhanced links appearance.

Two other Lancashire links — Hillside and Formby, count among the list of treed links. Indeed, several of Formby's boundaries are framed by firs and pines. While Formby portrays an inland look in spots, it retains the links stamp of approval — all the trimmings of links land terrain are present, with the added bonus that many holes are delightfully secluded.

BUNKERS HAUNT MANY LINKS: some of these hazards evolve through natural forces, others are man-made. At Dooks Golf Club, a greatly underrated links in County Kerry, Ireland, bunkers are unusually sparse in numbers. Until 1996, they had just eleven in total. With continuous improvement in mind, architect Donald Steel was called in to evaluate the links. Steel made a few suggestions for modernisation – add several bunkers here and there, fill in a few wasted bunkers, selectively plant furze to fortify fairways and toughen up of some entrances to the greens through various means. In his field visit evaluation, Steel referred to Dooks as:

> A gem of a links. As such, it has a special place in the annals of links golf and must be preserved at all costs. Its character typifies the true meaning of what this form of the game should represent. It exists to give enjoyment and challenge without resorting to undue length. However, the game has been changed by the inexorable advance in the manufacture of clubs and balls, a change that has a spinoff on our courses. Where possible, courses have to be adjusted to keep pace with this change. Periodic checks form part of enlightened policy.
>
> This is not to say that Dooks should become a playground for giants. Its strengths are more subtle, more imaginative, more permanent. It plays longer than its 6000 yards, even without Atlantic winds. This is on account of the angling and elevation of many greens but added interest is lent by the contouring of the putting surfaces and the variety of approach shots to be played from the undulating fairways. Positional play from the tee is also essential in order to set up the correct line for these second shots. There is a right part of the fairway and a wrong part.[10]

Not surprisingly, many golfers, when making their links pilgrimage to County Kerry in Ireland, become fixated on the well known courses of Tralee, Waterville and Ballybunion. The three beautiful but overcrowded inland golf courses at Killarney also attract much attention. For these reasons, as well as being 'slightly off the beaten track', the lesser known Dooks can miss out on the golf traffic. But take a little tip, Dooks deserves your support because the links is an excellent test of golf and well worth the deviation. Not only is it one of the most natural links (Dooks comes from the Irish *douaghs* meaning dunes), but one that has endured and overcome hardship. It was a target for a takeover deal by a continental hotelier who thought the area would be better served by a private golf course and beach. In 1963, the Club was served notice to vacate the links. A national publicity campaign was instigated to save Dooks and attracted much local, regional and national press interest. That one of Ireland's oldest golf clubs was in jeopardy startled many in the golf world.

Dooks upgrade – bunker proposals for the 3rd hole, 1996

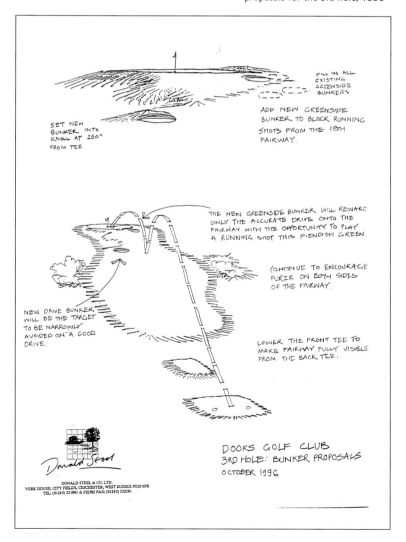

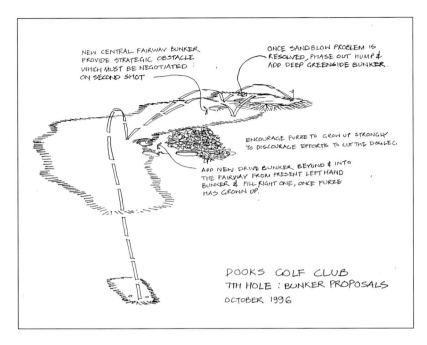

NEW CENTRAL FAIRWAY BUNKER
PROVIDE STRATEGIC OBSTACLE
WHICH MUST BE NEGOTIATED
ON SECOND SHOT

ONCE SANDBLOW PROBLEM IS
RESOLVED, PHASE OUT HUMP &
ADD DEEP GREENSIDE BUNKER.

ENCOURAGE FURZE TO GROW UP STRONGLY
TO DISCOURAGE EFFORTS TO CUT THE DOGLEG.

ADD NEW DRIVE BUNKER BEYOND & INTO
THE FAIRWAY FROM PRESENT LEFT HAND
BUNKER & FILL RIGHT ONE, ONCE FURZE
HAS GROWN UP.

DOOKS GOLF CLUB
7TH HOLE : BUNKER PROPOSALS
OCTOBER 1996

Dooks upgrade — bunker
proposals for 7th hole, 1996

The absentee landlord refused an initial club offer and would not accept any rent. He was adamant that the links must be vacated. For nearly two years the threat was alive, but with much relief, an offer of £7000 was accepted in 1965. The club was safe.

Basking in this new freedom, Dooks Golf Club turned their attention towards upgrading the links from a nine-hole to a regulation size eighteen-hole layout. Great praise must be given to the club for its initiative in allocating all nine committee members architectural responsibility for one hole each. The members were supportive of this measure and ploughed in to assist with the back-breaking chores. Remarkably, the upgrade from nine to eighteen holes, between 1967 and 1970, cost only a little over £2000.

As mentioned in the previous chapter, architects tended to route their outward nine along the dunal shoreline and then return inland to complete the circuit. Royal Dornoch, one of the oldest and very best links did exactly the opposite. Its front nine is on several levels (inland) with incredible elevation in sections. Many will recall, 'the long climb' after the par three 6th — Whinny Brae — aptly named for its grandstand of surrounding golden gorse. This stretch of gorse, which fairly blazes in summer, is at its most lethal between the 3rd and 7th holes. The first opportunity to find water will come at the par five 9th — a quick duck-hook into Embo Bay will see to that. Misadventure from the 11th tee will

Dooks upgrade — 14th hole,
new green proposal, 1996

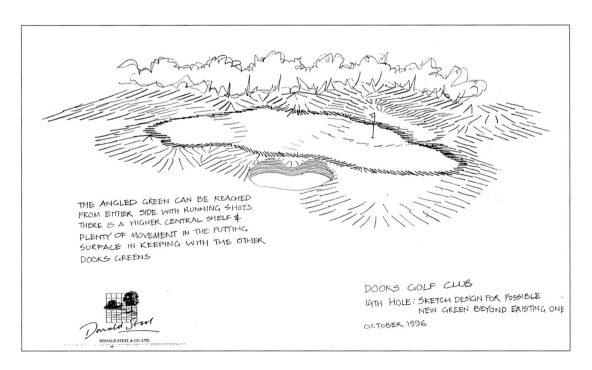

THE ANGLED GREEN CAN BE REACHED
FROM EITHER SIDE WITH RUNNING SHOTS.
THERE IS A HIGHER CENTRAL SHELF &
PLENTY OF MOVEMENT IN THE PUTTING
SURFACE IN KEEPING WITH THE OTHER
DOOKS GREENS

DOOKS GOLF CLUB
14TH HOLE: SKETCH DESIGN FOR POSSIBLE
            NEW GREEN BEYOND EXISTING ONE
OCTOBER 1996

Donald Steel
DONALD STEEL & CO. LTD.

also find the beach. Other than that, Dornoch Firth is highly visible but due to architectural routing is a visual attraction only. This timeless links is decidedly more strategic than penal and seldom disappoints the golfer of any standard. In fact, my recurring idea of a good time is to play here for a week in high summer, sauntering out each morning and evening whenever the mood takes hold.

When speaking to devotees of links golf, frequently they opt for dunes country as the most thrilling to play – getting to the heart of the matter. There are no links laid out entirely among dunes. Most of the dunal type seem to have, at best, one nine only. Royal Birkdale comes closest and is famed for its dunes – some gentle, others daunting. There are views of the sea at Royal Birkdale, but you will need to stand on the club house roof to get them. This links is the one most frequently associated with dunes, although Saunton, The European Club, Ballybunion New and Carne also conjure up images of formidable dunes.

The dunes and natural amphitheatres at Royal Birkdale, ensure exciting spectator viewing – among the best on the rota in this regard. Fairways appear trough-like below and the new swales by several greens have placed an increased premium on chipping. Many of the holes sweep gently around dog-legging corners, making one of the major tests of this links the blind and semi-blind recovery shots to the green.

When casting your eye over Royal Birkdale, it appears that the hand of man has intervened more often than at other links. It creates this impression on two counts: firstly, one feels the aura of target golf all around. Secondly, fairway stances are unusually level for a links and some count this as a blessing. Notwithstanding, there is little doubt that Royal Birkdale is a great links.

Murcar, a fine but less visited links in Aberdeenshire, is noted for its dunes, most of which confront you on the outward journey. A similar story can be told of nearby Royal Aberdeen – a real thoroughbred of a links.

Some links are laid out along triangular peninsulas and these are visually spectacular. They look brilliant from the air, surrender plenty of sea views on your journey and test your shot- making with fluky winds that quarter regularly from different directions. Such an example is best showcased by Portmarnock Golf Club, just out of Dublin. Different from the traditional out and in links, some believe that Portmarnock, along with Muirfield, is the fairest of all links. Many of golf's premier players have praised this magnificently natural links, and for years Portmarnock was thought to have the finest greens in Ireland. It regularly hosted the Irish Open.

Another triangular peninsula links – Castletown, on the Isle of Man, is not so well known but is highly regarded by those who have played it. The links here distinguishes itself by being set on a shoulder of land well above sea level. Ocean and majestic cliffs make for awesome views, while whins and heather frame the holes to make the links golfer feel at home. Without these features, perhaps elevated downland would be nearer the truth. Set out initially by 'Old' Tom Morris and later revised by Mackenzie Ross, the links is arranged so that due to ingenious routing the wind is not usually quartering from the same direction for more than two or three holes.

To fully quantify the links that 'Old' Tom designed, co-designed, redesigned, or merely advised upon is no easy matter. Record keeping in this era was sketchy and his inherent modesty did not help ward off the occasional architect who, in need of publicity, took the credit for Tom's work. But the work attributed to this great St Andrean is impressive.

Royal County Down Golf Club at Newcastle, Northern Ireland, is one club with which his name is inexorably linked. Regarding its architectural lineage, Royal County Down enjoys a privileged past. As well as Tom Morris, Harry Vardon and H.S. Colt each raised the standard of the course and

Seymour Dunn gave invaluable advice. Today, all successful golf clubs can isolate a turning point in their affairs when redesigning of the links ensured prosperity and recognition. Royal County Down can pinpoint two: the first of these was in 1889 when 'Old' Tom Morris visited to play a match on the nine-hole layout. During his trip he alluded to the possibility of an eighteen-hole upgrade, and shortly afterwards was engaged to build a links for a sum 'not to exceed £4'.

At this esteemed links, the members are truly blessed. Each time they set out, they do battle with an assortment of blind shots, menacing and unique bunkering, ridges, hillocks, defining sandhills, whins, bracken and tangly, grassy rough. These and other features, ensure that each round is an adventure. Of note, the golf is played upon true, crisp links turf.

The fairways are not desperately narrow, but neither are they wide enough to induce total relaxation. Suffice to say their width will enable you to appreciate why many nominate it as the finest layout in the portfolio of links golf.

As for the greens, they have become less intimidating with the passage of time, and today rely more on subtlety, both within the sites they occupy and their surfaces, to challenge the golfer.

Inter-hole variety is highly evident among the par fours where short, medium, medium-long and very long longs are represented. With three of the par threes stretching around 200 yards from the championship tees, variety in length is less apparent, but visually and shot making wise, they are completely their own entities. At any rate, the 4th and 10th holes are magnificent par threes. Contrasting sharply in length is the semi-blind and notoriously difficult to hold 7th hole at only 145 yards.

The dog-leg holes are loaded with interest, as best exemplified by the challenging 3rd, 5th, 13th and 15th holes. The 13th, in particular, is a showcase of eerie isolation. The other dog-leg holes throughout the layout are only slightly less grand.

EVERY OUTSTANDING LINKS can boast an impressive display of fine holes – Royal Portrush, Portmarnock, Ballybunion Old and the eight Open Championship rota links continually reaffirm this. My indelible impression of what sets Royal County Down apart is that it has fewer poor holes than any links I can recall. The 17th hole is their only obvious blemish and my reasoning is detailed later on in the book.

In addition to the superior golfing, a large part of Royal County Down's charm lies in the perfect union of the mountains of Mourne sweeping harmoniously down to Dundrum Bay. Set in this untamed panorama is the towering Slieve Donard Hotel with its distinctive redbrick appearance and spire. In a previous era, this site occupied golfing ground. A good friend of mine, Ken McNamara, has an interesting way of expressing his thoughts on the overall experience, 'Royal County Down is up there with breathing'.

The enlisting of H.S. Colt was the club's second turning point, for he modernised the layout in the late 1920s. The course, as it lies today, is very much a result of his creativity. He eliminated some elements of blindness as typified by his treatment of consecutive blind par threes to conclude the outward half. Until then, the 8th was played from low-lying ground (in front of the current 9th tee), over the gigantic hill to a billowy green, positioned at the base on the other side. The old 9th tee was in the middle of the current 9th fairway and golfers took aim blindly over another hill to the present 9th green.

These changes cleared the way for the creation of one of the most decorated holes in golf, but nevertheless, today's 9th hole still demands a blind tee-shot. Early twentieth century photographic

ABOVE: 17th hole – Saunton (East), England (*Images of Links Land* reproduced with the special permission of Barry King)

LEFT 11th hole – Ballybunion Old, Ireland

ABOVE: Opening tee shot –
Machrihanish, Scotland

RIGHT: Klondyke – 5th hole,
Lahinch, Ireland

ABOVE: Swilcan Burn and 1st
fairway – St Andrews Old,
Scotland

LEFT: Golden Gorse – St Andrews
New, Scotland

OPPOSITE: Putting out on the 9th green of the Shore Course at dusk with shadows forming along the dunes of Prince's Golf Club, Kent. The old clubhouse and Sandwich Bay are captured in the distance

ABOVE: The famous 'White Rocks' (5th hole) at Royal Portrush, Northern Ireland (this photograph reproduced with the special permission of the Northern Ireland Tourist Board)

OPPOSITE: Portstewart Golf Club sandwiched between the River Bann and the rolling Atlantic Ocean. This photo was taken high above the 2nd fairway on Devil's Hill and features the 3rd green in the foreground, which is the conclusion to a tough par three of 207 yards. Stretching away is the dog-leg par five 4th hole, which measures 535 yards. Reaching the green in two is rarely attainable, however, the real problem lies in judging the deceptive 3rd shot into a raised green. The blue Donegal Hills make a pleasant backdrop (this photograph reproduced with the special permission of the Northern Ireland Tourist Board)

LEFT: A delightful mood shot of Royal Liverpool

BELOW: The stately clubhouse at Royal Liverpool Golf Club, England. This once giant of the links game was a regular Open Championship venue until its swansong year in 1967. The links is commonly referred to as Hoylake

FOLLOWING PAGE: An example of the highly interesting bunkering at Royal Liverpool

A view of the glorious 10th hole at Royal County Down from behind the green

plates of the 8th and 9th holes depict their fairways as being devoid of framing whins. In fact, the widespread planting of whins throughout the entire layout was a relatively modern event and, when in full bloom, there are few finer spectacles in links golf. Having passed its centenary in 1988, most of the significant changes at Royal County Down occurred during the club's initial fifty years.

The awe-inspiring 4th hole, which is played over a plethora of whins, bunkers and broken ground, is another Colt masterpiece. Previously, the old 4th was around 500 yards long. Apart from this hole, many alterations included the lengthening of holes, which in hindsight was fortuitous with the advent of steel shafts just around the corner. One improvement to the links was the thoughtful remodelling of the 18th green and surrounds. This initiative was heartily applauded, for originally the ball needed only the merest trickle over the green to find out of bounds.

Royal County Down has always had a regal air about it, but in common with other links, things have not always been plain sailing. During the course of its existence committees have presided over horrific coastal erosion, insect plagues, compulsory fairway tee-ups, caddie strikes, heated debate over matters such as blindness and other progress-stalling issues.

In the annals of links golf, the year 1953 is remembered for Hogan's great triumph at Carnoustie. But it also marked the occasion of County Down gaining its Royal status. Place an asterisk against Royal County Down, for to play here is a treat.

Let me introduce you to the concept of the cluster. One of the great misconceptions about Great Britain and Ireland's shoreline, is that it comprises wall-to-wall links. Indeed, extensive areas of coastline exist where there are no links. Along the Shannon estuary for instance, countryside meanders a few hundred kilometres virtually devoid of sand – the topography is mainly green fields and marshlands.

When architect Pat Ruddy undertook his aerial survey of Ireland's east coast, the rarity of true links land became apparent to him. Brittas Bay in County Wicklow presented itself as the best land south of Royal Dublin. This discovery was the catalyst for his much vaunted project – the European Club. Travelling in a southerly direction, he found that the only comparable links land lay several hundred kilometres away in County Kerry.

ANY LINKS THAT SUFFERS FROM EXCESSIVE ISOLATION is at risk of being overlooked unless the links can boast similar qualities to Southerness in the south of Scotland or Carne in north-west Ireland. It has been no coincidence that with clubs and architects seeking the best available land, a multitude of links tended to spring up in close proximity to each other and within striking distance of the populace. In hindsight, it is clear to see the connection between the prospering railways and new club formation. When taking the Lancashire line for instance, one views a glittering procession of links, all lined up one after another.

Some of the best known clusters appear in Scotland. Fife's showpiece is St Andrews Old and its many adjoining links – all under the control of the St Andrews Links Management Trust. Despite an established reputation, the Old Course layout, shaped remarkably like a shepherd's crook, has frequently been the target of snide pot-shots from a long line of experts. On such occasions, these golfers are invariably greeted with benign conditions, play hideously above themselves and then lacking in grace, pronounce St Andrews Old as the most overrated examination in golf. It really rankles some, famous professionals and all. Others, when playing over its immensely undulating ground, say, 'Nice sizzle, what about the sausage?' This pinpoints the debate over what constitutes sound principles of course design.

St Andrews Old is synonymous with links golf and being the original links, is the master copy. The Old Course was created entirely by natural forces. An old saying suggests, 'It simply grewed'.[11] There have been consultant architects through the ages, but understanding that any modifications to this golfing institution attract widespread scrutiny like no other, they have had the good sense to leave well enough alone – save for the construction of some 'tiger' tees. Upon detailed study of the links, they must also reason, why tinker with a layout that under most conditions can still confound and embarrass the best?

Architecturally, the strength of the Old Course is that it can be courted by golfers of varying skill levels. The less skilled golfer may not score well here, but they may well get around without losing a ball. For many, that is a rather novel experience. In keeping with the shot-making values of Royal Melbourne and Augusta National, the golfer is presented with several alternative lines from the tee. One can contemplate the bold, medium or safety line. Commensurate with your courage (and ability) off the tee, you will be rewarded or penalised on your approach to the green. To illustrate this point, for a good deal of the front nine, the safe option is down the left side – giving the gorse flanking on the right-hand side a wide berth. This conservatism will cause much harder approaches, which in turn, invites a gaggle of three putts on the huge greens. The genius of this interrelatedness is sadly lost on many architects who pledge allegiance to the penal school of golf course architecture. Their philosophy dictates that it does not matter by how far you miss your target; if you miss, the penalty is the same regardless of the degree of error.

The double greens on the Old Course still remain the most talked about feature of the layout — some are so spacious the need for pivoting when putting will hardly turn a head. In Open Championships it is not uncommon for professionals to select their pitching clubs over their putters.

As the Old is a strong links, the top professionals can, on occasion, humble it. During the annual Dunhill Cup, it has surrendered a 62 to Curtis Strange and numerous scores in the mid-60s to others. And yet, many matches during the same week are won by quality players with 74 against a 76. The course that will not yield to great scoring is weaker for the blemish and, with the modern player in the right mood, most courses exhibit a degree of vulnerability.

The 1997 Dunhill Cup saw the introduction of new tees on the 3rd, 10th, 13th, 15th and 16th holes. The last two were primarily constructed to bring Sutherland and Principle Nose bunkers back in range. One suspects that the Millennium 2000 Open Championship was uppermost in mind with these new additions.

Unlike modern layouts, playing St Andrews Old is not a question of, 'Who can hit the most greens in regulation?' Common are the cries of 'having hit 15 greens for a miserable 82'. But wait. Remembering that elsewhere their distant putts would normally be chips, sand explosions and pitches, self-admonishment at three-putting every second hole is both unnecessary and avoidance of the real issue — poorly judged iron approaches. No golf course, links or otherwise, places such emphasis on this aspect of the game, nor the following approach putt.

JUST WHO OWNS AND MAINTAINS THE OLD COURSE? The links are the ancient birthright of the residents, but the St Andrews Links Management Committee is entrusted to maintain the links traditions. The Committee is comprised of eight members and similarly, eight trustees. Together, they rule under a 1974 Act of Parliament — the special Act of Parliament which determines how the links (both Old and New) are run. They preside over greenkeeping, starting times, green fees, and general operations. The role of the trustees is to ensure that quality decisions are made with regards to major developments and policy matters. They are also responsible for generating off-course income.[12]

There is so much to see and experience at St Andrews. The religious rejoice in an atmosphere befitting a city once known as the ecclesiastic capital of Scotland and the youth of St Andrews, students of its world famous university, lend an air of vibrancy and scholarly pursuit to an otherwise staid environment. Do make a point of paying your respects to 'Old' Tom Morris and Allan Robertson in the graveyard ruins at the far end of the city — the scene projects a constant reminder of a glorious but at times troubled past. And of course there is golf and, more recently, a golf museum.

Due to these diverse interests, the city has always been popular with visitors, and how the numbers swell during summer. One visitor though, is less likely to be welcomed with open arms — *the haar*. Once described as the chilly breath of the North Sea, the cold fog may descend at any time of the year and, not infrequently, disrupts starting times on the Old Course during the Dunhill Cup. Under these circumstances, the many ancient towers of St Andrews are shrouded, ghost-like, transforming a beautiful little city into a distinctly eerie landscape. Other well established Fife links are Elie, Leven Links, Lundin Links and Crail.

East Lothian, directly east of Edinburgh, is a vastly popular region for links golf. The golfing capital of this region is tiny Gullane, a village that virtually supports itself by golf alone. Found here is venerable Muirfield, known as the Honourable Company of Edinburgh Golfers since 1744,

The village of Gullane can boast a putting green, virtually in the main street

and Gullane number one, two and three. There is also Luffness New, famed for its peerless putting surfaces. By choice, Muirfield does not have a professional's shop, so Gullane gladly accepts custom from its neighbour's members along with their own. Other East Lothian links of note are Dunbar, North Berwick, and the historic Musselburgh.

The West links at North Berwick is a must-see destination if seeking old fashioned links characteristics: playing over and beside stone walls, putting on peculiar greens, blind shots, ample opportunities to find the beach and lastly, devilish approach shots that can send you twitchy. But you would not have it any other way at North Berwick. Necessity being the mother of invention, Berwick golfers were noted for their short game prowess; prior to the links being lengthened, there was little call for anything else but approach work.

North Berwick enjoys a reputation based mainly on nostalgia and sentimentalists do crowd the links. However, the holes are very good in their own right and famous the world over. In particular, the stretch of holes beginning on the 13th tee and finishing on the 17th green provide much enjoyment and summarise the Berwick round.

This stretch starts with the revered Pit hole — 365 yards par four 13th. Powerful players get silly notions of driving the green when playing downwind, but this is jealously guarded by a long stone wall running down the fairway's left-hand side. The height is just enough to intrude with nuisance value. From the tee, a perfectly played draw on the hard Berwick ground will often roll against the wall. Assuming a safe drive to the right, the green will accept a pitch, but it will need to be nipped just right; thinned approaches will gallop right on through. One of the great links holes.

The 14th hole is known as Perfection. The early pioneers who named these holes, were not afraid to telegraph their feelings on the sensitive issue of blind golf. At only 376 yards, its length is hardly severe, but in the golden era of links, negotiating the large hill from long-range must have been highly challenging, particularly knowing that the sea was lurking just yards over the green. Today, the influence of this hazard, both real and imagined, is just as strong.

At 192 yards, the 15th hole is known as Redan. Here, the tee-shot line is precarious. A bunker, best avoided, patrols the left side of the green while on the other side lies high ground. Once over its apex, the land slopes away distinctly. A much studied hole — one bold, straight iron will see you right. To 'sell it' among the better par threes in links golf is short-changing the hole. Some place it among the best in golf. Early architects often tried to cram in a Redan look-alike to their own designs and one transplanted Scot, Charles Blair MacDonald, succeeded when laying out the National Golf Links, Long Island, USA. Many other architects failed dismally with their attempts: namely by failing to consider important matters such as soil types, general topography and whether this sort of hole looked misplaced with the remainder of the course.

A most welcoming Bed and Breakfast — 'Hopefield House' owned by Sandy and Isla Knight, Gullane

1st tee at Gullane number one links

The 16th hole goes by the name of Gate. Its fame is derived by a brilliantly camouflaged green that at times looks indistinguishable from fairway. The green is set in two halves and the plateaux are punctuated by a deep gully — all this makes for some diabolical pin positions. Such a green could never be built, it is simply classic links land.

There was a time when both the 17th hole, Point Garry (in), and the 1st hole, Point Garry (out), shared the same green. Like the second shot on Perfection, this too demands a lengthy uphill approach to a glassy green. But then, a good deal of the golf at Berwick is fast running.

Though one of the acknowledged sporty holes of links golf, the 18th can hardly claim to be bracketed with the previous holes, but it has confounded many golfers over the years. Like the finishing hole at Prestwick, it is drivable, but here, the merest push will find out of bounds. And should the ball crash through a window in the car park, you would not be making history. In keeping with the 18th at St Andrews Old, a good score can be protected by aiming your drive down the left-hand side of this expansive fairway. Needing par for the club medal, this would be my first choice of hole.

The slicer's view on the 1st hole at the West Links, North Berwick. Note the prominent guide marker to assist the blind second shot

A touch of conservatism is called on for this testing drive — North Berwick, 2nd hole

The Ayrshire links on Scotland's west coast have long attracted the links pilgrim. The most famous of these include Turnberry, Prestwick, Royal Troon and Western Gailes. There are a host of other popular links in the region, including Prestwick St Nicholas, Prestwick St Cuthbert, Troon Portland and Barassie to name a few. The second links at Turnberry is one I have long admired. Despite its close proximity to Turnberry Ailsa, part of Arran's appeal lies with its vastly contrasting terrain and vegetation. Golden gorse is visually superb when in flower, yet its encroaching abundance only reinforces the need for straight driving. At the championship Ailsa links there is comparatively little gorse to speak of, although Jack Nicklaus came perilously close to finding some when driving from the 72nd tee during the 1977 Open Championship. His steel-wristed recovery from seemingly impenetrable rough will remain as an awe-inspiring moment in golfing history, as will the epic encounter with Tom Watson.

Angus in the Tayside region is heavily serviced with links land. While Carnoustie Championship represents their finest links, it is only one of three in the town. Monifieth, Arbroath, Montrose and Panmure round out the cluster.

THE SCOTTISH HIGHLANDS region boasts several clusters. In the vicinity of Aberdeen and heading northward along the east coast lies Royal Aberdeen, Murcar and Cruden Bay. From here, travelling westward along the Moray Firth will bring you to the next cluster. On this coast lies a collection of links and links-like courses which are often overshadowed by the appeal of Royal Dornoch. Yet Nairn and Moray (Lossiemouth) are famous enough in their own right.

Heading in a northerly direction to the Sutherland region Royal Dornoch, Brora, Carnegie Club (Skibo) and Golspie represent the next cluster of links and are all within easy reach of each other. Golspie is not strictly a links — but rather an interesting mix of heath and links style.

When thinking of English clusters thoughts first turn to Lancashire — arguably the most storied links region of all. Pre-eminent on this coastal stretch are the two Open Championship links of Royal Lytham and St Anne's and Royal Birkdale. In addition, Royal Liverpool (Hoylake) was a regular rota venue itself until its swan song year in 1967. Uncommonly, the second string supportive links of this Lancashire cluster are uniformly superb. Wallasey, West Lancashire, Formby, Hillside, Southport and Ainsdale can each boast a rich history and proud contribution to the links game. The Ryder Cup, qualifying links for the Open Championship and major amateur tournaments give credence to this assertion.

Another famed English cluster can be found in the south-east along the Kent coastline. Here, three revered links fall nearly on top of each other – Royal St George's and Prince's in Sandwich, and Royal Cinque Ports at neighbouring Deal. While Royal St George's is still actively involved on the Open rota, the other two have hosted the Open in earlier times.

Yet another English cluster of renown takes in the south-west regions of Cornwall and Devon. Royal North Devon (Westward Ho) is, of course, the jewel in this cluster but others to earmark include Saunton (enviable with two fine links), West Cornwall, Trevose, St Enodoc, Bude and North Cornwall. Another excellent links named Burnham and Berrow nearly qualifies, but for being half way between this cluster and a famous set along the south coast of Wales.

Wales is a country of unspoilt and under-promoted links. The southernmost coast of Wales presents a golfing cluster of real character and diversity – Royal Porthcawl, Pyle and Kenfig, Pennard and Tenby (the oldest of Welsh links). Another fine golf course in this region is Southerndown – not unlike a links it has views of the ocean but in many respects being elevated downland precludes it. Should the Open Championship one year come to Wales, and let's hope in the interests of fair play it does, Royal Porthcawl and Royal St David's would most likely vie for the

North Berwick's 14th hole – Perfection. This approach shot just narrowly managed to avoid the sea

The club house at famous
Portmarnock

Ballybunion's ultra modern
club house

honour. For golfers, where the mere sighting of the sea confers tranquillity, a visit to Royal Porthcawl is a must as every hole surrenders a magnificent view.

Ireland has four distinct clusters to entice the golfer: the Causeway Coast in Northern Ireland, Dublin's east coast region, County Kerry, in south-west Ireland and the remote but heavily links-populated north-west coastline.

First, the *Causeway Coast*. One of my personal favourites, Royal Portrush, is the standout links and quality wise, could be bracketed with St Andrews Old, Royal County Down, Ballybunion Old, Royal St George's, Portmarnock, Turnberry and Muirfield. In 1951, Royal Portrush was awarded the rare Irish distinction of hosting the Open Championship (the year of Max Faulkner's victory and Peter Thomson's Open debut). Only minutes down the road lies Portstewart Golf Club which each year continues to upgrade and impress. Their new holes have been met with widespread approval and have elevated a once very fine links into an excellent one. Two other popular and welcoming links, Castlerock and Ballycastle, complete the cluster.

The Dublin coastline and surrounding area is simply a golfing paradise. It houses over sixty courses and declaring my prejudice, most of the better ones are links. Portmarnock, as a regular tournament course, accepts the limelight, but Royal Dublin, County Lough (Baltray), the European Club, the Island, Seapoint, St Anne's (after the new holes matured), and Sutton also rate highly.

The brilliant 17th hole at
County Sligo

The 4th green at County Sligo, with the tip of Benbulben mountain in background. It is under the shadows of Benbulben that the remains of the great poet, W.B. Yeats rest. The area is commonly referred to as 'Yeat's Country'

Increasingly, it is being postulated that County Lough is fast becoming the equal of Portmarnock. Another well worth a visit is the new Portmarnock Hotel and Golf Links, financed by International Management Group (IMG) and designed by Bernhard Langer and Stan Eby. A challenging layout, it has incorporated some modern architectural treatment, but there is still plenty of authentic and stunning links land to catch your attention. Like Ballybunion Old, a graveyard presents itself on the right of the 1st fairway, and this is the resting place of St Marnock himself.

Eddie Hackett performed a minor miracle in routing a links through this typically rocky Connemara environment

When discussing the famous cluster of *County Kerry* in south-west Ireland, it should be stated that geographically, they are reasonably close together. This assumes we are talking as the crow flies. But due to spine-tingling narrow roads, beautiful scenery and stalled periods where strolling cattle seem oblivious to your tee-off time, the car mile in this region of Ireland is among the slowest anywhere. Do not be put off, the golf is glorious. Ballybunion Old leads the way and perhaps Ballybunion New may stake a claim in the future, while Tralee, Waterville, Dooks and a largely unknown but interesting links known as Dingle Golf Club (Ceann Sibeal) complete the list.

The north-west coastline of Ireland is remote. Comparatively few links enthusiasts have travelled to this region, and therefore rely on hearsay, when pundits refer to County Sligo Golf Club (Rosses Point) as one of the great links challenges. In 1995 I had the pleasurable experience of being paired with three sprightly seniors, all nearing octogenarian status. At some point on the inward nine, I passed comment on the impressive nature of their links and its fine scenery. In a collective chorus, they insisted, 'You've seen nothing yet, wait till you sample the 17th hole'. And when it unfolded, I could only agree. Many assume the Road hole at St Andrews Old to be the unchallenged pick of all links 17th holes. But anyone with the good fortune to have played County Sligo will agree that it is a worthy contender for that accolade. Noted English golfer, writer and commentator, Peter Alliss, is another to sing its praises and those of the links in general.

Other links housed in this delightful natural cluster include Enniscrone, Donegal, Rosapenna, Narin and Portnoo, North-West, Strandhill, Carne and Ballyliffin. Here, you gain access to two fine links – the Old Course and a recent Pat Ruddy addition, Glashedy. To include Connemara in this cluster is tempting but though definitely on the west coast, Connemara lies a good deal south of this group.

Preparing for the Open Championship

John S. Philp (Links Superintendent, Carnoustie)

In the build up to an Open Championship, to update design aspects in order to accommodate the modern game, planning must take place years in advance. Over the last ten years, we have toughened up the links in an attempt to present a challenge for today's best players; one in keeping with the hard won reputation the links earned in the 1930s. To achieve this, we have tightened the entrances to the greens and narrowed some tee-shot landing areas both at full driving distance as well as in the lay-up areas. This, it is hoped, will emphasise the need for much more thought and accuracy from the players.

To add to the shot-making requirement around greens, many surrounds have been re-contoured and at the same time turf quality has been improved by fescue and bent turf replacing ugly rye grass.

We have hollowed out swales and formed mounding. Now if players miss these greens, a variety of skills are required as not all surrounds are prepared in the same manner. Certainly in most instances, players will prefer the recovery from the greenside bunkers. Built with layered turf, 5-cm- (2-in.)-thick bunker revetments will typically last 3–4 years depending upon player frequency in bunkers and also the orientation to the sun. Some twenty of these will have sprinklers set into the turf walls during reconstruction.

A programme of improvement to bunker run-ins has also been in operation. It is typical on links courses for wayward shots to be funnelled into bunkers. This is not the case with Carnoustie. A gathering effect has been created on around sixty bunkers (there are 115 in total) including

another six we did last winter. Once these returfed areas are established, they will look considerably more natural and enhance the character of the relevant bunkers.

With some 46,000 rounds played annually and a multitude of club events generated by the six golf clubs using the Links, the Championship course has to be in top-class condition throughout the year. That, as you can imagine, is a lot of divots. Over-seeding on the fairways has become common practice due to a lack of suitable grass cover in the past. Greens are also over-seeded, although the large teeing grounds do not require as much in the way of seed.

The well drained, slightly acidic, sandy links soil favours the fine perennial grasses — browntop bent and creeping red fescues. Seed from the Dutch breeder Barenbrug is used extensively. The slender creeping red fescue variety, Barcrown, is exceptional in regards to tolerance to wear and sustained close mowing. The annual budget for grass seed for the three Carnoustie courses, including turf nurseries, runs to around £12,000.

Sand has to be purchased due to problems with coastal erosion and material dredged from the river Tay is used in the bunkers. Other sands are used for root-zone mixes, (usually 4:1 with fensoil) top dressing and divot filling purposes.

Little fertiliser is needed — nitrogen will be supplied by way of the monthly top dressings to greens from the fensoil and some from the liquid iron used in monthly sprays, along with liquid seaweed (either Maxicrop or Greentech). Dry processed seaweed is used as a turf dressing to maintain soil structure and aid plant rooting,

Finely demarcated division between rough and fairway at Carnoustie and gallery ropes placed in readiness for the Open Championship

moisture retention and nutrient release. Fairways and tees are treated similarly, although less often. However, in the build up to the Open Championship, sandy top dressings to fairways will be intensified. More than anything, the indigenous fine grasses are encouraged by the physical treatments that maintain a free-draining and well-aerated soil. The professional greenkeeping team at Carnoustie are continually slitting, mini-tinning, verti-draining and using high-pressure water injection to maintain a well-aerated medium throughout the courses.

Under a three-year arrangement, all of Carnoustie's mowing and other equipment is being updated with Toro machinery, supplied by A.M. Russell of Edinburgh.

First, a top-dressing programme will commence in spring at the commencement of growth and will be continued until early June. Our expectation is to apply three or four light applications of sandy compost to the greens, where improved trueness of surface is the goal.

Teeing grounds and fairways will receive 1-2 dressings in the spring period, and fairway verti-cutting will be more favoured (dictated by growth) in the month of June for the fine-tuning of fairway turf.

FINAL PREPARATION: heading towards the Open, there will be minimal surface disruption to putting surfaces after January 1999. We would like the links to play hard and fast. To help achieve this aim we need help from the weather, which is always the dominating factor in the timing of all treatments and cultural practices. Of all the management practices, it is obviously the mowing regimes that increase in intensity in the run-up to the event. Hand mowing of greens will commence in June and during the week of the tournament, greens will be mown twice a day and vibratory rolled as required.

Fairways will be mown at 5/16th with triplex mowers. We are aiming for a tight, firm close-knit turf from which certainly players can spin the ball,

Freshly revetted bunkers on the 18th hole at Carnoustie. Note the stabilising material in the bunkers and the new club house under construction

Fairway preparation at Carnoustie

playing to firm, fast-putting surfaces. We are not however, setting up the links to suit the players. The last thing we want in an Open Championship is a putting competition. The aim is to present a true challenge if perfect weather conditions prevail and therefore have control, whatever the

circumstances, to adjust tee positions or pin placements to offer a fair test in the event of more adverse conditions. We have, after all, over 7,300 yards to play with.

The course will be closed from 21 June to aid final preparations and disguise ugly divot scars, relieve traffic routes and establish mowing and other maintenance regimes.

Length, per se, will not halt the ever-increasing capabilities of the expanding school of top-flight golfers who have the game to win at the highest level. Many of the established championship courses on both sides of the Atlantic are being rendered obsolete by modern technology. Certainly Carnoustie in 1985 no longer presented a fearsome challenge to the elite players as it did in the thirties or even as in Hogan's time. I ask you, 'What's wrong with 70 being viewed as a very good score again, over a stiff yet fair test in good conditions?' As a measure of how things have changed, during the first four Carnoustie Open's (1931, 1937, 1953 and 1968) a score of 70 was only bettered on five occasions.

Remodelling in progress behind
Carnoustie's 1st green

If the regulatory authorities do not reduce the flight of the ball (which seems unlikely) then our championship courses, as we enter a new millennium, will be left seriously outdated. These courses will fail to deliver adequate shot-making and decision-making challenges commensurate with their status unless they are bailed out by poor weather conditions. This is surely not the way forward, merely leaving it to the elements to stiffen up the course in the hope that calm weather does not prevail over the championship days.

Golf courses, being dynamic, age like anything else and by necessity, need reviving to combat changes in other aspects of the game. But in doing so, our marvellous UK links must not lose their characteristics of real links golf.

The problems have been recognised yes, but the answers have often been to seek more length (perceived as the easy option) to redress the imbalance. It is hoped that such a futile solution will eventually run its course.

Returfing of 3rd green at
Carnoustie

CHAPTER FIVE

Links bunkering

During the golden era of links and prior to the inland spread, the significance of a bunker was vastly different to what it is today. With hickory shaft and gutta-percha ball in vogue, bunkers could be your ruination. They evoked fear and trepidation in the mind of the golfer; some of the most fierce being blind from the tee. Golf clubs became justifiably proud of their hazards and assigned them imposing names such as Hell, Road, Pandemonium, Maiden, Mann's and Cardinal, to name just a few. For an exercise in jaw-dropping astonishment, head to Royal North Devon (Westward Ho) and negotiate Cape bunker. Similarly, Cader bunker at Aberdovey links, prior to being remodelled, was a magnificent challenge to golfers – sleepered, proud and highly threatening.

In keeping with human nature, golfers have been only too willing to spread horror stories about being stuck in these bunkers – an activity that ensured their notoriety would grow with the passage of time. Some of these bunkers were so large, raking to any extent was ignored. They were true hazards.

Imposing in stature, links bunkers are not uncommonly fortified with railway sleepers and are frequently sod-revetted for support and insurance against wind erosion. On some links, there are sleepers galore, not only in bunkers but supporting the burns as well. For the inquisitive, the immediate question is 'Where did the sleepers come from?' Well, hardly any distance at all, for in most of the great old golfing centres, railway stations lay in close proximity. Discarded railway ties and sleepers were abundant. Their convenience made them highly prized but inexpensive assets to the golf clubs. A different modus operandi exists for the American courses of today – they bring the railway ties in first and build the course second. Pete Dye, a prolific American golf course architect, is masterful at this strategy.

The process of sod-revetting a bunker is intricate work and one that requires great craftsmanship and experience. Starting from the base, a solid foundation is moulded to the shape of the inside of the bunker. A layer of turf is then laid onto the compacted sand. This is continued upwards – the key is

OPPOSITE: The opening hole at The European Club

A good example of a bunker recently sod-revetted — the left hand Spectacle bunker at Carnoustie 14th hole

laying the next layer of turf slightly back from the previous layer. This system dictates the precise angle desired and prevents the bunker face from being too vertical. The more the ground crew sets the turf layer back from the previous layer, the greater the angle created. At all times during construction, backfilling is done with sand and soil to ensure compaction.

When deemed to be at the desired height to terrorise golfers, the bunker is then topped off with a collar of turf. For links that are most exposed to the elements, revetting is an important bunkering feature, primarily to keep the sand intact while combating strong winds. In general, revetted faces of bunkers last around four years. If a solid maintenance programme is kept up with a good deal of brushing and watering, they can last much longer.

At St Andrews a great system is in place and bunkers are worked on in rotation. Leading up to each Open Championship at the Old Course, all 112 bunkers will be revetted prior to the event. This necessitates the hiring of additional staff on fixed-term contracts. St Andrews Old is not unique in this – prior to each Open Championship, the bunkers of the host links undergo extensive revetting work. The net result of all this preparation makes them steeper, deeper and therefore more worthy of respect by the professionals.

On first sighting, one is bowled over by the cavernous bunker, Sahara, at Prestwick's famous 17th hole, Alps. Taking the primitive in-ground steps down to your ball is a fascinating experience,

Sahara bunker at Prestwick's 17th hole. When playing this difficult par four, you approach blindly over a large hill just short of the photo. To find the putting surface, this bunker needs to be carried

The infamous Cardinal bunker —
Prestwick 3rd hole

and for some, must radiate an aura of walking into your grave. Harry Vardon once stated, 'I have no hesitation in giving my judgement that the 17th is the finest hole to be found on any links. It is the best specimen of the really perfect two-shot hole'.[13]

No less eye-catching is Cardinal bunker on the 3rd hole at Prestwick. Played as a 500-yard par five today, it offers a good chance of a birdie four, if the deep Cardinal is avoided from the tee and the wind is favourable. When Prestwick regularly hosted the Open Championship, it was a constant threat and among the most menacing bunkers known to golf. James Braid, while leading the 1908 Open, was said to be 'playing a game of "racquets" by bouncing off Cardinal's sleepered wall'. Striving in vain for distance, he glanced two shots off the face into Pow Burn. Braid holed out in eight strokes but, ever calm in a crisis, recovered to win the event.

When playing Prestwick's 16th hole today, known as Cardinal's Back, the long hitter needs to be wary. With improved shaft technology and ball design, the chances of reaching Cardinal bunker with a single long faded drive are greater than ever. Earlier in the century, the obvious danger was finding it with a misguided second shot.

Apart from the massive bunkers found on the links of Great Britain and Ireland, there lurk some 'pot' bunkers, so tiny and steep lipped that your only escape is either backwards or sideways. St Andrews Old is full of them and due to the undulations of the general terrain, many are 'blind' to the golfer's eye. Players take on a comical appearance, not just at the prospect of getting out but at pondering how to best get in, in to order to get out. Golfers adopting one-legged, propped, contortionist stances are commonly seen.

The accepted St Andrews wisdom suggests that bunkers were at one time mere excavations made by sheep in search of shelter. Their urine killed grass, creating sandy waste in the process. With increased scraping, the size expanded literally to the point of being suitable temporary accommodation. Some bunkers were so deeply scraped they housed a small flock. *Voilà*, a bunker. Another theory is that divot marks, left vacant by players, were expanded over time by wind and rain. Yet another suggestion: some may have been formed by visitors to the beach, digging for shells prior to the sea receding.

In some cases, keepers of the green were pro-active – noting the difficulty of divot repair, where due to undulations, golf balls tended to pool time after time. A greenkeepers nightmare arose. The turf around this commonly pooled area would never get a chance to recover and so they reasoned, 'why bother – let's put in a bunker?' This, of course, relates to the man-made bunkers. The belief held in some quarters, that bunker formation was a result of war-time bombing or UFO activity, is quaint but highly fanciful. Royal Dornoch gives a portion of the credit for its bunkers to its cows.

Hell bunker at St Andrews Old

AN UNDERESTIMATED ELEMENT of links bunkering is the influence of the fairway undulations. Innocent on first sighting, they assist countless times in your ball's capture. By way of comparison, when playing inland golf, your ball generally has to be heading straight for sand to end there. Not so with many links – a ball in the general vicinity of the bunker line will often slew into a nasty trap, due to the feeding nature of the terrain. This further demonstrates the requirement for precise shot-making and judgement. Perhaps it is this very undulation which is the gift to links golf that first encouraged sheep to head towards the hollow depressions?

Today, golf clubs are collectively paying architects a king's ransom to redesign their own cherished holes – essentially bringing the bunkers back into play after an era of dormancy. My argument is not with architects as they merely respond to the call. I do object, however, to those who believe that every time a newer and fancier rare earth shaft material is discovered it must automatically initiate a course upgrade. Cause for celebration? I think not. It will put your playing fees up to pay for the redesign while intricate shot values are left as memories. Surely it is time to pause with these breakthroughs. Many courses lack both space and money to simply move tees back another twenty paces with each new discovery. The amount of classic links bunkers made redundant in the name of progress are too numerous to mention.

One, however, requires comment: Hell bunker. Today, golfers fly their ball over Hell like they can really play the game. Recently, two of us were on the front edge of this par five in two, while the others were within twenty metres of the green. Regrettably and all too frequently, Hell bunker is being reduced to a museum piece.

With Gene Sarazen's invention of the sand wedge, sand play guesswork has been largely removed. In modern hands and in response to pleas for perfect sand and texture, it is easy for the top notches to extricate themselves from most sand situations. In fact, they readily agree that under certain conditions, green-side bunkers are squarely aimed at; a far safer option than green-side rough. The severity of the US Open highlights this fact each year. Players work overtime in assessing how to make their ball land in bunkers should they miss the greens. Similarly these days, any fairway bunker devoid of a threatening lip poses only curiosity value to the advanced golfer.

Big Bertha bunker at Royal Portrush. Drives that veer to the right will find this 17th hole hazard

There is a simple but interesting story behind the bunkers that fortify the Postage Stamp hole at Royal Troon. At one time, the entire green was a large sandhill. It was flattened to what you see today, while the base was retained as flanking bunkers. Ingeniously, the teeing ground owes much to a similar levelling. At only 123 yards and often a mere flick, the hole requires protection. It receives this in two ways; firstly there is the very narrowness of the green and secondly, the remnants of the sandhill – should you come up short, push or pull your tee-shot. During Greg Norman's 4th round rampage in 1989, this seemingly innocent hole was responsible for halting his tilt. After six straight birdies and a par, the eighth hole (Postage Stamp) temporarily rattled him with a bogey – from sand.

An example of the punishing bunkers best avoided at Turnberry

OPPOSITE: Underclubbing or mishitting from the 11th tee at St Andrews Old will ensure a bogey four

Tommy Nakajimi has ensured his everlasting fame as a result of an encounter with Road bunker at St Andrews Old. This small indentation of links land, where natural slopes lure the ball towards it, has most likely terminated more good rounds than any other hazard in golf. Unlike other hazards, people experience anticipatory anxiety, not just early on in the round, waiting for the confrontation, but in speaking with golfers – months in advance. Is it any wonder it has such a hold. Despite being bracketed with Aoki and Osaki among Japan's best ever players, try as we may, we can only remember poor Nakajima splashing away during the 1978 Open Championship – on the putting surface in two, putting into the bunker and eventually recording a five over par nine. Brian Barnes, the genial pipe-smoking Scot putted into Road bunker as well. And there were others.

The riddle of the Road hole is easy enough to conquer in print, but more problematic during the heat of battle. How would you like your poison, the Old Course asks? Do you prefer instant death by avoiding the bunker but making an excursion on to the Road itself? Or is it to be a surprise outcome, where you purposefully avoid the Road but find the Road bunker? Finding a lucky lie and escaping is possible but most likely while in the vicinity, you will gain a little bunker practice and partake in trial by ordeal. Middle tees and a following wind can reduce the 17th hole to a short iron approach for powerful players, but usually the requirement is a medium-to-long iron. At times, golfers will raise their standard to find the putting surface on the Road Hole. After such fine tee-to-green playing, imagine the twisted feeling to then putt straight into Road bunker? It happens regularly enough, due to the prospects of a four and the intricacies of the green's slopes – not necessarily from a poor putt.

BIG BERTHA — NOW THERE'S A NAME. This massive bunker appears seemingly from the clouds, on the 17th hole at Royal Portrush. Is it sponsored by the Calloway organisation? One of the largest and deepest bunkers in links golf, it catches your drive if you happen to stray to the right. When finding this bunker, priorities must only be set towards getting out; you could stay in the chasm for an eternity. Home professional, Dai Stevenson, understands the talking point nature of the landmark and has printed it on to his laminated business card.

The best group of bunkers? Thankfully, as this is not a ratings style book, I am spared having to nominate. However, any links bunkering – either singular or grouped need only produce a dose of mental torment or wariness in the golfer's psyche to succeed in the purpose. Classic bunkering may or may not be aesthetically pleasing, but in all cases, a touch of intimidation will be apparent. The bunkers at St Andrews Old are superb and owe much of their bedevilment to canny placement. Many fine judges feel Turnberry's bunkers take a good deal of beating. The collection at Royal St

Bunkering designed to protect the dog-leg at Royal Dornoch's 17th hole

George's is impressive as are those at Royal Lytham and St Anne's. Ask any golfer's opinion who has played Muirfield, on its bunkering – 'first class', invariably is the response.

A marvellous group of sandy hazards lurk at Royal County Down Golf Club. As if shaped by the artist's eye, they are a grand mix of shallow and steep gradients with lips overgrown with fescue, whins and heather. Their strategic positioning is notable, and they do give off the appearance of being utterly natural. Several of these County Down bunkers have spouts, that could adequately pass for the pouring lip of a gigantic jug.

My caddie at Royal County Down, Jerry Tarade, taught me many things during our rounds together, some of which are better not disclosed. But he had a gift with bunkers and seemed in some mystical way to be connected with them. How he combed the bunkers for lost balls was masterful. As visitors, we dived in hands first, trying to separate the vegetation and spot the ball. 'Leave it me boys', he said picking up the rake and attacking the bunkers' outer edges with fists of fury. I could not help thinking that Jerry was like a garrulous barber in the company of a long-haired, spotty youth.

Welcome to Royal Dornock Sean. The result of this slightly pushed opening tee-shot requires a solid stance and a keen sense of humour

Links bunkering can be harsh on golfers, indeed it should be harsh. Pat Ruddy offered a very matter-of-fact opinion: 'Don't complain that they are unfair, they are not meant as pleasure beaches. They are places of penance. Why have them if they do not punish?' [14]

In truth, finding their clutches – hitting out backwards and sideways on occasion, serves only to remind us that our

game needs attention or maybe we were victimised by the bounce. In many instances though, the 'finger can be pointed' at poor club selection or dubious course strategy.

For those who may have developed a sand phobia, it is worth mentioning that there are many notable links holes where not a single bunker exists. The 1st and 18th at St Andrews Old are stealthfully protected in other ways; namely the Swilcan burn and Valley of Sin. At Ballybunion Old, the multi-tiered 11th fairway is supported by the hugging coastline, rough and dunes. One of my favourite links holes remains the strategic 14th hole (Foxy) at Royal Dornoch. This bunkerless double dog-leg hole swings firstly leftward and then around a large dune, culminating in a typically raised Dornoch green. It has never failed to elicit praise from golfers who play over the famous old northern links.

A delightfully natural burn at
Machrihanish – emanating from
the sea and bound for the links

CHAPTER SIX

Meandering Serpents – the wee burns

The true Scotsman may be a little sensitive in supporting his links heritage, but a sure way of offending him is to declare that your ball has landed in a pond, lake or creek. Utterances of the word stream may also arouse his ire. While these terms maintain their validity on the inland variety of golf course, they are misnomers as far as links terminology goes.

Burns or wee burns as the Scots affectionately refer to them, belong, along with bunkering, undulation, vegetation and the elements, as front-line defences mounted against the golfer. The proud Scot basks in their glories, but many visitors' utterances about them are unprintable. Eminent architect, Alister MacKenzie, was fond of an old story concerning player attitudes to them. A golfer visiting one of Scotland's well known links asked his caddie what the locals felt about all these burns running through the links? The caddie replied, 'Weel noo, we have an old Scottish major here, who when he gets over it, says, "Weel ower the bonnie wee burn laddie" but when he gets into it, says, "Pick ma ball oot o' thot dommed sewer".'[15]

Prestwick's Pow burn being re-channelled

Resembling meandering serpents, the burns wind insidiously this way and that, and, in accordance with many things natural, are asymmetrical. Emanating from the sea and bound for the links, these watery trenches confront the golfer as either completely untouched ditches, or as is frequently the case, fortified by man. This may be done by reinforcing them with concrete walls, stone surroundings, railway sleepers or corrugated iron supports. If the burns are damaged by storms, they may need re-channelling by the ground staff.

Nature, in all its wonderful and mysterious ways, has never made burns a mandatory feature of links. True, most have them, but several of the greatest do not. Muirfield does not, nor does

Man-made water hazard — 17th hole at Royal County Down

Royal Lytham and St Anne's or Royal County Down. But hang on, you ask. What about the 17th fairway at this magnificent Irish links? Well, that rather sad looking pond has caused much discussion and personally, I think it is the only aspect of the entire links not geared towards spectacular review. Among natural environs, the man-made pond looks totally misplaced. Royal Birkdale is an interesting case — water on several holes yet no burns arising from either estuary or sea. Their members seldom complain that it comes less into play than at other links.

DESPITE MOST BURNS BEING NARROW, they can exert a huge influence over the negotiation of a golf hole. At St Andrews Old, for instance, your opening tee-shot club selection and subsequent line is directly related to safe clearance of Swilcan burn and the pin position of the day. In keeping with the British tradition of naming holes, the first hole at St Andrews Old is appropriately named Burn. The most recognisable burn in golf begins its journey in St Andrews Bay and culminates abruptly near the road in front of the 18th tee. It has claimed many scalps over the years, but coming, as it does, at the start, there is time to recover should misadventure strike. Sadly in the 1984 Open Championship, Ian Baker-Finch did not recover. Co-leading at the time with Watson, his ball landed a few feet on the green, but strangely, spun back into the burn — an unusual feat given the crustiness of that portion of green. He, like everyone else was totally dumbfounded by the incident. Rumour had it that someone unwittingly watered the part nearest the burn, but this is all supposition and rub of the green stuff. Despite a late round surge, Baker-Finch finished well down the list.

During the same Open, the amount of approach shots landing short of Swilcan, then jumping over it, was amazing. Still, the green has been driven several times over the last hundred years so this act of good fortune is not surprising from time to time. Those who fail to negotiate Swilcan, face the additional strain of a delicate pitch over the same territory, once your ball has been fished out. A front pin position compounds the difficulty, especially if played from a typically tight links lie.

Considering the massive expanse of green that lies beyond Swilcan, you feel silly for having ended up in water (assuming benign or following wind conditions). But when encountering a lashing in your face, pitching clubs are dispensed for much longer irons and woods. Notwithstanding the inevitable nerves that playing at the home of golf can produce, the burn is frequently visited for an entirely different reason. Unusually for the Old Course, both green and fairway are at the same level, appearing indistinguishable – in essence, giving rise to dead ground and confusion with club selection.

Turnberry's 16th hole on its outstanding Ailsa Course is known as Wee Burn on the card, but is colloquially referred to as Wilson's burn. At only 409 yards, it could, save for the burn, lay claim to being a birdie hole. Into any wind though, forget such foolishness. Wilson's burn is very much a different species from Swilcan at St Andrews. It cuts a swathe through a deep-sided ravine and your ball can be claimed in four ways: by rolling into the burn, landing outright in it, landing over the burn but short of the green then running back down the steep slope, or lastly, by clearing everything but spinning backwards from the tilting apron of the green.

Constant exposure has Swilcan deeply etched into our minds, but Wilson's burn is really a more daunting prospect. The green's surface is considerably smaller than at St Andrews and the demonic ravine seems to stare at the golfer during preparation for your approach. To further distract the golfer's eye, a bridge lurks ominously on the right side of the green. Another point of differentiation, Swilcan need never be carried from rough. On the other hand, Turnberry's 16th fairway may be bordered with deep rough during the Open Championship, making the lay-up a very sensible option.

If you discount the tiny carry off the 18th tee, only once does Swilcan exert any influence. By contrast, Wilson's burn gets into the act three times. Initially, it frustrates the high handicap golfer when driving from the 7th, then winds onto the 16th hole as described, and finally its passage culminates on Turnberry's other links, Arran. By coincidence, this is also the 16th hole (Lea Rig) but being well away from the green, poses more of a fairway challenge.

When nature provided links land as ready-made for golf, little was known of the economic advantages of utilising natural water hazards. But they have proved to be so beneficial. By the sea, burns often double-up or triple-up to act as hazards on other holes — one section may come into play on the inward nine, another bend may confront you on the outward half. Whereas water hazards on inland golf courses are usually incorporated specifically to strengthen the challenge of that hole in particular.

On the opposite side of Scotland, Carnoustie's strenuous finish owes much to the presence of Barry burn and the way it dominates the whole landscape. At every Carnoustie Open this burn has never failed to influence the outcome. Gary Player, for

A side view of Wilson's burn — 16th hole at Ailsa Course, Turnberry

Barry burn guards the front of
Carnoustie's 18th green

example, displayed an almost paranoid stance here in winning the 1968 Open Championship. So desperate was he to avoid Barry, he taunted the 525-yard par five 18th hole with three seven irons — each time carrying a different section of the hazard. The hole has since been reduced to a long par four and become even more burdensome.

Carnoustie's 17th hole, known as Island, is notorious for testing a golfer's shot-making and club selection under pressure. Depending on wind direction and strength, there are several confusing ways of playing it. Dubbed Island for good reason, you must drive out onto a sort of island in between the bends of Barry burn. If you drive too far, or stray too far to the right, you will be in the burn. However, overly conservative golfers who choose to lay-up excessively will not get home in regulation figures. As burns go, Barry is a work of art — the most renovated and manicured you will encounter.

The same burn looms large on Carnoustie's 18th hole. It places the right-handed hooker on notice, as does the out of bounds fence. Barry then crosses the fairway, 30 m (33 yd) or so in front of the green. When playing downwind, this portion of burn causes little grief, but into anything stronger than a gentle headwind, it can require a super-human effort to carry the hazard.

The closing stages of the 1975 Open Championship are worth retelling, for Barry is never more threatening than in the context of championship conditions. Feeling he needed two pars to win, Jack Newton drove off the 17th tee with a long iron — no doubt to lay up. By forcing the shot, his ball was pushed badly, missing the clutches of Barry by inches. Standing awkwardly with his right foot balanced precariously on corrugated iron, it was a miracle Newton did not topple backwards into Barry. He managed to hack a mid-iron towards the green and then his punched nine iron found the target. Newton subsequently bogied the hole.

South African golfer, Bobby Cole, who triumphed nine years earlier at Carnoustie in the Amateur Championship, was in a position to challenge. Leading after three rounds, he came to the 17th, requiring two pars for a play-off. In an attacking mood, Cole slashed a wood from the tee, but he too was wayward. He narrowly avoided the burn and was greeted by a shocking lie on the steep bank of Barry. A commentator of the day suggested his fairway lie resembled an aeroplane taking off. Attempting a most ambitious three wood, Cole's ball squirted along the ground, well short and right of the green. Like Newton, Cole also bogied the hole.

Earlier, and playing in front of Cole and Newton, a young Tom Watson was displaying the temperament that was to stand him in good stead for the next twenty years. After a safe drive onto the Island, he produced a magnificent three wood that finished 6.5 m (20 ft) from the hole, sealing his par and picking up a stroke on the leaders. Johnny Miller, playing with Watson, and just one from the lead, bogied the hole by badly under-clubbing his approach.

Running in the opposite direction meant that the 18th on the final day was playing downwind. Hypervigilant at avoiding Barry, Miller pushed his tee-shot into a bunker, and on his first attempt, left it in. The body language from the crest-fallen Californian suggested a shattered golfer. He pulled his next shot just left of the green and from here, he nearly chipped in but it was one too many.

Miller waited only one year to atone for this disappointment – he won at Royal Birkdale in 1976 when his greater experience proved too good for the precocious talent of Sev Ballesteros. But Miller did not leave Carnoustie empty-handed. The bunker flanking the 18th fairway where his hopes were dashed has since been named Miller's bunker.

Like a meandering serpent, Barry burn wends its way around Carnoustie. This photo shows the 17th hole. In 1953, Ben Hogan referred to Carnoustie as 'burn happy'

Watson meanwhile, following a cracking drive on the 18th, and after his ritualistic brisk waggling, hit a short iron into holeable territory and made his birdie. The list of Open Champions at Carnoustie to date had been impressive – Tommy Armour, Henry Cotton, Ben Hogan, Gary Player – and yet a finish displaying this brand of courage and aggression was noteworthy.

Newton, needing a birdie to win, found the 18th green in two, albeit a long way from the cup. In the end, he holed a gut-wrenching three footer to make the play-off. Cole's makeable birdie putt slid by, as did his chances to join the play-off and a rare opportunity of achieving the Double: the Amateur and Open Championships on the same links. Tom Watson went on to win the play-off, 71–72. Again, the final two holes settled the contest. Watson recorded par-par in the presence of Barry, as opposed to Newton, par-bogey.

Twenty-four years later at Carnoustie, there had been changes: a magnificent modern club house had been erected, the links had been further lengthened and the entrances and surrounds to greens had been tightened and modified. However, there was no lessening of the influence of Barry during the 1999 Open Championship. Consider how three of the four leading players coped with the final hurdle. Justin Leonard, playing in front of Parry and Van De Velde, was two shots behind at the time, and realistically needed at least a birdie to tie. Despite a poor lie in the left-hand rough, he brandished a fairway wood and duly found Barry burn. Little could he have envisaged that a par would have won the tournament outright.

FOLLOWING A WAYWARD DRIVE Jean van de Velde did the sensible thing knowing that his worst case scenario was being either short of Barry in long grass, or in Barry itself. Cruel was his fate for his second shot was sufficiently long enough to take trouble out of play, but by ricocheting off the side of the grandstand, landing on the stone section of Barry, and then rebounding 30 m (33 yd) backwards, he found the very territory he had attempted to avoid. Appearing to decelerate on his next shot, Van De Velde's ball came to rest in the water. The remainder of his saga is too painful to go through in detail.

Let none of this take anything away from one of Scotland's favourite golfing sons, Paul Lawrie. To finish the Open Championship in 67 strokes is some achievement, as was his astonishing birdie-birdie finish on the 17th and 18th holes of the play-off. But it is worth remembering how he got into the play-off in the first place. Needing a finishing par to be club house leader, Lawrie's approach landed well short of the burn, and as providence would have it, his ball jumped the burn and skipped into the left-hand green-side bunker. A beautifully played splash, a bold putt and par was safe. But surely with Van De Velde and Parry on the 11th green at the time, their lead of 3–4 strokes would be too great? If not, Leonard was poised to take advantage. Well, none of this eventuated, and what a proud moment it was for the traditionally minded Scots, when one of their own prevailed on the toughest of all links. There is no fluke about Lawrie's play: the Ryder Cup only a few months later, confirmed the class of this golfing latecomer.

On the other side of Scotland at Royal Troon, Gyaws burn crosses the third fairway. Being a short par four, it adds protection to an otherwise innocent hole; the lay-up making its length a bigger issue than the card suggests. From the tee, it can barely be distinguished from the fairway and many first timers drive into it – unaccustomed to the fast running links game and the premium on judgement. Wise counsel from a good caddie can justify half their fee right here.

On double duty, the same burn traverses the par five 16th and promotes much second-guessing from the tee. Fortunate golfers with length at their command, attempt to get as close as possible to

This highly soothing photo was taken at Dingle Golf Club (Ceann Sibeal) in Ballyferriter, Co Kerry, Ireland. The Blasket Islands lie proudly in the Atlantic Ocean (all photographs in this section reproduced with the special permission of Michael Diggin)

The goats at Lahinch have long
been a curiosity for newcomers to
links golf. Inside the clubhouse,
an old barometer has lost its
weather-forecasting hands; the
wording, 'see goats' has taken
their place

ABOVE: The majestic 8th hole at Tralee, Ireland

LEFT: The wildly undulating 13th green at Dooks, Ireland. It is affectionately known as 'The Saucer', where four putting is a common occurrence

OPPOSITE: This photo shows the view from the 17th tee at Ballybunion Old. The right-handed golfer will do well to play for a draw. A hook, however, will finish in deep trouble among dunes and rough

ABOVE: More evidence of the splendour of Ballybunion Old. Many people rate the 11th hole, known as 'Herbert's Fancy', among the finest par fours in the world

Named 'The Gabions', the par three 15th hole at Ballybunion Old is outstanding and universally admired

Everyone who plays at Dooks Golf Club, Co Kerry, Ireland, enthuses about the peaceful scenery and overall golfing experience. This photo depicts the 8th green and dark furze in the foreground, plus Dingle Bay in the background

An aerial view of Waterville Golf
Club, Co Kerry, Ireland

Pow burn at Prestwick — looking back down the 4th fairway and towards the 3rd green. Braid's bunker is visible

it, and in a favourable wind, go for the green. A good strategic links hole, those who lay-up off the tee will usually attain par figures with straight hitting. But Greg Norman was not content with nursing. During the final round of the 1989 Open Championship and after a safe throttled back tee-shot, Norman hit a towering driver onto the heart of the green and birdied, en route to a closing 64.

Fifteen minutes away from Royal Troon lies famous Prestwick, a links where a celebrated burn known as Pow lies in residence. It was not always a major hazard — only when the links was upgraded from the original 12-hole circuit to its present 18. Pow burn first terrorises the jittery slicer on the tee of the par five 3rd, a great links hole known as Cardinal. A dog-leg hole to the right, the slicer must ponder the possibilities of finding it again with his second shot. Beautifully positioned, Pow follows the hole for its entire trip.

For many golfers, the presence of Pow burn on the 4th hole (another dog-leg to the right) changes the talk from possible capture on the 3rd, to probable on this tee-shot. For those prone to fits of slicing, it signals that little voice inside to get active, as does the effect of a brilliantly conceived bunker by James Braid. The hole is not especially narrow, unlike Prestwick's 15th, but it does tempt the greedy to drive close to the burn and steal distance. The golfer, who can apply this with any certainty, is of the champion class; if you try and fail you cannot help looking reckless.

At the European Club in Ireland, owner Pat Ruddy's philosophy on his treatment of water is both fascinating and frank:

Bluidy burn at Cruden Bay
(6th hole)

Water — what fun. We have a nice strong stream about 4-m (12-ft) wide running along the left hand edge of our par three sixth hole and along the right edge and I mean the very edge of our par four 7th hole. The beach is in play on holes 12 and 13. The 15th green was lifted up 1 m (3 ft) and out (15 yd) onto the very edge of a cliff and a lot of balls now trundle over that one and into the sea. All good fun. But when they come to the 18th, a few American purists throw their hands up in the air. When they find an old swamp cleaned up into a small lake in front of and to the left of the green, 'There should be no water on a links', they cry, having just passed by, without demur, our other water hazards.

'Where was the first water hazard in golf?' I ask them (having unfortunately, let two years supply of these fellows through before I thought of the answer). They fall silent and wait for the answer. 'On the very first hole at St Andrews Old itself', I tell them, and then the debate gets really hot. 'Okay, I agree, I will fill in my lake whenever they fill in the Swilcan burn at St Andrews, or the Barry burn at Carnoustie — both converted sewers for God's sake — or the Wee burn at Turnberry or the Suez Canal at Royal St George's.' And I mean it, because the shot over water has become one of the most wonderful shots in the game and a course without at least one of these lacks something just as much as does the course without a bunker; and when it comes to a really strong finishing hole, when the bets are on the line, water is at its most delightfully pernicious.[16]

THERE ARE TOO MANY FAMOUS OLD BURNS to describe in detail — you could write a separate book on them. But for those unafraid of encountering water hazards, try the remote and greatly underrated Southerness links in Scotland. It has burns on the 5th, 6th, 7th, 11th and 15th. Lundin Links is another with no shortage of burns, and its neighbour, Leven Links, has an 18th hole that prompts comparisons with Carnoustie's. Being over 400 m and frequently played into the wind, Scoonie burn can only be cleared with a wood or long iron. During winter, there are few tougher finishing holes in links golf.

Eil burn must be safely negotiated at North Berwick's 7th hole and Cruden Bay's glorious Bluidy burn on the 6th needs little translation. It positively makes the hole and has remained a vital feature, despite advancements in technology. Dunbar's interesting and wide-mouthed 6th hole burn, Broxburn, has captured many, as has a huge burn, Rubicon, which patrols the front of the 1st green at Deal. Sometimes likened to Swilcan at St Andrews Old, it differs by allowing more leniency in regard to ground between burn and green.

Few issues surrounding the traditions of links golf have the capacity to arouse such heated debate as the presence of water on a links; be it natural, converted or contrived. To many enthusiasts, any water that emanates from the sea is bona fide. Incorporating prudent usage of rivers, estuaries, natural running streams and inter-tidal marshes also meets with widespread approval. Invariably, this is because important architectural considerations are made due to the existence of water, not so that preconceived notions can be acted upon after water has been included. Those who advocate artificially placed water on a links suggest it is a modernism designed to enhance the skill requirement and progress golf into the next century. Be your own judge.

The Machrie Hotel and Golf Links, Isle of Islay, is a delightful and uncrowded links. In Scotland, though, a burn is never far away. This photo shows the 2nd fairway and its troublesome burn, with the hotel and lodges in background

BELOW: Dunbar's distinctive burn — Broxburn (6th hole)

A worm's eye view of Klondyke –
left–hand side of 5th fairway and
hill at Lahinch

CHAPTER SEVEN

Traditional blind shots

In many respects, inland golf courses and seaside links are as foreign as chalk and cheese. One marked difference lies with the prevalence of blind golf at the older links centres. The occasional blind shot will be tolerated when inland, but no more, mind you, for underpinning the whole experience is an expectation that everything be neat and perfect – predictable golf is sought, a minimum of surprises, and definitely no bad bounces to stir up the reflux. A poor lie on the fairway provides a ready-made excuse for the next shot. The great shame of this prevailing attitude is that golfers fail to grasp the true adversarial meaning of the game. But when it comes to links golf, by and large, links are neither fair nor unfair – they just are. Ardent links golfers are more tolerant of things beyond their control, and understand that blind golf is character building and only bolsters the challenge.

Too many golfers short-change themselves in the pleasure stakes by harbouring a dislike for blind golf. Last century, a golfer with a low tolerance of this prominent early links feature, must constantly have thought of giving up the wretched game. These shot-making challenges were as common and integral to the links game then as long carries over bunkers and water hazards are to the inland variety today. One teasing question is worth pondering though, had mechanisation in the form of bulldozers been discovered during the golden era of links golf, would these blind holes have survived?

Today, architects must tread on eggshells when contemplating the design of a blind tee-shot – they could be lynched for the mere suggestion. As time passed, golfers began to lose touch with the sporty element of golf and at the same time, the amount of blind shots being included in architects' new designs began to wane. Consequently, this particular links feature has been much reduced by way of removal or modification. But who was influencing whom? Interestingly, even some architects of note were quick to lead the chorus of doing away with all semblance of blindness.

Two famous blind holes at Royal St George's have suffered at the hand of the scalpel – Sahara and Maiden. At Burnham and Berrow, there are remnants of blind golf today, but at one stage, this feature was present throughout the entire links.

View from the 5th tee of Prestwick's Himalaya hole. The aiming point is a small white disc on top of the hill, centre-left in photo

'No man is an island' is a reasonable truism, but not in the case of Ireland's Eddie Hackett. This prolific links architect, revered as a saint in Ireland (and rightly so), shunned overseas opportunities for fame and wealth, preferring to ply his trade with native Irish links land. It has been no coincidence that in his layouts, blindness has been either totally removed or greatly minimised. One, however, at Ceann Sibeal was spared and even now continues to receive much comment. It also gives an insight into the architect's justification for the occasional blind element. The hole in question is the 10th — uphill and nearly 200 yards over an intimidating expanse of rough. Hard enough, you may say, but even harder considering that the green slopes alarmingly from front to back and is blind from the tee. Given Hackett's well-known dislike for blind holes, it was only natural that he would be queried. Said Hackett in response to the question of fairness, 'It is what was there, you see'.[17]

Another Irish architect to endorse Eddie Hackett's philosophy of minimal blindness is Pat Ruddy, owner, designer and president of the European Club, Brittas Bay. He passed on his thoughts to me:

> I have never been an admirer of blind shots and believe that the old masters would not have tolerated these, if they had modern machinery available to do an occasional nip or tuck. Or if 'Old' Tom Morris had spent more than the one day he did at Royal County Down, for example. I would love to see Jack Nicklaus trying to collect his $1.5 million fee for that one.
>
> While loving links golf, I have never been one to justify some of the nonsensical things left behind by men who were in a hurry in the good old days. I don't like windows without glass, toilets without water or going out to fetch the coal either. So, at the European Club, we can see tee-to-green on fifteen holes. On the remaining holes, you see your fairway target, and following a half decent drive by an eighteen handicapper, you will see your second shot target.[18]

A close-up, near the green view of Himalaya. Uphill and blind, a good caddie will insist upon an extra club or two. Note the wiry vegetation

ONE OF THE MOST FAMOUS of all blind holes, is the 5th at Prestwick. Himalaya is an uphill par three of 206 yards over a white disc. This is some hole — not quite the backbreaking challenge of yesterday, 'Brassies galore', but still a long-to-medium iron, depending on wind strength. Around the turn of the century, the massively inclined hill in front of the green was predominantly sandy, ensuring the blind recovery shot was a lottery for golfers. Today it has more or less grassed itself over — effectively reducing the penalty for a miscue or gross under-clubbing. Many of the early Himalaya photographs capture the caddie standing close by his master, quizzically pondering the chances of clearing the hill. But under a by-law of 1892:

> Players will make it a rule, before striking off, to send a caddie forward to the top of the ridge to signal when the party in front have left the green.[19]

The second shot to Prestwick's 17th hole is another fine example of why committees need second opinions before they bulldoze the blind holes. Over a gigantic hill, the finalising of many a famous match has culminated here with sound judgement. At 391 yards, the wind may dictate an approach shot with anything in your bag, but is usually a medium-iron of sorts. Golf balls that make it safely over the hill do not automatically find the green — there is the huge Sahara bunker to be cleared. Depending on your view of links golf, you will either love or hate this hole. Sadly for Prestwick, this type of excitement and other quirky antiquities led to the links being removed from the Open Championship rota. In fairness though, the links was also considered too short for the very best professionals.

No less famous are the two blind classics at Lahinch: Klondyke on the 5th and Dell on the 6th. This is links golf supreme, made famous by tiny white rocks perched on high ground to guide golfers on the correct line. The 5th hole is a short par five of 441 metres and, when played downwind, is easily reachable by medium-to-long hitters. The drive is of the arresting links variety, needing to be threaded through defining dunes. Balls that veer left tend to stay up on the hill, while those sprayed to the right will often feed back to the fairway. A small, white stone lies perched on the hill for second shot guidance, and any slightly thinned ball will surely not make it over — it can even plug into the hill. The hole would never be built today because of the potential legal trouble associated with blindness (the 18th tee-shot traverses Klondyke and raises the possibility of golfers getting hit).

ONE OF THE ANOMALIES of British links golf is the degree of empathy shown by club management in respect to blind golf. There are no hard and fast rules — tee-shots may or may not gain assistance from guide markers and the same can be said for approach play. Regardless, being resourceful and tapping into your intuition or caddie's advice is wise.

The par three 6th at Lahinch is precious to the members and viewed as a National Irish Monument. Totally blind, the green at Dell is surrounded by enormous banks on all sides — yet another testimony to the unsurpassed role and skill of nature itself. Only 142 metres and uphill, the green is hidden from view. Each morning, the greenkeeper climbs up the hill to move the white indicator stone in accordance with the pin position of the day. Were it not for the sandy soil, this type of green would easily be prone to flooding.

The blind holes of Lahinch have long been a talking point, yet over the years, a good deal of blindness has been removed through the levelling of its sandhills. In 1920, these sandhills played a part in saving the lives of Lahinch residents. The village was under attack and many of the town's houses were burned by the Black and Tans. An ambush followed, and one afternoon, four Royal Irish Constabulary officers were

A frequently discussed blind par three is Dell — 6th hole at Lahinch. Each morning, the greenkeeper climbs up the hill to change the white stone guide, in line with the new pin position

Named Dell for good reason, this is the view from behind and above the green

shot dead in the town of Rineen, close by Lahinch. Later in the evening, uniformed men made their way to Lahinch and terrorised the streets in motor lorries, hell bent on revenge and burning everything in sight. Many of the panic stricken locals fled to the safety of the sandhills nestled among the links, with children and household necessities in hand. What must have been a chilling night was spent under the moonlight.[20]

For many years, a much discussed and admired feature of Aberdovey links in Wales was their blind 4th hole, known as the Cader. The links has been redesigned three times since 1892, where Cader as a par three has ranged anywhere between 130–165 yards. To the members though, their precious 4th hole was always a sacred institution.

The hole embodied much of the pioneering links spirit – an uphill blind shot over a commanding sandhill with eye-catching sleepers rising above. The sleepers were more than mere intimidation; they assisted with stabilisation of the sandhill. Years later when they were removed, much of the hole's terror was lost, along with the hill.

In the heyday of Cader, the enterprising Colonel Ruck installed a clever device to avert the potential danger of a blind par three. Electricity was put to good use when in 1909 it powered a periscope apparatus on the teeing ground. At a glance, this showed whether the green was clear. If it was not, the apparatus showed DANGER. Upon the green becoming clear, the golfers pressed a button and the signal, ALL CLEAR was recorded. With that instruction, the players on the tee hit their blind shots and on reaching the green pressed the button to record DANGER to ensure their safety while putting.

Ruck's periscope was non-operational after 1913, chiefly because nobody could repair it once the device was damaged. Naturally, the sensible idea of installing a bell was mooted, but surprisingly, this was years away from adoption. Another periscope was erected in 1927 and remained until 1965 — the same year a bell warning system was introduced.[21]

You are hardly into your stride at Cruden Bay before driving blindly at the short par four 3rd hole. At only 286 yards (Medal tee) it proves that length does not the hole maketh. With trouble flanking both right and left, the fairway must be hit and, from there, a delightful heavily sloping punchbowl green awaits your short iron. The intrusive mound, just short and right of the green, does much to preserve the allure of this hole.

ONE OF THE THRILLS OF PLAYING CRUDEN BAY is its retention of early twentieth-century-style sportiness. Many experts have offered opinions, and much of this has been unsolicited, but in the main, the club has resisted tampering efforts. As a result, Lahinch, Prestwick and Cruden Bay exemplify what the term — old-fashioned links values — has come to symbolise. The lengthy uphill approach to the 14th (Foxy) is classically blind, where an errant shot can easily disturb golfers on the 15th tee — an even worse shot can finish right out of the links entirely.

Two intriguing par threes demonstrate this sporty Cruden Bay aspect. At 239 yards, the 15th hole (Blin Dunt) is such that your only assistance is a guide post perched high on the diagonal brow of the hill. If taken on face value this hole is too onerous to enjoy, but if your reference point is akin to the pioneering spirit of adventure, you will never play a more enjoyable hole.

Blin Dunt is thoroughly blind, but the following hole, Coffins, at 182 yards is nearly as much fun. Though more conventional, a slight glimpse of the top of the flagstick precludes it from being totally blind. Consecutive par threes of this calibre, interest and blindness are highly unusual.

There is a good deal of blindness at Ballybunion New and some have downgraded the links as a result. Ballybunion Old presents less of the feature, but many of the stirring shot-making challenges are partially blind. The uphill and narrow approach to the Old 18th green remains an exhilarating experience — the outcome of approach shots being delayed until peering over the brow of the hill. But in 1995 Tom Watson's architectural team effected a slight and well thought out modification. Cutting a notch from the Sahara enabled drives that split the fairway to gain some view of the green. It was always regrettable that, given the exciting nature of the hole, members inside the club house were blocked from viewing proceedings. Yet Tom Watson advised Ballybunion's administration that he had no intention of changing the character of the hole, merely adding to what was already present. Instead, to fix this, a

Aberdovey's famous Cader (the Chair) hole. Today, this 3rd hole has lost most of its nightmarish reputation but still requires a semi-blind shot that can be stretched to 173 yards. Ruck's periscope is not needed anymore. In the background lies Cader Idris, the largest mountain in the area

Blin Dunt — a totally blind par three at Cruden Bay requires an adventurous diagonal drive over the hill. Once finished putting, a bell is rung to signify all clear

The exciting uphill approach to the 18th hole at Ballybunion Old

small section was carved out of the hill between the green and club house. The front portion of the green is now visible. Ballybunion Old has always been a marvellous links but these and other subtle improvements have enhanced the famous destination.

Elie is generally thought of as a windswept and generously open links. But you would not think so, if your opening tee-shot were any indication. It requires a blind drive over a ridge — but not before gaining the starter's nod when his periscope convinces him of safety ahead.

One hole that epitomises the feel of blind golf is the frequently photographed 9th hole at Royal County Down. The tee-shot is again blind and having cleared the crest, the fairway drops off alarmingly, with the remainder of the hole being relatively flat. And yet, with all the pre-game build-up, many visitors express surprise at the generosity of the landing area (once safely away). Consensus is difficult, but this is one of the greatest and most cherished links holes. At the very least, it is among the most talked about.

Those who condemn blind golf may reflect upon its prevalence at Royal County Down — half a dozen or so tee-shots plus several long-iron approaches. The thought to ponder though, is how often these critics turn a blind eye to their pet hate when singing the praises of Royal County Down. It happens all the time.

Not uncommonly, a links hole will not need to be stamped blind to bear this feature — misplaced driving can bring it to life. A good example is the strategic 1st hole at Carnoustie. From the tee, the braw line is down the left-hand side and with adequate distance this opens up the view to the green appreciably. But in gaining this elusive sighting, Barry burn must be avoided, along with penalising

OPPOSITE: The awesome view from the 9th tee at Royal County Down. One of the most revered of all blind shots

OPPOSITE: Once over the crest of the hill, the splendid scenery of Royal County Down continues

1st green at Carnoustie, looking back down the fairway and catching a glimpse of the caddie who looks less than excited about the coming round

rough. By contrast, a similar length drive that is pushed to the right will leave the golfer with a totally blind approach over exacting terrain and a sandhill. The concept of blind golf following misplacement — now that is something even the non-conformists can embrace.

Clearly, golfers are evenly spread in their tolerance level of blind golf. Some as we know, down-right despair of the tradition, while others embrace the concept with childlike glee. Of the one hundred and sixty genuine links, it may interest you to know that around twenty have only two par fives on their layout. A coincidence perhaps? I doubt it. Finding links land that can extend for appproximately 550 yards amid undulating terrain that does not include blindness is difficult. This, in part, explains architects' dilemmas with routing issues. Among the great links this phenomenon applies to are: Royal Birkdale, Turnberry, St Andrews Old, Royal St George's, Royal Dornoch, Machrihanish, Montrose, The European Club, Prestwick, Cruden Bay and Carnoustie. At Brora, the 8th hole is their solitary par five.

A Good Walk

Michael Wolveridge

At some time in the eighties, during an inspired late afternoon stroll over the Old Links and walking home via Grannie Clarke's Wynd, I found myself overtaking an elderly gentleman wrapped up in a light tweed suit, coat and scarf and passed the time of day with him. He was pleasantly disposed towards me and turned out to be Laurie Auchterlonie, octogenarian and revered professional attached to the Royal and Ancient Golf Club, also the unofficial Keeper of the Green for St Andrews. What a piece of luck.

Strolling gently on, we chatted about the day and the courses as I explained my particular interest in the Links, whereupon he invited me to complete the short walk to his shop in North Street and join him for some tea.

Laurie Auchterlonie lived above his golf shop which also contained an impressive and precious gallery displaying old clubs, trophies and photographs, prints and paintings of ancient golf. It was a time when the golfing world was awakening fully to the importance of golfing memorabilia and Laurie was already in demand to appear on the speech circuit in the States, a chore he seemed to relish.

He was, of course, interested in golf architecture and listened patiently to some of my stories of golfing works in strange and far off lands. Time passed pleasantly and tea was replaced by something stronger. I had the ear of the great man and questioned him about the Old Course. I spoke of my partner in golf architecture, Peter Thomson, and his own early misgivings regarding some of the maintenance practices which had taken place on the Old Links over the years. This warmed Laurie up and he let fly. He spoke of the previous greenkeeper 'adopting ruinous maintenance policies for a links by fertilising and top-dressing with soil and peat and building the turf from the top. He had allowed greens to shrink to accommodate sprinkler coverage and over-watered excessively. Road bunker at the 17th green had been destroyed by refacing without first removing the old face and then realigning the bunker to face the fairway instead of the road as it used to'. Laurie was clearly no fan of 'that man from the South' and set off for the Scotch, for this was thirsty stuff indeed. 'The new mon knows what he is about. He's top-dressing with sand and blood and bone to restore the links turf quality. He's drastically cut back on the watering and goes back to the sand when refacing the bunkers.'

The 'new mon' was Walter Woods who had been at St Andrews for twelve years at the time. He consulted with Laurie Auchterlonie from time to time and was observed to be mowing the greens again to almost full size. It takes time to achieve the low cut but he was getting there. I asked Laurie how he would like to see the greens on the Old Course kept and he said at once that he would like to see them square again. I, who had learned to make an art form of a random, natural look for putting greens, was appalled at this pearl cast before me.

'Auch, no laddie, in the early days the finest turf was on the putting greens and this was achieved by placing a post at each corner of the greensite and running a wire between them to keep the sheep off and give rabbits free reign to mow and develop the velvet turf for putting. The sheep mowed the rest — it was a bonny arrangement. After mowers were invented, the course was hand-mowed by four greenkeepers to give the fastest and truest surfaces imaginable — any ball finishing beyond the flag on the 11th green needed the putter to be merely waved at it for the ball to stay above the whiskers which clumped just above Shell bunker at the bottom of the slope.'

I asked him about the whiskers and he agreed to take me out there the next day as it was getting on and his supper was being prepared. We met at his shop in North Street next day just after lunch and commenced our stroll. As we walked along the pathway beside the 17th fairway, he opened up. 'You know laddie, the early course was played in reverse to the existing layout and is still used at times during winter. The idea is to allow the approaches to greens to rest as they become "carry" areas for tee-shots played across them from the other direction. That is why there are so many bunkers that you may think are unnecessary and which, in the Reverse Course, suddenly come into play.' How very interesting.

Our perambulation had by now arrived alongside the 16th fairway and Laurie explained on the spot how the Principal's Nose bunkers were typical of the versatility of the Old Course, doing service being played from both directions. Laurie said he preferred the Reverse Course: 'More broken ground to play across and many greens like the 14th easier to play at as the slope favours the approach shot.' Sure enough, as we drew abreast of this famous green, there it was with the prospect of a much better approach shot played from the reverse side across broken ground containing small whins, tall fescues and heather to a green set beneath the large mound that today's golfers playing from the normal direction have to negotiate. I asked him how the Reverse Course worked at the start. 'The 1st tee was where it is now, the 17th green was the 1st green and the Road bunker was easily seen from the reverse side. The 2nd hole saw Cheape's bunker in play at the corner and the second shot was a pitch across more broken ground to the left side of the current 16th green, making an

excellent hole. On the 3rd, the Principal's Nose bunkers faced the player teeing from the left of the 2nd green and applied as they do from the current 16th, except the railway line was on the left or hook side.' And so our walk continued. We found a few whiskers at the 11th but they were far from the vexed place they used to be and long mowed out by modern machinery. The grand old man muttered into the wind. It seemed hours later that we came finally back to the Swilcan burn. 'The 18th tee was on the left of the 1st from that flat patch of rough over there and the hole played to the 18th green as is. The green needs to be enlarged still further to the left to take the green in front of the steps. Still, it is a good green and the only green to be devised and built by man on the Old Course. It was done by 'Old' Tom himself.'

We had arrived at Grannie Clarke's Wynd at last. Laurie was tired. There was no tea. The Royal and Ancient Keeper of the Green had completed another inspection of his famous links.

A sketch of the 11th hole at St Andrews Old by Michael Wolveridge

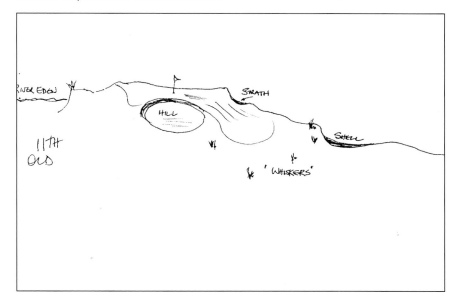

A caddie job well done, deserving
of a decent tip

CHAPTER EIGHT

The links caddie's lot

The introduction of the feathery ball in the early 1600s effectively ended the reign of the crude beechwood ball. As yet though, there were no professional golfers. The caddies assumed great importance on the golf scene – juggling the combined duties of dispensing professional tuition with their regular chores. Often these all-rounders were clubmakers as well. They understood the intricacies of golf and strode the links as if they owned them. A good number of caddies were inclined to believe this, some to the extent of sleeping on the links in sheltered enclaves and bunkers. The small matter of drink, no doubt, would have contributed.

Like most things in golf, the caddie has evolved from rudimentary beginnings. Originally, one of their duties was to build a tee from sand to match the individual requirements of the golfer. Try doing this yourself with dry sand, and you'll quickly appreciate the difficulty in caking it up to an adequate driving height. On the tee-boxes, many clubs provided wet sand but all too quickly, it dried out. Out of necessity and, as an example of self-sufficiency, caddies began wearing a container full of wet sand around their necks.

In the feathery era, ball production was laborious and thus, costly to golfers. To lose a ball was unthinkable and, not uncommonly, fines applied to caddies. To further reduce the incidence of lost balls, the forecaddie evolved. The aim was to station the forecaddie at the point where the drive would most likely finish. This great innovation served some important functions. First of all, it sped up play and who could complain about that. Secondly, the stitching of a feathery ball upon finding a water hazard would easily unravel under the influence of dampness – essentially making the ball useless. The forecaddie could quickly retrieve the ball, dry it and its viability was maintained. Another role for the forecaddie was the safety issue and placement on blind holes.

From time to time, a forecaddie would find himself distracted and be in danger of getting hit. When it appeared that the master's ball would strike the forecaddie, a loud shout of 'forecaddie' would resonate in his direction. Somewhat cumbersome, it was felt that harm could be averted by shortening the warning to 'fore', and as you know, this system is still in vogue.

CADDIES DO NOT RUN ERRANDS, but in the seventeenth century, certain people who hung about the streets of Edinburgh did so. Over time, the word caddie became synonymous with being a porter. Eventually, caddie became confined to purely golfing lexicon as someone who carried clubs but not necessarily fetched. In this connection, Robert Browning's *History of Golf* retells a famous caddie retort after the golfer discovered he had left his jacket in the club house and wanted the caddie to go back for it, 'Go back for it yersel. I'm paid to carry — no to fetch and carry'.[22]

The first account by name was of one Andrew Dickson who caddied for the Duke of York (afterwards James II) in 1681 and 1682 when a respite from the stresses of court was required.[23]

There is much speculation that this is the same Andrew Dickson who was honoured in Mathison's classic poem, *The Goff*, published in 1743. As golf book collectors know, it continues to be the grand prize in any serious collection. A caddie, alas unnamed, found his way into the household accounts of the great Marquess of Montrose in 1628 and similarly, a recording of 4 shillings against the accounts of Sir John Foulis, Ravelston in 1672 showed up 'for the boy who carried my clubs'.[24]

Prior to the formation of The Royal and Ancient Golf Club, the Code by which the Society of St Andrews golfers played, revealed a formalisation of caddies' tariffs in 1771. Should they perform caddie duties to the Hole o' Cross (13th hole), they would receive four pence and if proceeding further than this hole, six pence but no more. An old minute book records, 'Any of the gentlemen of this society transgressing this rule are to pay two pint bottles of claret at the first meeting they shall attend'.[25]

Around the middle of the nineteenth century gutta-percha as a malleable material was adapted for golf and the reign of the feathery ball was over. This coincided with an era of epic big money grudge matches. Each of the links, few in numbers as they were, had their own local champion. These demigods were elevated in status, and challenged the heroes of other Greens. The main venues were the links of Musselburgh, St Andrews, Prestwick and North Berwick.

Protagonists, Willie Park and Tom Morris Snr were perhaps the most notable contestants to hound each other, the usual stake being £100. The caddies would often introduce the players on the first tee, along with the need for 'keepin weel back off the greens and giein the players elby room'.[26]

By the late nineteenth century in Scotland, the employment of caddies, their conditions and general well being was being brought into question. They had nationally been allowed to run amok and skulduggery was the order of the day. Many clubs reported disharmony in the relationships between players and caddies, where at the bottom of matters, a good deal of mistrust was pervading. In 1890, the Royal and Ancient Golf Club on behalf of fifty or so golf clubs attempted to improve and formalise things by way of permanency and standards. One such inequity saw the St Andrews caddies being paid at a higher rate than at any other Green — apart from Musselburgh on the eastern side of Edinburgh.

It was not uncommon for St Andrean residents to employ their favoured caddie by the month. They fed, clothed and assisted them during the harsh winter months when pay opportunities were scarce. Unfortunately though, caddies gained a reputation with golfers for being ungrateful and abusing the relationship. The remedy lay in appointing what was probably the first ever caddie-master of sorts. The club employed Mr Nicholas Robb to sort things out. A highly respected man, he had been in retirement after 23 years service in the navy. Due to impeccable personal qualities, including citations for bravery and impressive testimonials, Mr Robb was viewed as the man to keep a reign on goings on. His duties included acting as hall porter, engaging caddies and paying them to look after members' clubs, keeping a register of caddies and generally keeping order among them in the vicinity of the club. Various tariffs were introduced and importantly, a benefit fund was instituted for the purposes of looking after invalided caddies or those who ran into strife. In addition, the Royal and Ancient Golf Club was invited to participate in the fund. Thereafter, their caddie donations and various grants were gratefully received. As a two-way deal, the new order suggested that caddies themselves would contribute to the fund, should they wish to avail themselves of the benefits at a later date. Finally and with slight modifications by the caddies, the scheme was adopted after consultation with both parties.[27]

ONE OF GOLF'S OLDEST TRADITIONS thrusts the St Andrews caddies into the spotlight once a year. Each autumn since 1806, the Captain-Elect of the Royal and Ancient Golf Club has driven himself into office, amid much pomp and pageantry. This involves heading down to the first tee, whereby the honorary professional tees up his ball and on the stroke of 8.00 a.m., a tiny cannon explodes into action — signalling the Captain-Elect to drive off. In no way a private affair, the townsfolk turn out to welcome the new Captain and line the 1st and 18th fairways. Past Captains and distinguished Royal and Ancient Golf Club members are in attendance, as are the caddies.

Part of the ceremony dictates that local caddies are strategically placed up and down the fairway, some short of Grannie Clark's Wynd (the road crossing the fairway) and others over it. The lucky caddie who retrieves the Captain's ball runs excitedly back to him and as tradition demands, receives a golden sovereign for his trouble. Gaining the edge, the truly astute caddie, will make it his business to observe the Captain's ability prior to the big day, and position himself accordingly on the fairway. In 1922 for instance, when the Duke of Windsor drove himself into office — writer Sir Guy Campbell noted that some of the caddies stood disloyally near the tee.[28] Gold sovereigns are in short supply now but the Royal and Ancient have managed to secure a supply that enables the tradition to continue. To commemorate the term of Harvey Douglas, who in 1996–97 became the first South African Captain of the Royal and Ancient, the successful caddie was presented with a golden Krugerrand.

During its formative years, Machrihanish Golf Club had much trouble with its caddies. As most of its members in the late 1800s lived in London, Glasgow, Edinburgh and overseas, it was their custom to play the distant and secluded links in high season. The demand for caddies in these few months was constant. In 1897, a caddies charter was drafted and, by all accord, had quite a pompous tone. A shelter was to be erected for them, payment of 9 pence a round and lunch: 6 pence for nine holes or ten shillings for a week's work. The charter contained a few other items that raised the hackles of the caddies, so much so they went on strike. For several days, they refused to carry and in the process earned the wrath of their superintendent.[29]

Sandy Munro was the superintendent's name and he enforced discipline in quite a bizarre manner. By carrying a dog whip and using it on the boys' bare legs, he ensured that arguments were few and far between. In time though, Sandy tendered his resignation and things settled down around the club again. Many of the striking caddies went on to become fine golfers and respectable characters upon reaching manhood.[30]

It is interesting how some reputations refuse to be shaken off, once legend takes hold. I refer to the dubious reputation which caddies down the ages have cultivated: hard drinking, hard living, humorous and at times sarcastic of their masters' abilities. But equally true are their less acknowledged qualities such as persistence and loyalty, the style of which was ably demonstrated by Fred Matsell of Hunstanton fame in the early twentieth century.

Fred was a village boy who began his caddying duties at age eight. By the ripe old age of twelve, he was a member of the ground staff. Each day, along with other village caddies, he would sprint along the tops of the cliffs where their aim was to intersect with golfers walking down from the railway station. 'The fastest runners got all the jobs', he recalled.[31] A natural born leader, Fred became spokesperson for the caddies, and on their behalf began asking for an extra penny per round. The club was embarrassed by this activity and put Fred on suspension. Refusing to accept the decision, he staged a clever protest. There was a public roadway by the first tee, and defiantly, he blew a bugle every time a golfer attempted to drive off (no doubt, he timed the act to coincide with that precious period, straight after the waggle). In a hastily convened meeting, the club secretary, realising that Fred was more trouble off the links than on it, cancelled his suspension.

Fred Matsell continued to be an identity around the links and in reform, became a loyal servant of the golf club. In 1915, the ex-caddie was appointed head greenkeeper and served his beloved Hunstanton links for over fifty years.

DURING THE GLORY DAYS OF HOYLAKE, a caddie by the name of Alexander Campbell plied his trade with great distinction. An exiled Scot, his presence on the links was unmistakable — slightly stooped, swarthy and grizzly. He developed a lifetime habit of wearing a heavy coat, come winter or high summer and his weather-beaten face was invariably covered in sweat. For nearly twenty-five years he faithfully carried the bag of a very good local golfer, Michael Pearson. Campbell was never one to refrain from counselling his master; an inseparable team, they could have been joined at the hip.

Members of Hoylake rarely if ever saw old Campbell's forehead — a dirty old cap saw to that, as did his black gypsy-type curls usually plastered down by sweat. Campbell was a friendly soul, whose greeting to members was constant. 'Arl the best Mr So-and-so, arl the best.'[32] During one period of club house reconstruction, a fondly remembered Hoylake golfer, 'Nobby' Roberts, said, 'I've just seen Campbell in Meols Drive en route to the station and, believe it or not, he's carrying one of the club house doors on his back'.[33]

During another period, the pleasurable Hoylake round was threatened by a plague of crows that delighted in stealing golf balls. On one festive morning alone, they swooped up twenty three balls as the golfers' cries of foul play mounted. The club's response was to erect a giant wire cage which had a very narrow entrance — just enough space to allow an inquisitive crow in, but difficult to retreat from. To entice them in, meat was strategically placed alongside a range of old golf balls. The bait was set. Strangely, not one crow was fooled by the scheme. Campbell, however, was sighted looking longingly at the old balls, conjuring up ways to fill up his ample pockets with them.[34]

He could not bear the thought of his spacious coat pockets being empty. At every opportunity he filled them with silver paper, cartons, string, tees, golf balls, odds 'n' sods and anything else found floating around the links. In this regard, he must have been a great friend to the ground crew. Deep within a pocket, it was not unusual to have a kipper, destined to be his evening meal.

For a short period, Campbell found himself as caddie-master. One day, the pro shop was closed during lunch, prompting a group of visiting South American golfers to approach him with, 'We need some new golf balls'. Said Campbell, 'Got no Dunlops, only 'effin Goblins'.[35]

Among caddies, the art of accurate club selection is a highly prized asset. Campbell was noted for this skill and he once assisted local champion, Allan Graham, in defeating Bobby Jones in the

Amateur Championship. On another occasion, Michael Pearson was faced with a long second shot to the home green and lent on Campbell for inspiration. 'Give it timber Mr Pearson, give it timber'.[36]

While caddying, he occasionally incorrectly called the outcome of Pearson's putts in midstream. Long putts, that to Campbell were obviously short, would be angrily muttered at, 'It it, it it'.[37] Pearson's putting style obviously imparted much top-spin and sometimes those putts, appearing to be short, would confound Campbell and roll into the cup. Then there was a deathly silence.

Campbell loved his craft and invariably direct opinions on golfing matters would be curt. To illustrate this, once Pearson was feeling rather pleased with himself for dispatching a naggingly difficult opponent in a match. Said Pearson, 'Well what about that, Campbell?' 'Aye', replied Campbell, 'But you shudder had the bracelets on 'im an hour ago'.[38] As an Open Championship venue, Hoylake was no stranger to big events. At one such tournament, Campbell's opinion was sought concerning a golfer reputed to be putting poorly, ''im, 'ee couldn't putt butter on bread'.[39]

Campbell wove himself into the fabric of club life and even the pro shop attendants had need for his services — filling his massive pockets with coins and asking Campbell to exchange them at the bank for a fiver. A natural wit, Campbell was once heard to observe after a slow day on the links. 'Been a bit slow sir, been a bit slow. Why, even the bloody worms wuz overtaking us down the seventeenth'.[40] Around Hoylake, the passing of Alexander Campbell was greatly mourned.

Cunning and wit are prerequisites for the links caddie — entrepreneurship, an added bonus, in promoting one's services. But sometimes, this attribute can get out of hand, as was the case with Snead's caddie at St Andrews Old in 1946. Not long after it became official that Snead had won the Open Championship, his caddie let loose his renowned charm. He presented a heartfelt case to Snead, as to why he, the caddie, should keep the winning ball and how it would be treasured all his remaining days. Acknowledged teasingly in many quarters as still having his original dollar note, Snead begrudgingly handed the ball over, obviously impressed by the boy's sincerity. The caddie promptly sold the ball for a princely sum.[41]

At Prestwick, genial Stan Craig related to me a story of a well known local caddie, Charlie. He was carrying clubs for a wealthy American and at the 5th hole (Himalaya), thrust the six iron into his hands and without a second glance, walked away. Charlie began loping away up the steep hill, seeking a vantage point to view the tee-shot outcome. When he was nearly half way to the hole, the American hollered out, 'Do you think I have enough club?' After a short pause and considering his age, Charlie yelled backed down to the tee, 'You'll be right ... just hit it harder'.

Strong evidence of the reliance
between club and rail connection
— 1st fairway at Prestwick

CHAPTER NINE

Paying a debt to the railway companies

Today we take travel by rail for granted. It goes overland seemingly forever and some cities like Singapore and London base much of their culture on the underground variety. But in the nineteenth century this new form of transportation revolutionised the way of communication, reduced emphasis on the horse and buggy and positively influenced the movement of goods. Postal services became more reliable and, like never before, populations took to travel – some for business, others for pleasure.

Beginning in 1840, a railway line operated by the Glasgow and South Western Railway Company linked Glasgow and the coastal town of Ayr. En route, it ran through Prestwick. For years afterwards, this opened up the Ayrshire coast, bustling with golf courses, and assisted the revenue of both towns and links. Barassie, Troon, Prestwick, Turnberry and Gailes were just some of the beneficiaries of the new technology. The company was quick to capitalise on, and to see the potential of, advertising such pursuits as the Eglington tournament and the Land of Burns.

In the 1800s, Ayrshire was a fashionable destination for Glasgow people, and many with poor health from living in industrialised cities made the journey in search of fresh air. Others sought the fine coastal beaches renowned for their sea-bathing. Various Glasgow golfing societies, keen to escape typically boggy inland courses, filled excursion trains to sample the firm textured and bouncy coastal links. Transfers were highly convenient due to the close proximity of stations to the golf links.

Few find time to reflect upon the influence of rail in popularising golf. By way of promotion today, many hotels advertise their wares as being 'Only ...minutes from ...golf course'. In the early days of rail, golf courses advertised themselves as 'Only ...minutes from ...station'.

The influence of rail extended beyond mere transportation. On many links throughout Great Britain and Ireland, railway lines serve as timely reminders where not to aim your golf ball. In earlier days, one could never be sure; some of the railway lines were deemed out of bounds, others were in play.

CRUDEN BAY GOLF CLUB has a grand story to tell, for their creation in 1899 by Tom Simpson under the supervision of Tom Morris Snr was the inspiration of a great rail man, the nineteenth Earl of Erroll (Chairman of the Great North of Scotland Railway Company). Highly influential, he cabled 'Old' Tom Morris to visit the Grampians and lay out a links. As a visionary, he foresaw Cruden Bay as a pioneer golf links and hotel complex – the first in Scotland. Aberdeen was already linked to London by rail and so the Earl felt that extending the line to Cruden Bay was routine enough. When the golfing eventually began, all were quick to praise the peaceful and inspiring rolling links land. Standing guard over the links was one of the most impressive hotels in Scotland with its stunning view of proceedings. The facilities were promoted by the golf club, hotel and rail company as 'the Brighton of the North'. Sadly though, within fifty years of its opening, the rail line had closed. The mansion-like hotel, known as the 'palace in the sandhills' was demolished, and the splendid golf links is all that remains today. Should you play here, you will leave feeling it is one of the finest and most interesting non-rota links in Britain.

The story of Turnberry's development reflects the best known example of effortless integration of railway, hotel and first-rate golfing facilities. In accord with the 1896 Light Railways Act, an application was made for permission to build a passenger and goods railway line along the Carrick coast between Ayr and Girvan. The line was designed to run by the village of Turnberry, where a luxury hotel was planned in conjunction with a championship style links. In 1899, rail construction got under way.

Without the enterprising work of the third Marquess of Ailsa, it is doubtful that Turnberry would have seen the light of day. Combining a busy life of landowning and a directorship in Glasgow and South Western Railway Company with a healthy golfing appetite, he recognised the potential of his privately owned land as classical terrain ready for golf purposes. Following the commissioning of the Troon professional, Willie Fernie, the links was laid out in 1901 and this enabled Turnberry Golf Club to be instituted in 1902. Within a short space of time, the Glasgow and South Western Railway Company took over the development of the golfing facilities, where the Marquess' directorship was a key factor in assisting negotiations.

In 1906, the scenic coastal line was completed, running from Ayr to Girvan specifically to service the needs of the new Railway Hotel at Turnberry. Despite the single track covering a mere nineteen and a half miles, it had taken an arduous four years to complete. In an orchestrated act, the railway line and Turnberry's hundred-bed hotel were both officially opened on the same day.

In 1926 British railway companies were amalgamated into four main groups. Turnberry became the property of London, Midland and Scottish Railway Group and fell under the direction of a very keen golfer, Arthur Tawle. He christened the two courses Ailsa and Arran and appointed James Macdonald as head professional.

The London, Midland and Scottish Railway Company felt confident that a combination of their own hotel and golfing facilities would ensure sizeable profits, but as since proven, golfers alone could not sustain their dreams. In 1930 amid an era of increasing competition from cars and buses, the passenger service from Alloway Junction to Turnberry was withdrawn, although the Turnberry to Girvan section remained open. For the affluent, this included a London–Turnberry sleeping car which was maintained in connection with the hotel and golf courses until 1942. All good things come to an end and the last Turnberry passenger train ran on 28 February 1942.[42] Turnberry today tends to be seen as the yardstick for this type of joint ambition between rail, course and hotel, but few realise that Cruden Bay was the first to succeed at this type of venture.

Golfers with a keen sense of history will be well aware that Prestwick hosted the first twelve Open Championships beginning in 1860. The progressive railway companies made this possible by providing the necessary transport for hordes of spectators. Many golf clubs collaborated with the various rail companies for this event. As an example, Prestwick advertised their Open Championship meeting of 1908 thus:

> The Railway Companies will issue First and Third Class tickets at a single fare and a quarter (min. charge 1s), to Prestwick, or Ayr, to competitors and certified members of golf clubs, on production of a certificate, which can be obtained from the secretaries of The Royal and Ancient, The Hon. Company of Edinburgh Golfers, Royal St George's, Royal Liverpool, Prestwick Golf Club and Cinque Ports. *April 1908.*[43]

Railroad companies were particularly active in Ireland competing heavily for the patronage of golfers. Northern Counties Railway Company, for example, offered free tickets to Royal Belfast golfers to visit the new links at Portrush. Upon its opening in 1888, the railway company did everything in its power to attract golfers, including changing timetables to suit and offering them reduced fares. Its generosity to fledgling golf clubs was well known and included transporting free of charge sods for greens to Greenisland Golf Club, a five-year grant to Larne Golf Club and financial aid to Portstewart Golf Club towards its first club house and links upgrade. Royal Portrush Golf Club, which lies on the Causeway coast, was leased by Northern Counties Railway Company from Lord Antrim right up until 1928.

The Great Northern Railway Company wasted no time in targeting its market, offering discount fares to travel south and play Royal Dublin Golf Club during its first competition. Showing great initiative, they took to sponsoring club events at Portmarnock, Sutton and County Lough Golf Clubs. The company also had close ties with Bundoran Golf Club, as recorded in the 1897 Sportsmans Holiday Guide, advertising the course as '19 hours from London via Kingstown'.[44]

The Great Southern and Western Railway Company was actively involved in the region of County Kerry. Through its hotel connection, it built a nine-hole course at Caragh Lakes in 1895 for the use of guests. The company did much to promote the recently laid out links at Lahinch. The Belfast Newsletter, 12 November 1895 records:

> The Great Southern and Western Rail Company have agreed to give golfers Friday to Tuesday tickets from Kingsbridge to Lahinch, Co Clare, a distance of 175 miles for one guinea first class return. As Lahinch links are one of the best in the country this concession will be a decided advantage to the golfing public.[45]

London and North Western Railway Company formed a great alliance with one G.L. Baillie. At one time joint Secretary at County Antrim and County Down Golf Clubs, he did much for the promotion of Irish golf and was said to be instrumental in the laying out of many clubs. Thought to be on a retainer with several railway companies, this pioneering man was credited with one of Ireland's earliest golfing tour advertisements: Holywood, County Down and Portrush Golf Clubs in 1899. Greenore Golf Club, originally a twelve-hole layout, had its course and club house constructed by this company in 1896.[46]

The Listowell and Ballybunion Railway Company owes much of its early prosperity to a patented invention of a Frenchman. Ballybunion's line became known as the Lartigue line, in honour of Charles François Marie-Thérèse Lartigue. He is credited with inventing the monorail system and, everywhere he travelled, promoted it as a cheaper alternative to conventional rail, albeit at a slower pace. The inaugural run took forty minutes on the nine and a half mile line, at a speed of only 15 mph. Some countries acted quickly by taking on the quirky invention – USA, Brazil and half a dozen or so on the Continent. The novelty of the Lartigue line lay in it being the only monorail operating in the entire British Isles.

Fortuitously, the Honorary Secretary of Ballybunion Golf Club, Mr P. McCarthy held the post of general manager of the rail company, and the station master, one William Shortis, was a founding member of the club. Not surprisingly, an especially tight bond between the golf club and the railway was forged.

The influence of the line was highly positive in Ballybunion's formative years, but a chain of unsavoury events soon conspired against the rail service. By 1916, the government had stepped in to take control of the line. It was, however, returned in 1921. Trouble persisted – in 1920, a 4.48 p.m. train out of Ballybunion was held up by masked bandits. In 1922, the Ballybunion Station was blown up, and increasingly, mail robberies were becoming tiresome. Added to this, the 1922–23 Irish Civil War was causing great unrest.

These were problems from outside forces but the monorail system also faced problems from within. These were mainly a question of balance. As author John Redmond points out in *Ballybunion Golf Club – an illustrated centenary history*:

> One lady wanted a piano delivered to Ballybunion, causing consternation in that there was unlikely to
> be a second piano on the same train. The solution arrived at was to counter-balance the piano with
> two calves. For the return journey, one calf was placed on either side.[47]

Eventually, the run of adverse events weighed too heavily on both town and line, heralding its closure. An unsuccessful attempt was made to integrate the line in the 1924 Great Southern Railway merger but by order of the High Court of Dublin, the line closed permanently.

The Dublin, Wicklow and Wexford Railway Company was another to throw its weight behind the promotion of Irish golf. It gave discount fares to golfers who played at Leopardstown Golf Club, and donated cups to Foxrock and Greystones Golf Clubs at the end of the nineteenth century.[48]

THE ROMANCE OF THE RAILWAYS has long disappeared yet a links enthusiast would be remiss in ignoring their everlasting influence. The first hole at Prestwick golf club, with its lurking railway line ready to gobble the right-hander's slice, is reminder enough. Should your ball manage to find this wickedly narrow Prestwick fairway, most approach the green with similar unease – aware of the line running the entire length of the hole.

From his starters enclosure, Stan Craig recalled the day his ball sailed over the railway line wall, not once but twice (yet he still secured par figures). Expecting a punch line at any time, I asked, 'How was that Stan?' 'The wind was so strong (right to left), it rescued me both times. Actually, I missed a "short 'un" for my birdie'. The respect Stan held for the railway line was clear to see, and I do believe his eyes glazed over. A friendlier starter and better ambassador for his links club, I am yet to meet. 'Come inside Paul, you may appreciate another pearl', said Stan. 'It concerned the lady golfer playing the first hole at Prestwick. As she was hitting her second shot to the green, the

A timeless scene on the 1st tee at Prestwick — Prestwick station, stone wall which runs the entire length of hole and a few timely hints on etiquette

Glasgow train pulled into the Prestwick station. The driver got up and moved about a bit, settling into another cabin. Her wayward shot, a shank, was heading out of bounds. The ball narrowly missed the driver's head and hitting the train, bounced back on to the fairway. Looking appropriately concerned, she inquired after the driver's health. Gratified but looking somewhat sheepish, he replied by asking was she playing the next day? Puzzled, she asked why do you inquire? "I'll make sure to be in the same place, same time".'

At Formby, due to the rail proximity, their members are well used to the threat of being three off the first tee. When playing Carnoustie you will get your chance to see the trains run by, as you will at nearby Monifieth links. For the majority of the outward nine, slicing will find the railway line and out of bounds — more evidence that most golfing trouble hounds the right-handed slicer. At Royal Lytham and St Anne's the railway presence can really make your flesh creep while steering off the 2nd, 3rd and 8th tees.

One of the most dreaded golf shots on any links occurs at Royal Troon. Here, the drive off the 11th has abruptly finished many competitors' dreams in the Open. The railway line runs down the entire right-hand side of the hole, with gorse in abundance. Just like Prestwick's opener, the railway line needs squaring up to again on your approach — as your legs are reduced to jelly. Depending on which tee is used, it is interchangeably a par-four or five hole. Golfers overly intent

The narrow 1st fairway at Prestwick — sandwiched between deep rough on the left and the railway line to the right

Train whistling by Carnoustie links

on avoiding the railway line and out of bounds, risk equally threatening rough and gorse flanking the left-hand side. Jack Nicklaus scored a ten during the final day of the 1962 Open Championship. Arnold Palmer, the winner, played it better than anyone in his typically brazen manner. More recently, you may recall Tiger Woods coming to grief here during an early round of his 1997 Open campaign. Amazingly, by the end of the tournament he fought back to finish just one stroke from a play-off berth.

At Brora links the railway line runs alongside the 10th hole. Hootie Baillie, who can always be relied upon as a good source, told of the day he partnered Monsignor John Taylor in the qualifying stages of a local four-day event. Pushing badly off the tee, Hootie's ball landed on the rail line and hit a tie at the precise angle. This caused his Dunlop 65 to rebound back onto the fairway. His reaction to the good fortune was, 'John, he must have thought you had teed off'.

Another time on the 10th tee, even his rank could not spare the Duke of Sutherland the acid tongue of his caddie. Said the Duke, 'What's the best line off the tee, caddie?' He replied, 'For all the good you doing here, you might as well take the Wick–Thurso line'.

The rail connection at St Andrews has been significant. In 1845, a proposed railway line and threat of encroachment had caused much concern for the Royal and Ancient Golf Club. The survey carried out by Northern Rail supported their commercial interest, despite it cutting through the links

The terrifying 11th hole at Royal Troon, depending on tee location, is interchangeably a par four and five. The railway line lurks to the right

BELOW: A view of the 11th hole at Royal Troon nearer the green

at the Burn hole. The net effect would mean a separation of the green from the remainder of the links. After much flurry and negotiation, the Royal and Ancient Golf Club was successful in getting the line re-routed. In 1851, the railway line was constructed alongside the links, south of where it was originally intended.[49]

At the St Andrews Open of 1905, James Braid was simply running away with the title. He was so far in front, only a calamity could retard his charge. In the form of a railway line, it came. Twice his ball found the line, once on the 15th and again at the following hole. For this Championship, the railway line was not out of bounds, although penalties in the form of nervous energy expenditure and club head damage from sleepers and steel lines were real enough. Sparing you the details, Braid double-bogied both holes but, with stout golf to follow, won by five strokes. One marvels at the constitution of such a golfer.

This section of the Old Course line no longer exists. Until 1969 though, steam trains travelled past the end of the 15th hole, then leisurely chuffed along the 16th hole and green. Steeped in the ways of golf, local train drivers observed basic golf etiquette, often doffing their hats, and stopping while putting was in progress — even tooting their whistles for a good putt.

Lundin Links is unique in that a railway line used to run right through its centre. Trains no longer operate here, but this narrow patch comes into play for a good deal of the round and is out of bounds.

Links land fortification showing
careful placement of sea gabions
at Ballybunion

CHAPTER TEN

Threats to the viability and survival of links

There is no more ominous and constant threat to coastal links land than the battering effects of the weather. Coastal erosion, aided by the ceaseless pounding and crashing of waves, has in many parts of Great Britain and Ireland caused sections of links to literally sink into the ocean. Ballybunion, one of the hardest hit, experienced the effects of particularly violent winters throughout the mid-1970s. During one tragic night alone in 1973 more than 18,000 square feet of fairway, cliff and rough were devoured by the Atlantic Ocean.[50]

Ballybunion's future was in jeopardy during these worrying times. Far from taking the impending disaster lying down, the club instituted a 'Save Ballybunion Golf Links Fund' which at first had good local support and soon other Irish clubs weighed in with financial help. Finally, when news spread around the golfing world that a pre-eminent shrine was losing the battle against the elements, money poured in from all over the globe. It was confirmation of the esteem and awe in which the club had long been held, but even still, the overseas generosity surprised and touched the club immensely.

The money was primarily used to strengthen the seashore. This was done in quite an ingenious way by taking advantage of sea gabions (rectangular baskets) made of steel wire mesh and then filled with layers of stones. These were strategically placed along the seashore at varying heights and positioned according to their particular construction details. As waves crashed against the sea gabions the menace to a large degree was blunted, the net effect being accretion, not the dreaded depletion, of sand and surroundings. The essence of their success lies in being both flexible and strong.

However, at Ballybunion the battle has not yet been won. As a measure of due vigilance, Ballybunion's committee budget £100,000 per annum to this alone.

Royal County Down Golf Club has fought a long and bitter battle with coastal erosion. For many years, sandbanks above high water mark had been vulnerable to coastal lashings. In 1938 groynes were added to fortify the shoreline. They were partially successful but by 1960 things had worsened and an approach was made to government for assistance, as erosion kept rearing its ugly head. The club records a fierce four-day storm in 1961 that in hindsight served as a turning point in the club's affairs. In an effort to quantify the effects of erosion, Club Secretary, Arthur Jones, had previously left markers near the third tee. He discovered that by the fourth day of the storm, eighteen square feet were lost. The fate of the Medal tee on the third hole was assumed grave.[51]

This sparked urgent attention by the town council. Over the next two years the ground staff dug a trench, 1.5 m deep and 70 cm wide over a stretch of 900 m. More than 3000 sleepers of 3 m length were inserted into the beach (half buried and half atop). By 1963 the barricade was completed after untold man-hours. The idea was to insert the sleepers 6 cm apart, each acting as a breaker and to allow shingle to be trapped behind by the receding undertow. This method has proved relatively successful for the time being.

ROYAL PORTRUSH GOLF CLUB, like so many Irish clubs, has also been at the cruel mercy of coastal erosion. In 1976 the Coleraine Borough Council commissioned an enquiry into the problem and made some urgent recommendations.

Regrading and re-contouring parts of the dunes along the east strand was the top priority, and intensive planting of marram grass and brushwood fencing to assist stability would follow. Unfortunately, government cutbacks prevented any such work from going ahead. During the particularly bad winter of 1982 the consequence of not proceeding with the work became evident — approximately 8 m of ground on the 5th green and 6th tee were eroded.[52] Club members were deeply angered by governmental inactivity.

Emergency steps were taken with the laying of four and five tonne boulders at the base of the damaged area. It was feared that should a similar fury to that of 1982 be unleashed, more damage to this area would surely follow. The council was also concerned for their second course (Valley Course), due to much of this links lying below sea level.

The leading engineering firm, Lewis and Duviver, from London, was hired. Following their investigation, they submitted a two-part scheme for committee approval. Coastal erosion was the urgent focus. An estimated £200,000 pounds was required to pay for Lewis and Duviver's scheme. As with Ballybunion, a coastal erosion fund was instituted. Local fund-raisers assisted, but without the financial support of many clubs from the British Isles they would never have reached their goal. Help came from overseas, via the club offering life memberships to overseas golfers who contributed US$500 and a suitable application.

Phase one comprised work in the affected areas around the 5th and 6th holes. It consisted of laying black basalt and white limestone armour stones (each four to six tonnes) upon material of a smaller size. This was designed to dissipate the wave action and adapt to beach level fluctuations. A good deal of the ground surrendered in the previous winter's assault was reused as filling material.[53] The struggle at Portrush with coastal erosion is ongoing and there can never be any room for complacency.

Close-up view of Ballybunion's sea gabions. The top section is grassed to provide a natural appearance

Royal Birkdale 11th hole (408 yards). The raised teeing ground and ever-present wind promote a difficult tee shot challenge, where bunkers on either side must be avoided. From there, a lone bunker guards the green which slopes well away to the right (this photograph reproduced with the special permission of David Kelly and Eric Hepworth)

Royal Birkdale, 7th hole (177–yard par three). A new elevated tee, some 50 yards left of its original position has changed the character of this hole. The golfer's aim is now squarely down the length of the green and you must negotiate an array of greenside bunkers (this photograph and opposite above reproduced with the special permission of David Kelly and Eric Hepworth)

ABOVE: The opening hole at Royal Birkdale is 449 yards long. Your tee shot calls for a high degree of precision to a fairway that sweeps first left, then veers slightly right towards a tightly protected green

LEFT: The famous Spectacles bunkers occupying high ground on Carnoustie's 14th hole. It has been freshly sod–revetted in readiness for the Open Championship

ABOVE: Cruden Bay 5th hole. This type of dunal countryside really gets to the heart of the matter

RIGHT: The 4th hole at Waterville is just one of the quality par threes they possess. Frequently the wind is quartering from right to left, making your starting line out over the dunes

An aerial view of Carnoustie
which features the 14th, 5th and
6th holes – from left to right

ABOVE: Safe driving at the short 3rd hole at Carnoustie is the main priority, where penalising fairway bunkers place a premium on accuracy

RIGHT: This photo depicts the new mounding behind the 15th green at Carnoustie

ABOVE: Once the bunkers have been avoided from the tee, the next hurdle at Carnoustie's 3rd hole is Jockey's burn. Though one of their shortest holes, bogies are common

LEFT: The most southerly aspect of Great Yarmouth & Caister Golf Club, Norfolk, England. This photo depicts the trouble around the 5th green

ABOVE: An excellent finishing hole at Aberdovey, Wales. At 443 yards, it presents the golfer with a challenging and lengthy carry from the Medal tee. In addition, the hole is bordered for most of its journey by a series of ditches

RIGHT: Despite being only 288 yards in length, Aberdovey's 16th hole demands a 'safety first' approach from the tee. Straying left will result in finding the railway line, which is out of bounds

In County Wexford, Rosslare links has been much affected by coastal erosion. At the other tip of Ireland, Donegal, lying perilously close to the Atlantic on headland, has been a constant target of the environmental turbulence. Here, great chunks of the 8th and 9th holes have disappeared.

The Royal and Ancient has much upon its plate, however, it remains vitally interested in preserving the links heritage of clubs such as historic Montrose. This grand old Scottish club gratefully accepted an R&A grant (interest-free loan) for the purpose of overcoming the violent ravaging by the North Sea. In the middle of the 1990s the sea was not visible from any part of the links, but it has advanced and there are now two fairways from where it can be seen. Well-positioned signs on the outward nine warn golfers in no uncertain terms about cliff fragility. On the other side of Scotland, Turnberry's dunal region is considered unstable, and similar stories abound all over Great Britain and Ireland.

PESTICIDES AS A THREAT? As far back as 1934, Dr Alister MacKenzie criticised the use of alkaline fertilisers. He stated, 'The rabbits have been killed off. Alkaline fertilisers, fit only for agriculture have been used, with the result that the sparse velvety turf has disappeared and is now replaced by plantains, daisies, clover, and luscious agricultural grasses, which need an enormous amount of mowing, weeding and upkeep.'[54]

Today, one of the benefits in limiting the use of chemical sprays can be the sudden reappearance of vanished bird life, insects of interest and yes, even weasels which return to the fold. Much to their delight, Royal Troon has been witness to the re-emergence of this fauna. Over the last few years, the Ayrshire Club has embarked upon a programme of a light ammonium sulphate spray, three times per year. Being careful to avoid excess, the Superintendent, W.D. Lachlan has done much to eradicate the excessive growth of leaf and fairway colouring – the latter being a tell-tale sign of earlier over-exuberance. Where areas are deemed to be weak or overly thin, pig and chicken manure comes to the rescue with a light hand.

Ballybunion maintains magnificent links turf on Pig Swilly – an entirely natural fertiliser. During the latter part of the 1800s and right up until relatively recent times, great herds of sheep roamed over many of the links, providing natural fertilisation along the way. They have all but disappeared, however, Royal North Devon (Westward Ho) keeps them going, as does Brora links. At one time, Lahinch was also heavily populated by them.

In 1978 we saw the highly controversial introduction of fairway watering at St Andrews Old, altering its intrinsic playing value and style. The most distinguished of all links is traditionally in peak playing condition when browned off and running fast. Par becomes a severe test, but not with artificial watering essentially removing the venom. Venom is speed. Fast links will run the ball into trouble. Hence, the chess mentality of, 'Do I blast away with driver or play a three wood or long iron into position', is lost. Excessive watering serves to lush up the fairways at many links and give them an overly manicured appearance. It signals a major departure from the mean Spartan lies that are synonymous with links and that helped establish their reputations. So what does it all mean? Essentially, too much fairway watering encourages foreign weeds and produces fairways which encourage excessive back-spin – one of the key elements of inland golf.

A positive move is underway at St Andrews as I write. They are purchasing a Toro watering system which will provide their links with the right amount of water on demand (which of course may not be much at all). It is hoped that a return to traditional playing characteristics will result, and that other administrations follow their lead. It was gratifying to hear the proud boast from an offi-

A warning sign at Montrose — certainly to help protect their links but also to ward off litigation in the event of an accident

cial at one famous old Scottish links, 'We are getting back on track, Paul. Every other links around here is lusher than us'.

All manner of things have conspired against the links game over the last fifty years. To go through each issue individually would be exhaustive, but as many of the problems are inter-related, this is not required. In the era of Robert Trent Jones (especially prolific with well over 400 course designs), he hit upon the concept of water hazards as the ideal hazards. This radically changed the prevalent thinking towards golf course design to accommodate water hazards and make them integral to strategy — one decidedly penal. Regardless of your opinion about water as a hazard, there is a certain finality about its effects on a golf ball. The rising eminence of Trent Jones coincided with the television era, which led naturally to television executives being obsessed by presentation and aesthetics issues for their viewers. The end-point for the stations is high ratings to justify their continued investment in golf.

At one and the same time, funding for professional events continued to grow, which in turn had tournament sponsors demanding low scores. Companies were putting up huge sums of prize-money and in many instances had a mandate to voice opinions and dictate certain things. Uppermost in their minds was that birdies were needed to attract crowds. Low scoring requires birdies, and birdies en masse can only really be achieved by golfers who exhibit advanced control over their shot making into the greens. A sound swing technique, when coupled with receptive greens, will do much to promote the modern ball behaving as though on remote control. In essence, everything becomes automated. The professional requires only one swing, and the predictability factor is high. At the conclusion of one tournament site, the tour follows the sun to the next location, where an identical set of preordained conditions greet the golfers. This is in stark contrast to the glorious uncertainty of links golf.

Arising out of these coexisting chains of events target golf was born. That it is still around today proves that it is not short on popularity. The purpose here is not to criticise the American ideal or Trent Jones, per se, but merely get you thinking about the ramifications of imposing similar ideals on British links golf. In Britain, where climate, selection for the poverty grass species and undulation encourage the unique fast-running links game, conditions are not conducive to target golf. For those of us who have made a study of links golf, any thoughts of a cross-pollination of the golfing forms are repugnant.

Inland golf courses and links must be treated separately. But all too often they are not. Nature itself will dictate what is acceptable practice. The sooner this simple but powerful fact is recognised and acted upon, the sooner links can return to their former glory. In some quarters, the concern is that a few treasures have been sacrificed due to zany experimentation.

One of the greatest beneficiaries of typical bouncy links conditions, was the late Bobby Locke. As a four times Open Champion few could match his canny judgement, nor the consistent draw that combated ever present winds. His ability to bounce the ball onto the greens, invariably pin high, became legendary. Yet, in a strange twist of logic, it was he who campaigned for the adoption of watering practices. Like the man himself, his word carried considerable weight, and was thought partially responsible for many golf clubs heading in new directions. In 1953, his controversial thoughts were released:

> I want to digress here for a moment, as the watering of the greens is one of my pet subjects. I believe that British golf will never challenge the supremacy of the Americans until clubs all over the country adopt the watering of greens during dry spells. All American greens have watered greens, and nearly all have well watered fairways. The result is that American golfers learn to pitch not for the green, but for the flag. On too many British courses you cannot do that. When they are in dry condition and you play for the flag, your ball is liable to go bouncing yards over the green. You have to play short and to a great extent, trust to luck. I have played on British courses when the greens have been like concrete. For top-class players, this is grossly unfair. It is like asking a snooker player like Joe Davis to play on a well-worn carpet. Because of this, on too many British courses luck counts almost as much as ability. It is imperative, in my view, that a golf course should reward good shots and punish bad ones. Too often on British courses you have to pitch short of the green and even then you do not know what is going to happen. I am deliberately labouring this topic because I believe British golf clubs in general must adopt the watering policy in the interests of the game. It has been my unhappy experience to play in the British Open on a course that, in my view, was not at the time in good enough condition for a local club competition. As I have said, the greens at Troon and Berkshire are outstanding exceptions and for me those courses are a joy to play.
>
> It would seem that Americans reduce the element of luck in the game to the absolute minimum — with rare exceptions. On the best American courses a good shot is amply rewarded but a bad shot is ruthlessly punished. It is universal practice there to water the greens. Their idea of golf round the greens is that you go for the flag — the run-up shot is rarely played. And because the greens are so well watered you can go for the flag every time knowing that when your ball hits the green it will quickly stop. I wish golf clubs all over the world would follow this American example and do away with the high element of luck that enters the game on courses where greens, and approaches to greens, are hard and your ball can kick in any direction.[55]

Tom Watson proposes that architects should spend time studying the great links prior to construction of their own courses — links or otherwise.[56] He cites Ballybunion as the ideal model and many prominent architects give credit to St Andrews Old for rounding up their education. It follows then that architectural revamping done in haste and without great study of the master links centres will cause much distaste.

The welfare of future links designs and upkeep is less concerning, for due to long-range predictions of links land restrictions, preservation and conservation orders, the best is most likely with us already.

The members are the lifeblood of any club, but activity stemming from ignorance of links matters can be threatening. In discussion with several prominent secretary/managers in Britain, it became apparent that members were having too big a say. A disturbing undercurrent is the push for the Augusta National syndrome of beautification. Brilliant though this course is, it necessitates the artificial dying of creeks, coloured sand for divot replacement, overly green fairways and amazing flora. During the US Masters we look forward to seeing the professionals using their drivers and, in its own deep south setting, I fully concur that this style of course is beautiful. The point of the comparison is to distinguish between the ideals of two different styles of golf – target inland as opposed to fast-running links golf. With the convenience of air travel, many links members are being exposed to lush courses and upon their return, bend the ear of committees. Trouble is afoot when members start inquiring about similar trimmings, after having reassessed their own links as 'too dry, too unpredictable, too bouncy – let's spruce it up'.

Interestingly, some committees happily buy into the argument. They too travel and can be influenced by the comforts of foreign inland courses. The silent problem is the insidiously short election span of each committee. But with tenure as an extended period, change happens as a consequence of considered planning and not under the assumption of limited time. Continuity with the members is enhanced and costly errors are less likely to be repeated.

At the risk of being politically incorrect, several of the world's greatest golf courses owe much of their prosperity to dictatorships, where one man has overseen a club's progress through its formative, growth and mature years. Alarming, yes, but food for thought. It is because of this very feature that the European Club has a chance of becoming something quite grand.

SAFE-GUARDING AGAINST VANDALISM and dune fragility are issues I am surprised have not been raised more often. As links lie so close to the sea, anyone of unsound mind or inquisitive nature can just wander on to the links and run amok. Dunes are preciously frail. Marram grass, their protector, has the unusual ability to put out roots from its stem, which means it can climb, step by step, up the growing dune, binding the sand together as it grows and encouraging the dune to expand. Any trampling or uprooting of the binding web of plants by thoughtless holiday makers or picnickers exposes the sand to the wind which, if constantly attacked in its bare state, will destroy dunal habitat and encourage shifting sand.

Intrusion via the beach is hard to guard against. However, Ballybunion in other ways is reasonably well placed: a 3-m high fence borders the roadside of both Old and Cashen links, while the Shannon estuary provides a degree of deterrence elsewhere.

All links administrations endure sporadic events sent to try their patience. Prestwick, for instance, reported a firebug who took great pleasure in setting alight areas of whins. As an encore, the guilty party proceeded to burn down the 4th hole hut.

At Carnoustie, the general well being of the 13th green is returning to normal. In 1997, this green was seriously vandalised during the month of December. A spade was brandished, causing malicious damage and much disruption to play. The restoration work saw the employment of over one thousand repair plugs before a satisfactory outcome was reached.

The St Andrews Links Management Trust tell of a different variety of vandalism – one more akin to a time-honoured tradition. Being a university city, the students can cause problems by engaging in high jinks. During most of the year, orderlies roam the links to ensure that any inapppropriate activity and loitering from others is kept to a bare minimum.

Pests, in the form of insects and grubs have played their part and from the superintendents' point of view, are definite threats. In the early 1930s, the pestilent Leatherjacket targeted Royal County Down and wreaked havoc in the process.[57]

In 1976, the same grub held Prestwick to ransom and converted this fine links into a dust-bowl. Known as Crane Fly, or *Tipula Olerace*a for the biology students, this pest eats away at the joint between the grass leaf and its root. Turf cannot survive the assault and dies. A particularly badly affected fairway was the 14th, eaten away for two years. During the time of recovery, members were

Vandalism on the 13th green at Carnoustie

forced to play from the rough and fairways were re-seeded under the careful eye of agronomist, Jim Arthur.[58] Thankfully, the links has since recovered.

Selective weedkilling has done much to relieve Brora links of the nuisance of stinking willies — better known as ragwort. Though picturesque, its demise was mourned by few, as its rough stems could strangle the real rough. Since the mid-1970s the problem has been under control.

Overuse is something that causes much concern to club managements. On many of the great links, a second course, or at some like Troon and St Andrews, a multitude of courses lie in wait. But who wants to use them? Not many, I'll wager. Visitors travel half way around the world with stary eyes to play over the number one links. Part of the problem lies with the short golfing summer season. As a rule, visitors come over from mid-May to September and crowd out the popular links.

Those who have little faith in the St Andrews ballot system write months in advance for a game on the Old Course. When booking, they signal their intention of playing it twice in the one day. The written reply from links management will come back: *'Not our policy, but you will be granted one round on the Old and one on the New, Jubilee or Eden Courses'.* In reality, who can blame the Links Management Trust for taking this protective line? Another method of protecting St Andrews Old against wide-scale scarring is the use of fairway mats in the quieter March to April period — an important consideration when coming out of the winter chill and ensuing frosts. A further protective and partly religious consideration is disallowing golf on Sundays. 'Old' Tom Morris was

In early 1995 tidal flooding reared its ugly head at Carnoustie. This photo shows the 18th fairway

apparently fond of saying, 'You may not need a rest but the links does'. Ballybunion Old is also spared on Sundays.

Carnoustie Links Management suffers the tourist demanding the championship links, as does Ballybunion Old. Royal Troon has an innovative system in place to reduce the pressure and expose golfers to Troon Portland by providing a quality hot lunch included in their day ticket.

Two hoary old chestnuts are as alive on the links as they are for inland courses. Widespread lack of divot replacement and repair of pitch marks on the greens proves that golfers do not suddenly undergo personality changes just because of coastal air. The clubs are becoming increasingly piqued at pug marks as evidenced by several first tee signs – 'It takes nature fifteen days to repair your pitch-mark'. Enough on this, it has been said a million times before.

THE BIG THREE – not the Mark McCormack marketing exercise of Nicklaus, Palmer and Player in the 1960s, but the ball, club head and shaft, pose a pretty fair threat to links traditions and golf in general. The ball goes too far and too straight. Flattering shafts see embarrassed seniors as long as they were in their prime, and the oversize club heads are too forgiving – granted though, a welcome advance for the weekend golfer. If the short-sighted trend of being able to purchase a golf game continues, courses will be lengthened to the point of absurdity. The professionals will find a way to meet the challenge, but the club golfer will surely become disenfranchised. Let us hope our golf ruling bodies, the Royal and Ancient Golf Club and United States Golf Association act soon to dissuade future discoveries and restore a balance.

By comparison, one need only look at the game of cricket – here the battle between bat and ball remains as riveting and intriguing as ever. Depending on climate and pitch conditions, batsmen and bowlers take turns at dominating the other. But with golf, where the modern ball and shaft have complete ascendancy over the course, the contest has become uneven. In many instances, the hands of the ruling bodies are tied; for with the manufacturer's threat of action should their livelihoods be threatened, things are far from straightforward. And so, we are left with the ridiculous situation where major championships courses are artificially strengthened by growing suffocatingly high rough and devising wickedly narrow landing areas for driving. If this fails to blunt the professionals' attack, nobbling can easily occur by preparing overly slick greens. But why is all this necessary? Have empathy with a superintendent when he is under attack and relegated to the role of villain. Incorrectly, these men shoulder the collective flak when higher authorities abdicate their responsibility. Hopefully in the near future, with regular dialogue between all interested parties, a satisfactory solution will surface. The words of outgoing Royal and Ancient Golf Club Secretary, Sir Michael Bonallack, make interesting reading but his despair is hard to misinterpret:

> Technology, and the way in which it advances at such an incredible rate, is a problem. Equipment manufacturers are like car manufacturers. They change their models every year now and sometimes more frequently than that. People can't afford to change clubs every six or nine months just because a new model has come out. I hate changing once I've got clubs I like. But people feel they're dropping behind if they haven't got the latest technology. That is why we're concerned about some of the new materials which are coming out on the market. We don't want a new club coming out next year which hits the ball fifty yards further. We'd like to stabilise the whole thing. We can't put the clock back but we're aiming to hold it at where it's got to. It's only a matter of time before the ball won't hook or fade and won't be affected by the wind. The game is easier for high-handicappers to play and in some ways that's a good thing because it encourages people to take the game up. On the other hand, it's too expensive. So we've got a catch-22 situation.[59]

There are some who campaign for the production of an etiquette card on the first tee. This may be going overboard but it does point to the heightened level of frustration that stumbling across a half-smoked cigar will produce. It sickens me to relate that far from an isolated event, the British coastlines are littered: tees, fairways, aprons of greens, gorse and heather, all too commonly with these man-made pests.

To comment on another man-made disgrace, imagine as you search for your missing ball it plays a game of hide and seek. 'Ah, it must be lodged in a rabbit scrape'. And so you place your hand down the scrape, and in the process narrowly avoid cutting your hand on a compressed soft drink can. Many links endure this unscrupulous behaviour. Brora officials call it 'a damned irritation'.

ABOVE: A close-up look of the Leatherjacket's pupae

After waging a two-year war on Prestwick Links, Leatherjackets turned the 14th fairway into a dust bowl

Dune formation and management

Alistaire Gilchrist

Simply stated, a sand dune is a mound or ridge of drifted sand. To fully understand the problems of management of such landforms though, it is important to be aware of just how sand dunes are created. The two basic requirements for their formation are, first, a good supply of dry sand and secondly, wind to move it.

Coastal dunes have usually formed after heavy deposits of sand have built up along a coast as a result of sea action. It may not always be clear where the sand has come from, although it is safe to assume that it will have eroded from some part of the coastline. When the height of the beach deposits build up above high tide, it will rarely be inundated with water. Such occasions would usually be due to extreme storms or exceptionally high tides and might only last a few days in two or three months — as would be the case over normal summer months. Over these extended dry periods the combined action of wind and sun makes the sand extremely dry. Now, with the sand dry, it only needs wind to move the particles which are blown along until some obstruction is encountered. This slows the wind and allows the particles to drop. Beach debris and vegetation are commonly encountered obstructions, but man-made obstacles in the form of brushwood fencing are frequently used to facilitate the establishment of dunes, or alternatively, provide protection against erosion.

It should be noted that dunes will only occur where the land form behind the beach is fairly flat. They will not form where the beach backs onto cliffs or other rigid structures. As wind is the other main factor in dune establishment, it helps to understand the mechanics of wind on dry sand.

Tests have shown that a constant wind speed of about 16 km (10 mph) can lift sand grains from a smooth surface and move them. These grains move in a series of short hops and each time they land, they disturb other grains of sand, which in turn, move forward in the wind in the same manner. This multiplying factor can be readily appreciated. The resultant sand movement can build up very quickly, but equally, erosion can occur by a similar process. It only then needs a relatively modest rise in wind speed to greatly increase the amount of sand moved.

The foregoing refers to the establishment of dunes, but of course, the reverse is true in the case of erosion of dunes. It is this problem which now poses the greatest concern to many of the well established and famous golf links of Great Britain and Ireland. Many of these golf clubs are now around one hundred years old. However, due to an almost total absence of records, it is virtually impossible to gauge the rate of change along their coastlines. What is certain is that there are now a considerable number of these links that have imminent or serious erosion problems. In the past, many clubs simply attended to these problems as they arose and did not consider early preventative measures. A few of the more enlightened clubs have, within the last ten years, initiated regular coastline checks, thereby containing their problems to a manageable degree.

The following case studies provide examples of action taken to combat erosion and include some problems which have been identified but not yet resolved.

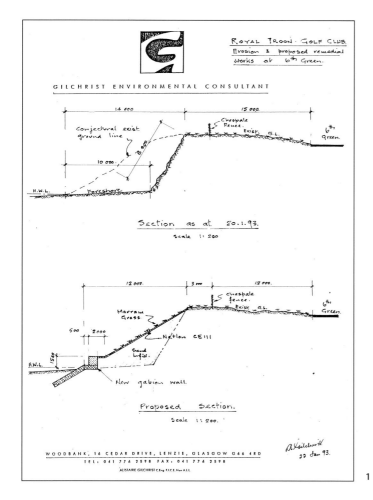

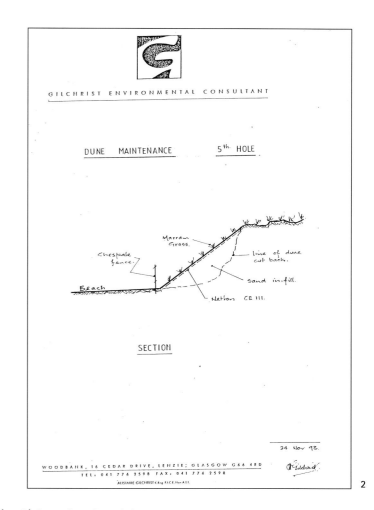

Royal Troon Golf Club have been aware of their problem areas for more than a decade and, following major storms in 1991 and 1993, have carried out successful protection works. A careful monitoring programme has also been set up.

The January 1991 storms caused substantial erosion along the largely unprotected coastline on the edge of the first two holes. Earlier attempts by the greens staff to protect the 2nd tee were washed out by the storm. The adopted solution was to use a 6-m (20-ft) gabion mattress toed into the beach at a slope of 2:1 with a box gabion on the landward end (photograph 3). This has successfully withstood two major storms — in 1993 and 1997 (photograph 4).

The 1993 storm, however, seriously jeopardised the 6th green and left an 8-m (26-ft) semi-vertical face just 15 m (50 ft) from the edge of the green (photograph 5). In the repair stage, my company adopted the same strategy that proved successful on the first two holes using gabions rebuilt at high water mark. The void was back-filled with sand and finished to a gradient of approximately 22° (illustration 1 and photograph 6).

Photograph 7 depicts a slope which would remain stable and sustain marram grass without being eroded by strong winds. To ensure that erosion to the slope was minimal a geogrid plastic mesh was nailed into the slope which encouraged vegetation to grow.

Royal Troon now undertake an annual coastline survey and any areas of concern are noted and duly acted upon. The 'blow hole' phenomenon is clearly shown in photograph 8. This occurs where

(3) Gabion mattress and box construction

(4) Royal Troon 1st fairway protection during storm conditions

the vegetation surface of the dunes is broken by what is usually pedestrian action, allowing the wind to blow out the dry and unprotected sand. If not acted upon, this will lead to a progressively larger excavation and inevitably, destruction of the dune. Sand fencing across the entrance to this hole should trap blown sand and enable the hole to refill which will augment dune re-establishment (illustration 2).

The problem highlighted in photograph 9 shows how erosion can occur at the end of a previous protection scheme. Appropriate sand fencing and marram grass establishment should successfully solve this problem.

As quickly as possible, vegetation should be encouraged to grow on exposed dune faces, as this becomes an essential feature of dune stability. At North Berwick the problem of motorcycle scrambling on the dune is evident and has completely removed all vegetation (photograph 10). Remedial action to replant this slope is now a priority.

Protection of steep grass slopes above a pebble beach is shown in photograph 11. Timber logs which are wired together, provide reasonable protection but will eventually fail, principally through rusting and failure of the wire.

The previously mentioned examples have been concerned with relatively low level dunes. Erosion

(5) Eroded dune behind 6th green at Royal Troon

of higher dunes is considerably more problematic and this can be appreciated by the following examples.

Major dune erosion has occurred on a stretch of Aberdeen coastline where the dunes are approximately 12 m (39 ft) high (photographs 12 and 13). On relatively flat slopes, grass will remain and maintain the dune, but where vegetation fails, erosion will occur. Both photographs portray the effect of mainly wind erosion aided by sea action, while photograph 12 specifically reveals the deleterious effects of erosion on a teeing ground. From a baseline photograph taken in 1991, it is estimated that the rate of erosion in this area is about one metre per annum. The estimate is confirmed by the fact that the toe of the dune is now about 20 m (66 ft) inland from a drainage pipe outlet which is twenty years old. Presumably, this outlet was originally situated at the edge of the original dune. Of added interest, there is no evidence of excessive sand deposits up and down the coastline from this location. Work is ongoing to develop a stabilisation scheme for this troublesome area.

These case studies have opted for particular solutions to their particular requirements. There are, however, a number of treatments which have been used extensively in dune protection and which should be considered when deciding upon the most appropriate solution for any given situation. They fall into two distinct categories:

(6) New gabion protection and slope stabilisation at 6th green, Royal Troon, summer 1993

(7) The 6th green at Royal Troon
— vegetation stabilisation on
slope. Photograph taken in
summer 1995

(a) hard and (b) soft techniques.

Hard techniques are generally used when the dune is affected by tidal waters and consist of either rock armour or some arrangement of gabion basket. Photograph 14 demonstrates a scheme where both techniques have been used. Rock armour has a semi-natural appearance once vegetation has established and sand has partially filled the voids in the stone. It is easy to construct

and can be regarded as a medium-cost solution. Gabion protection schemes are much more artificial in appearance but this depends upon the arrangement selected. The stepped box wall will generally remain exposed, whereas the mattress and box arrangement chosen for the Royal Troon works will eventually be covered in sand and sustain growth of marram grass and other beach binding plants. In time, the construction will be virtually obscured from view. With both cases, some movement of the hard elements is tolerable before compromising their effectiveness.

Soft techniques fall into three main categories; all of which aim to produce the same outcome, and are used where the surface is not subject to any wave or tidal action.

1. Sand fencing (photograph 15) is used to trap blown sand and usually consists of chesspale fencing with either brushwood or geogrid netting. It is often used as a first stage treatment, prior to the dune's stabilisation by vegetation. The benefits are twofold: it is relatively cheap and most find it a visually acceptable method.

2. Sand stabilisation using either brushwood thatching or geogrid netting will generally

(8) Typical 'blow hole' along
Royal Troon's shoreline

(9) No room for complacency, erosion can occur at the end of a previous protection scheme

(10) The menace of motorcycle scrambling at North Berwick has completely removed all the dunal vegetation

prevent wind erosion of newly planted surfaces. In addition, it is a relatively low cost solution (netting was used in the Royal Troon scheme as depicted in photograph 4). Also effective can be a system using chemical binders which need only survive long enough to allow vegetation to establish. These artificial aids are soon hidden when vegetation takes hold.

3. The ultimate objective in all protection schemes is to re-establish vegetation, whether it be natural dune turf or the coarser more robust marram or sea-lyme grasses. On the seaward face of dunes these coarse grasses are the most common initial growth to establish. Once their binding forces take root, they spread rapidly to provide a relatively cheap solution.

Protection of our links requires a constant vigil and speedy action to remedy failures as they begin to appear. Good maintenance will pay dividends in the long term and avoid the catastrophic damage that can so easily occur. This damage, as we have witnessed, can occur over a very short period of time. The old adage, 'time and tide will wait for no man', most certainly applies to those who take responsibility for tending to the needs of our coastlines.

(11) ABOVE
Wired log protection works at North Berwick

(12) BELOW
Aberdeen — progressive erosion affecting the upper tee level

(13) LEFT
Aberdeen — major wind erosion

(14) ABOVE
Arran — an example of gabion
wall adjoining a rock armour
protection scheme

(15) LEFT
Arran — anti erosion fencing

The impressive tumbling terrain
of Royal Birkdale is demonstrated
by this photo of the 2nd and 3rd
holes (reproduced with the
special permission of David Kelly
and Eric Hepworth)

CHAPTER ELEVEN

The Open Championship and masters of the links

Quite simply, the rota is the collective name given to golf clubs that regularly stage the Open Championship every six to eight years. The townships and club committees of each Open site are well used to the disruption and for most members the Open is a welcome and highly prestigious event.

Any links honoured by inclusion on the Open rota has earned its stripes — the type other less successful links would die for. The acclaim does not end there, for those previously honoured but since removed from the rota can for all time say, 'We've hosted the Open Championship', thereby attracting the golfing pilgrim like a magnet. Prestwick's current fame owes much to this phenomenon.

The following circumstances have signalled the chorus for links disappearing from the rota: antiquity, diminishing shot values and club facilities that fail to keep pace with modern requirements. The second point, in particular, was made inevitable by the coming of the modern Haskell golf ball. As for rota inclusion, poor roadways or inadequate transport access has also led to stalling — Royal St George's was a late rota entry due to unsuitably narrow roads from London to the Kent coastal haven of Sandwich.

For rota links, their biggest enemy is complacency. This was clearly the case with Carnoustie — a municipal layout on Scotland's east coast. The malaise saw it run into the ground and subsequently removed after the 1975 Open. Stung into action, a diligent and sustained fightback effort by the Club and town council paid off — the reviews by the Open Championship Committee were favourable and prompted discussions for future reinclusion. The good work of current Links Superintendent, J.S. Philp, and his team, were largely responsible for creating this change of opinion. It has since forced its way back for the 1999 Open Championship, having performed well at Scottish Opens in recent times. By general consent, professionals consider it the most stringent of all Open Championship venues.

The venerable club house of
the Royal and Ancient Golf Club,
St Andrews

Being on the rota entitles the club to a privileged position when it comes to the setting of green fees. It is no coincidence that these clubs tend to be the dearest to play, and visitors, keen to say, 'I have played so and so', simply pay the required sum and dine out ad infinitum on the highlights. Whereas you can try until you are hoarse to tackle Cypress Point, Pine Valley or Augusta National, the Open Championship links of Britain will welcome your advances, if you give them a combination of notice, a decent letter of introduction and a signed handicap certificate.

Today, the rota includes eight links. The Scottish ones are St Andrews Old, Muirfield (the Honourable Company of Edinburgh Golfers), Royal Troon, Turnberry (Ailsa) and Carnoustie (Championship). The English ones are Royal St George's, Royal Lytham and St Anne's and Royal Birkdale – the latter in 1954 being the first new addition after World War II. In 1977, Turnberry became the latest addition to the rota and, thanks to the great shootout between Nicklaus and Watson, it will not be disappearing in a hurry. Greg Norman and Nick Price have since proved, with their victories at Turnberry, that only players of the highest rank can win on this difficult links, a links where unpredictable weather is taken for granted.

Such is the enormity of running an Open Championship that each year a host of other courses (usually links) come to the fore, through their role as qualifying courses. Clubs such as Western Gailes, Lundin Links, Gullane No.1, Kilmarnock Barassie, Prestwick St Nicholas, Montrose, Scotscraig and others have the chance to raise their profile in the golfing world. As a measure of the growing complexity of staging the Open Championship, only two qualifying courses were used in 1969. For the 1970 Championship, the qualifying courses were increased to three. Only two years later it became necessary to increase this to four and by 1976, five courses were on duty for full-scale qualifying.

Though still a joy to play, the following have for one reason or another departed the rota. Prestwick hosted the first twelve Opens, the last in 1925, won by American James Barnes with the neatly rounded off score of 300. Musselburgh, to the east of Edinburgh, once a giant in links golf,

hosted six Open Championships between 1874 and 1889. Hoylake (Royal Liverpool) staged ten Opens but none since 1967 when Argentinean Roberto de Vicenzo finally triumphed, and Deal (Royal Cinque Ports) on the richly abundant Kent coastline, staged the 1909 and 1920 Opens.[60] Though a thoroughly fine links, it has always tended to be swamped by its more famous neighbour, Royal St George's. Another fine Kent links, Prince's, has also departed the rota.

Regarding Royal Portrush, speculation was rife that the club may be awarded the 2001 Open, marking a neat fifty years from its initial entry. What could have been a major political and marketing boon, has sadly fallen through. In the meantime, the venue never fails to impress the professionals during the British Senior Open Championship. This exposure can only assist any future push for reinstatement.

From the beginning of the Open Championship in 1860, it was played eleven times consecutively at Prestwick until 1870. Of significance that year Tom Morris Jnr won the Championship belt for the third consecutive occasion and, under the rules of the event, made the belt his exclusive property. In 1871 the Open was held in abeyance for one year.[61]

Upon its resumption in 1872, the tournament was back on familiar turf — that of Prestwick Golf Club. A major change was the winner receiving a cup, as a result of the Championship belt residing

One of the most famous short holes in golf — the par 3 8th hole at Royal Troon — commonly referred to as Postage Stamp

An elevated shot of Lundin Links which is a regular qualifying course for the Open Championship

Montrose is a widely underrated links. This photo shows the 140-m (154-yd) par three 3rd hole from behind the green, looking back towards the tee. It is known locally as Table

in the Morris household and never to be replaced. The year 1872 marked the first of a remarkable period in the Open Championship, whereby three leading Scottish clubs rotated in hosting the prestigious event on a once-in-three-year basis from 1872 righ through to 1891. They were Prestwick, St Andrews and The Honourable Company of Edinburgh Golfers, then based at Musselburgh.[62] For several reasons this was the golden era of the Open Championship: small but passionate fields, committed railways, the gutty ball, rampant patriotism and lots of bad weather. In addition, the era of big money challenge matches had not yet come to pass.

In 1892 the rota was extended to include Muirfield Golf Club — a new home for the Honourable Company of Edinburgh Golfers. It has since hosted the event regularly, fourteen times in total.[63] With the success of this venture, other prestigious clubs continued to be added to the rota. To date, a total of fourteen clubs, all links, have been used. Including the 1999 Open Championship, the frequency of Open rotations is as follows: in order, St Andrews Old leads the way with twenty five appearances, Prestwick with twenty four, Muirfield fourteen, Royal St George's twelve, Hoylake (Royal Liverpool) ten, Royal Lytham and St Anne's nine, Royal Troon seven, Royal Birkdale seven, Musselburgh six, Carnoustie six, Turnberry three, Deal (Royal Cinque Ports) two, Prince's one and Royal Portrush once in 1951. Play was of course suspended during the two World Wars.

Wales has yet to stage the Open Championship despite the amount of very fine links and the presence of a couple of classic links — Royal Porthcawl and Royal St David's. Surely the time has come for a premier Welsh links to take its rightful position on the rota.

The British Open is correctly known as the Open Championship and is a major championship in every sense. The gallant victors have won because of an ability to adapt to the rigours of links golf — bumbling the ball forward and down rather than forward and up, coping with inclement weather and holding their nerve when it most counted. Of course, being naturally gifted never harmed their chances.

The Open is by far the most International of all the four majors, where a three-ball pairing may feature a leading Japanese, Australian and American golfer or many other interesting possibilities. For this reason alone, no other major championship can hope to match the television viewing audience appeal, with the possible exception of the US Masters.

Historically, the Open Championship organising committees have exercised great caution in ushering in structural change, but their initiatives have usually been well received as positive, progressive and forward looking.

Initially there was much informality, when the tournament was a 36 hole affair with small Scottish fields. Playing over the Prestwick links of 12 holes, contestants were required to make three circuits of the layout. Between 1860 and 1891, the Open Championship was a

A Medal tee amid golden gorse at the far end of Montrose links

contest over 36 holes and it was not until 1892 at Muirfield, that the modern format of 72 holes was introduced.[64] It was at this Open that entrance fees were first collected from players.

With the format firmly fixed at 72 holes, it was played over three days; the first two being single 18 hole rounds and culminating in 36 tension-filled holes on Friday. The 1966 Open Championship at Muirfield again broke new ground when, for the first time, play was over four days of single 18 hole rounds.[65] The tournament concluded on Saturday and fourteen years later in 1980, the tournament experimented with the logical step of ending on a Sunday.

ONE OF THE MOST SIGNIFICANT CHANGES to the Open format was dispensing with qualifying rounds for the leading players, two days prior to the event – even the defending champion was not excused. One now sees the ridiculous nature of qualifying. Including the four rounds in the main event, the tournament was played over six rounds. It was too much and obviously the players, given a choice, would have preferred to rest or practise. The change in 1963 was welcomed, especially by the leading contingent who knew in all probability that they would qualify.[66] From this tournament onwards, only non-exempt players have been subjected to qualifying.

In the same year, another first was experimented with, and subsequently retained; doing away with any qualifying play on the Championship rota links of the tournament. The playing conditions during the Championship proper improved significantly as a result.

Many golfers have received a lucky bounce off the wall towards the flag on this Dunbar hole, East Lothian, Scotland

Play-offs were dreaded at the Open Championship, for up until 1964, 36 holes were the order of a very long day. There had been a few since 1892 when the 72-hole format was introduced. The great Harry Vardon won twice in this manner – 1896 and again in 1911, Jock Hutchison in 1921, Denny Shute in 1933, Bobby Locke in 1949, Peter Thomson in 1958 and Bob Charles triumphed in 1963.[67] Charles won the last of the great 36-hole play-offs and most agreed that an 18-hole replacement made good sense. The first play-off under the new scheme took place at the Old Course in 1970, when Jack Nicklaus narrowly defeated Doug Sanders in an epic encounter.

By 1989 the amount of spectators who attended the Open Championship had grown immensely. There were important and hard commercial decisions to be made and most surrounded the desire to complete the event on schedule. The announcement was made that a new format was to be trialed – a four-hole play-off. In 1989 at Royal Troon, Wayne Grady, Greg Norman and the eventual winner, Mark Calcavecchia played over the 1st, 2nd, 17th and 18th holes. Despite Norman starting with successive birdies (making ten for the day), Calcavecchia had one of his own, plus another on the 18th, where the golfing world watched in horror as Norman self-destructed after driving into an unreachable bunker. Throughout the play-off Grady never threatened and was relegated to being a supporting cast member.

The four-hole system has recently had another opportunity to claim validity, and this occurred when Mark O'Meara outlasted Brian Watts at Royal Birkdale in 1998 on a brilliant summer's evening. No play-off system will appease all interest groups, however, the current one seems to be meeting with considerable approval.

One of the most controversial changes to the world's oldest golf championship concerned the size of the golf ball. Up until 1974 competitors were at liberty to choose between the small 1.62 in. British ball, or the large 1.68 in. US Ball. Gary Player won this Lytham and St Anne's Open – the first time the large ball was obligatory.

GIVEN THE SPECIALISED PLAYING SKILLS and patience required to win the Open, the high number of multiple winners comes as little surprise. Harry Vardon, who popularised the Vardon grip, leads the way with six victories, followed by his fellow great triumvirate members — James Braid and J.H. Taylor with five wins apiece. Peter Thomson won five times in twelve years, and during this hot spell, and for an extended time afterwards, was always thought to be a legitimate chance. In seven consecutive Opens between 1952 and 1958, Thomson never finished worse than second.

Equally impressive has been the great run of Tom Watson, winning five times in nine years. The 1984 Open won by Seve Ballesteros was of special interest, for when playing the 71st hole, Watson was tied with Ballesteros and threatened to equal Harry Vardon's record. Alas, the Road claimed another one. Still wearing the look of Huck Finn, Watson continues to strive for that elusive sixth win.

Five golfers have won the title four times. They are Tom Morris Snr and his son, Tom Morris Jnr, Willie Park Snr, Bobby Locke, the unflappable South African golfer, plus the flamboyant American, Walter Hagen. No account of any Open Champion compares with the tragedy of young Tom Morris. Seemingly, all zest for life was drained out of his system following the early death of his wife. Only in his mid-twenties, but with the will to live gone, he too passed away. The golf world collapsed into inconsolable mourning.

On three wins, are the incomparable R.T. Jones who won thirteen major titles as an amateur, British maestro, Henry Cotton, Jack Nicklaus and a revamped Nick Faldo who for many years has been on intimate terms with Misery Hill. Seve Ballesteros has won the coveted trophy three times, and confounded golf watchers with the manner of his victory in 1979 at Royal Lytham and St Anne's. It has since been dubbed somewhat to the Spaniard's annoyance 'The Car Park Open'. His other victories were loaded with flair, conservatism when required and masterful golf at crucial stages. Gary Player, the globe-trotting South African golfer, remarkably won once in the 1950s, 1960s and 1970s. To conclude the list of golfers on three victories, Bob Ferguson and Jamie Anderson won three times each in the nineteenth century, consecutively.

The dual winners are Bob Martin from St Andrews, who in 1876 won the Open in bizarre circumstances after his play-off opponent simply refused to play.[68] His other victory was more conventional to say the least. Willie Park Jnr, from the great golfing family at Musselburgh won twice, as did Arnold Palmer during his formidable years of 1961 and 1962. Lee Trevino's low-ball flight was ideally suited the British conditions, and his chipping was devastating when winning consecutively in 1971 and 1972. Lastly, Greg Norman converted his awesome talent to triumph in 1986 and 1993. By adhering strictly to his fitness regimen, another championship in the next five years is not out of the question.

The Open Championship presents an ideal opportunity for the Royal and Ancient Golf Club to showcase its wares. However, the massive event serves an equally important secondary function — the income generated from television rights provides their major source of income each year. Other championships are thereby funded from this income, such as the Amateur, Boys and Seniors along with grants to clubs.

This breathtaking view captures a
relatively new addition to the
links portfolio — Tralee Golf Club
built in 1984

CHAPTER TWELVE

New links developments — beyond World War II

There have been remarkably few genuine links developments since World War II, for a variety of reasons. First, increasing mechanisation and the need for employment has forced people into the cities away from potential new developments. Consequently, quality city-based inland golf courses have experienced waiting lists. Secondly, with the advent of the conservation movement, gaining co-operation among interest groups to develop sensitive coastal areas has become increasingly less straightforward. As modern day Irish architect, Pat Ruddy says, 'The environmentalists have closed in'.

But added to this, the early links architects were no fools — they recognised and utilised the best land, making quality links land less readily obtainable today. Nevertheless, the ones that have materialised are well worth detailing and add a modern layer to the rich but threatened links heritage. Given the ancient nature of links land, new links, in this context, means those developed within the last fifty years.

Southerness Golf Club

After the cessation of wartime hostilities, the first links development began at Southerness in the Dumfries region on the Solway Firth, southern Scotland. Construction got under way in 1946 and its official opening was 29 June 1947.

A wealthy and good-natured landowner, Major Richard Oswald of Cavens, Kirkbean, was the driving force behind the project. He came to realise the suitability of his own property, being sandy based, complete with rolling undulating terrain and colonised by fine wiry bents and fescues grasses. In short, ideal links land. The Major was aware of the miracle (reconstruction) work architect McKenzie Ross was performing at Turnberry and so it seemed logical and convenient that his services be sought.

Upon sighting the land, Ross emphatically declared his intention of not wanting to destroy the natural beauty or character of the tract of land. Designed along traditional Scottish lines, the new links had nine outward holes to a distant point, and nine holes returning inward. Its measurement was 6,250 yards, although this could be stretched with the addition of tiger tees to 7,000 yards. Throughout its short history, the par of Southerness has remained fixed at 69 with the standard scratch rating, four strokes higher — clear endorsement of the challenge for golfers. Remarkably, the construction costs were little over £2000. The greens were sown from quality fescue seed and speed wise, were inherently fast from the beginning.

As a bonus to members, Ross laid out an additional nine-hole miniature course. The theme of this was to recreate many of the famous links holes, such as the Postage Stamp of Troon fame, the 11th at St Andrews Old, 13th at Muirfield and so on. Alas, the course where many promising juniors gained their start has not survived.

INITIALLY, THE SOUTHERNESS LINKS was much harder than it is today. Rough extended a considerable distance out from the tees and when the wind was unfavourable, some fairways were only reachable by the mightiest of hitters. Of little solace to the timid steerer, its fairways were tightly framed with bracken and heather. In recent times, the bunkers at Southerness have been reworked with sod-revetting, but for many years were entirely natural and fringed with tufted grasses. Though less severe, much of the original tightness remains.

Right from the outset, Southerness was blessed by having two great men of vision — Major Oswald and the renowned agronomist, Jim Arthur, who for many years supervised the preparation of links to be used for the Open Championship. Arthur's forthright links commentary and memories of Southerness are educational and, where appropriate, damning in places. He states:

> Southerness represents so many things to me personally and indeed to the game of golf that it is hard to know where to start. As a young adviser, straight out of the services, I benefited inestimably from the truly valuable education in golf course construction that it provided.
>
> It is hardly believable that when Major Oswald proposed to build the links it was reported as being the last course likely to be built in Scotland. There have been a few since — but none surpassing McKenzie Ross' superb design, made even more magnificent by its unspoilt surroundings of links and heathland between the wide sweep of the Solway River with its skyline of the Lake District peaks and the backdrop of Criffel.
>
> Southerness has survived as a natural links where others have suffered almost a complete loss of links character due to chopping and changing of management policies. There have been many reasons for this — one being that in the dicy days of the 1950s and 1960s when so many heretical ideas were being promoted, initially to sell fertilisers, by those who should have known better, three factors stopped them being adopted at Southerness. The first was the continuity of direction rigidly imposed by Major Oswald. The second was a management policy based on traditional links methods, which with one or two lapses from grace has continued to this day. The third was lack of money which actually served to limit mistake making.
>
> I well remember a new greenkeeper (who shall be nameless but I still know his sons) who came from an inland course. I sensed trouble and within a year, one green started to show a change in grass type. I mentioned my fears to Major Oswald, who tackled the culprit. Under pressure he admitted to giving that green a touch of a popular complete (NPK) granular fertiliser. On being examined as to whether he agreed with the established policy of nitrogen only and very little of it once

a year, he stated that he did not agree with me or my methods. 'Right,' said Major Oswald, 'You can go on Friday' and go he did. I have never forgotten this incident in a long advisory career and have always subsequently avoided greenkeepers being dismissed.

Two greenkeeping adages are proved by the excellence of Southerness when all around are succumbing to the green is great school of greenkeeping. First, that the poorest clubs have the best courses and secondly, that in greenkeeping one should ask a farmer what to do and then go and do exactly the opposite. I am aware of the benign influence of a certain noted farmer-patron, but he did see that diametrically opposed aims demand diametrically opposed methods. It was he who recruited the redoubtable Peter Clement, with whom I enjoyed a most rewarding partnership, and fought with tenacity and ferocity every attempt to interfere with his course.

Southerness to me represents the essence of links golf. I was there from its conception — and how rewarding it is to know a course from the start before it comes into play. Especially, as so often has happened in the intervening fifty years, when one has to correct problems caused by someone messing things up because they had not the slightest idea of the needs of those two fine grasses, fine fescue *(Festuca)* and bents *(Agrostis)* which give courses their character and indeed dominate the whole links at Southerness.

I was very lucky indeed to have two mentors in my early learning days. I had joined Bungalow as it was invariably described, from six years in the Army, having graduated in 1939. Their then director said three things to me on appointment, 'First, you have an agricultural degree. Forget everything you learned, as greenkeeping is the opposite of grassland husbandry. Secondly, you are going round for the first year with (the then senior adviser) Richard Libbey — botanist of international renown — and you are going to keep your mouth shut and your eyes and ears open, though I realise even on short acquaintance that will be a hardship'. His third admonition was that I would make mistakes as they all had 'but please do not copy the ones we have made earlier'.

Richard was an inspiration as he treated golf greenkeeping botanically not chemically and taught me to learn from nature — 'the only fertiliser which links get comes from a passing seagull or sheep'. He was the first to point out to me rabbit scalds dominated by coarse and ephemeral grasses as a result of local overfeeding to prove his point.

All this lore he and I put into practice in bringing McKenzie Ross' superb design into play, on a shoe-string budget. Indeed during construction, links techniques were used — no fertiliser, the use of local peaty deposits and indeed turfing where feasible with local turf from fields near the Paul Jones. This in itself was a milestone because not only had few courses been built in the past decade, but those that had, were on inland sites at the height of the fertiliser era.

One limiting management factor at Southerness was mowing and manpower. They were big greens and the lone greenkeeper, Mr Anderson — he did get a boy to help part-time in the summer — had only a hand pushed (not a conventional powered) machine to cut eighteen greens. If we fed, there was no way he could cut all the greens even in two days. From the start these were superb fescue greens needing no fertiliser but only top-dressing, to produce fast, firm, true putting surfaces, to impart drought resistance and provide slowly available nitrogen.

In those days the top-dressing was prepared by stacking black peaty deposits (a layer exposed as tides cut into the shallow dune structure to the west of the course) with local sand. Nothing could have been more local and it worked. Today we use exactly the same type of material (an alkaline peaty deposit from East Anglia, overlaying gravel on the site of long since drained lakes) known as fen peat over thousands of UK courses. Another thing I learned from my early days at Southerness.

Aeration was not so important in those days because there was so little play, but it was still done. Hand forking (no machines in those early days) was a daunting, never-ending drudge, but in those days greenkeepers flexed their muscles and got on with it. I am not sure whether they would do the same today but in any case the intensity of play vastly increased the need for more frequent and deeper aeration and more play meant less time for such greenkeeping operations, which perforce had to be mechanised to keep ahead of play.

Thus Southerness provided doubly valuable precedents by the development of MacKenzie Ross' architectural concepts with sound construction and first class traditional management. Its excellence on a shoe string made big impressions on some other Scottish courses who noted the philosophy and changed their management back to traditional lines. What a pity that Turnberry, being restored by Ross at the same time — on sound lines — was nearly ruined by the gross overfeeding and overwatering made possible by the deep purse of British Rail, leaving me with a Herculean task in restoring links character to an annual meadow grass in the run up to their first Open Championship. In the three years prior to that 1977 Open, by dint of literally monthly visits and a massive budget from BTH, we succeeded in restoring some semblance of links character by emulating what was routine management at Southerness.

It is just possible to run a golf course on sandy links in a drought without irrigation, providing there is virtually no golf and the few golfers accept a steadily deepening shade of khaki on the greens to match sere conditions over the whole course, but clearly limited irrigation makes life easier for golfer and greenkeeping staff alike. However, it should be stressed that drought does not kill grass which rapidly greens over again with rain. Indeed an old adage has it that 'a good drought gets rid of a deal of rubbish'. On a strictly limited budget, there was no possibility of a piped water supply to greens. Pop-ups had not even been dreamt of then, even in the States. They were not employed on golf courses here until 1964–65 though used more and more widely in the States a decade earlier.

The solution was to dig a series of pits down to below the water table and to use 'surplus' NFS pumps to hose the greens. By a combination of restricted supply (over-extraction caused the sides of the pits to collapse), limited manpower and the logistic problems in getting water to the greens, over-watering (the cardinal sin of greenkeeping) was avoided.

Thus, by a combination of dedicated hard work by a devoted green staff, working on a sensible traditional pattern of greenkeeping and the natural advantages of the site so ably developed by McKenzie Ross, was Southerness created — living proof of the effectiveness of following, not fighting, nature and providing only what the links grasses require, not what some fertiliser salesman thinks they should have.

All this modern 'green' emphasis on conservation was predated and implemented by good greenkeepers looking after their courses and the fauna and flora therein. I played a good deal of my early golf at Southerness; my recollection is that it cost five shillings for a day's golf then, but holidays at Paul Jones were not all golf. Listening to the myriads of natterjack toads talking to themselves in the still of a spring evening was something I will never forget. The flora of the heather and links land produced countless surprises, agronomists are often botanists at heart, while the bird-life varied wildly with the season as I am certain it still does. A pair of oyster catchers nested for three years on the back of the short 7th green and reared their young in the first two seasons after the course was opened. For two years after that, a solitary bird having presumably lost its mate, scraped a hollow on the same site but did not lay eggs. This is not a tribute to the attachment of birds to a nesting site but a comment on how little play there was.

Certainly Southerness ranks high in my list of favourite courses. Many of them being links but all examples of how superb golfing conditions can be created by dedicated and skilled work, by devoted and hard working greenkeepers, without which golf would be a shadow of its traditional face and far less of a challenge. Here's to those stalwarts from first to last, whose energy and enthusiasm pointed in the right direction have been so responsible for the establishment of a truly wonderful links which developed from such inauspicious beginnings, essentially the consuming hobby of a landowner, whom over many years of co-operation and response to challenge, I am very proud to have claimed as a good friend and mentor.[69]

When taking into consideration the isolation of Southerness and its relative infancy, that it has gained prominence by hosting national championships where more established links have been overlooked, confirms its quality. To date, the Scottish Amateur Championship has been played there twice, and it has been honoured with the Scottish Ladies Championship, the British Ladies Stroke-play Championship and the British Youth Championship once apiece.

Carnegie Links

Built in 1992 Carnegie Links is considerably more than just a links development – it is part of the original 3,035-ha (7,500-a) estate of steel magnate, Andrew Carnegie, at Skibo in the Scottish Highlands. After he died in 1919 the property remained in the family until 1990, when an English entrepreneur by the name of Peter de Savary, simply made an offer too good to refuse. His master-plan was to create an all-encompassing retreat.[70] Let's not lower the tone by disclosing the nightly fee, suffice to say it is pitched at an exclusive market, has a well honed aura of privacy about it and the surrounds are exceptional.

Greg Norman is one to agree, having found his nirvana here while preparing for the 1995 Open Championship at St Andrews Old. Norman's aims were to enjoy some relaxing privacy with his family and sharpen up his golf game without the usual throng of backslappers. Despite these aims being met, the Great White Shark did not have complete run of the place. He requested the greenkeeper to mow down a green so he could experience championship firmness and speed during chipping practice. The 11th green was chosen, albeit reluctantly by the man in charge of greens – 'the course is new, I won't cut any green to its roots, not even for him'.[71]

A feature within the complex is a magnificent tenth-century castle which was renovated by Carnegie in the 1890s to go along with guest houses, fishing grounds, riding stable and swimming pavilion. Under the direction of de Savary, many experts were hired and assigned to upgrade each part of the estate. Our focus is the golf links, and for this he engaged the highly respected architect, Donald Steel. In keeping with the modest nature of Steel, his reticence was noted when called upon to comment on his links, 'I hate talking about my own courses, I'm not very good at it'.

There had been a prohibition in Scotland against building seaside golf courses, necessitating some fancy politicking to see the links come to fruition. What sealed the approval process was an argument put forward by de Savary that his proposal was just a reworking of the original but dormant Skibo course built by Andrew Carnegie in 1898. For the best part grassed over, it had lain fallow since the 1930s. Nevertheless, while flying authorities over the land on a selling mission he was able to indicate sufficient evidence of original tees and greens to make the argument stick – and so work could begin.[72]

Laid out upon a sliver of land and surrounded by water on three sides, ecological preservation was very much required in the planning process. On one side lies Loch Evelix which is filled with salmon and continues to be a haven for aquatic bird life. Architectural routing also took into consideration a rare and protected lichen heath.[73] Today this is apparent when playing the short 6th hole. Empathy of this kind, enabled Skibo to win a national award that assessed where golfing matters and complex environmental issues were best handled sensitively and coexisted in harmony.

This thought process continued off the links and even the club house remained in character, achieved by modelling it upon the farmstead it replaced. Unlike several other links developments, Skibo was spared the task of hiring an army of bulldozers (Donald Steel is well known for his light-handed approach at construction time). Among delightfully natural links land holes were simply placed advantageously. In keeping with a true links, the Carnegie Links topography includes much grassy rough, sandhills in places (though lower than most), gorse, heather and a series of shot-making challenges, that if failed, will amount to a watery grave. Of note, the water holes are entirely natural and play alongside or over, inter-tidal salt marshes, an estuary, a river and the Dornoch Firth.

Sixteen of the holes could broadly be described as running along an east–west axis.[74] As the wind is a constant companion, you can therefore expect to play a good deal of downwind or into-the-wind golf. To cater for a range of playing abilities, Carnegie Links has five tees on each hole, which stretches the links from 5,436–6,671 yards. Despite the presence of many worthy and challenging holes throughout the entire links, the last two are arguably the best of a very good collection.

The par-four 17th hole, at only 267 yards, provides the golfer with a tantalising choice. Drivable by the adventurous, it plays slightly downhill and the prevailing wind is left-to-right. Those with visions of eagles will need to start their golf ball out over the Dornoch Firth and pray it honours your bravery. Should a mis-hit occur, steep revetted bunkers await to penalise you. However, a sensible lay-up from the tee will secure a par easily enough.

To conclude your round at Skibo, the dramatic 18th hole tee-shot beckons you to chew off as much territory over a salt marsh as your nerve and skill will allow. A leftward swinging dog-leg par five, it has much of the Pebble Beach look about it. At any stage of the hole, a right-handed-golfer's hook will find water. This visually magnificent hole culminates in a green perched right out on a point, where proceedings can easily be viewed from the club house.

Ballybunion New

Of all the new links, none has aroused such a spate of divergent opinion as Ballybunion New. The high profile American architect, Robert Trent Jones, was commissioned to construct the second links at Ballybunion, despite the original plans being drawn up by Irishman, Eddie Hackett. At Jones's disposal was stunning land to work with, and this made him the envy of many architects. Ballybunion Old was suffering from ceaseless pilgrimages and it seemed the natural thing to take advantage of the abutting sandhills. It had been mooted for years.

In 1984 the links was completed and within a short time frame, Trent Jones pronounced that the New was among his top five most favoured creations.[75]

Opinion is divided, and some suggest he failed to deliver a links that lived up to its advance billing. American architect, Tom Doak, states, 'You either love it or hate it – because that is exactly how it treats your golf shots. If you are not hitting your irons within 7.5 m (25 ft) of the hole, through a stiff breeze at that, you will need strong legs to finish the round. I don't see how any sane man can rate it superior to its sister'. He adds, 'In the end though, it must be admitted that the New course is one which gets the pulse going quicker, and the pioneer spirit in me says that is a mark of greatness. It is too bad the recent softening has taken some of the grandeur away, since it may have been the only thing the original design got right'.[76]

Others, such as ex-Ballybunion professional Ted Higgins have claimed, 'Although in certain respects it may be too early to tell, I have a strong gut feeling that the New Course here at Ballybunion may just possibly turn out to be one of the most magnificent links that the world has seen'.[77]

Noted golf writer Peter Dobereiner, who has since passed away, was in no doubt: 'Gradually the sheer excellence of the course and the exhilaration of playing through an "Andes" of dunes, will win over the critics, or most of them. Today, the people who know it best, the members, rate it better than the Old by a considerable majority. And that means, quite simply that it is the greatest links course in the world'.[78]

Donald Steel offers a different perspective: 'It is full of fine drives and the dunes lend an imposing, custodial look that in conjunction with the superlative coastal stretch, makes it every bit as scenic as its neighbour. It is more a test of stout legs but some of the greens are far too small, particularly with the presence of so much wind. The greens are the focus of every hole on every course and must also blend well with the landscape but, in this vital respect, the New cannot compare with the Old'.[79]

My own feeling is that Robert Trent Jones was a brave man to accept such a commission. No matter how well he performed the New was apt to be seen as somewhat controversial, if for no other reason that many golfers harbour the sentiment of Ballybunion Old being their favourite links. Any links, let alone one right next door, was bound to suffer by comparison. Despite the arduous leg work, in a gentle Kerry breeze, it is quite possible to appreciate on face value. But in anything stronger, let alone extreme adverse weather, the links becomes unplayable quicker than any other I have encountered. Most likely, it is upon these occasions that golfers let fly with comments that may appear a little harsh. There is no shame in admitting that sometimes a golf course is too penal and despite best intentions, needs further refining. That is my hope for Ballybunion New.

Waterville Golf Club

Two hours south of Ballybunion, a fairy tale story emerges of Waterville Golf Club's development. Who among us can honestly say that in our quieter moments we have not fantasised about laying out a links? Wealthy Irish-American Jack Mulcahy had long dreamed of such an eventuality. The result of much forethought is the breathtaking Waterville Golf Club towards the southern tip of the Ring of Kerry in County Kerry, Ireland.

It must be stated that this links is no place for the tap and run golfer. Architects Jack and Eddie Hackett are well known for their good work, and with Waterville, which opened in 1973, their reputations have only been enhanced. Apart from incessant wind, Waterville is brutally long, as evidenced by seven par fours over 400 yards, two par threes around 200 yards and two of the par fives at 595 yards and 582 yards respectively. It demands a combination of both very long driving and accurate shot-making to succeed here. Greg Norman's game would be ideally suited to Waterville.

Waterville is frequently discussed as among the most testing course in the British Isles. Sam Snead played it and commented, 'The Beautiful Monster – one of the golfing wonders of the world'.[80] Raymond Floyd was so impressed during his stay that he thought, 'Waterville is one of the most beautiful places I have ever seen, with the finest links holes I have ever played'.[81] Tom Watson who

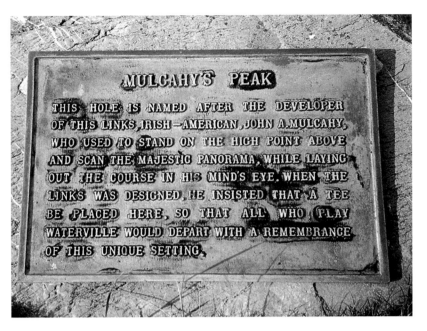

MULCAHY'S PEAK

THIS HOLE IS NAMED AFTER THE DEVELOPER OF THIS LINKS, IRISH—AMERICAN, JOHN A. MULCAHY, WHO USED TO STAND ON THE HIGH POINT ABOVE AND SCAN THE MAJESTIC PANORAMA, WHILE LAYING OUT THE COURSE IN HIS MIND'S EYE. WHEN THE LINKS WAS DESIGNED, HE INSISTED THAT A TEE BE PLACED HERE, SO THAT ALL WHO PLAY WATERVILLE WOULD DEPART WITH A REMEMBRANCE OF THIS UNIQUE SETTING.

A self-explanatory plaque on the 17th hole at Waterville

has for many years had a love affair with all things linksy and Irish, stated, 'Apart from anything else, Waterville possesses the best collection of par threes I have ever encountered on the same golf course'.[82]

Owner Mulcahy got it right when he named the first hole Last Easy. To test your lumbago, consider that the first three holes measure 430, 469 and 417 yards respectively. I have never adhered to the school of thought that 'all that is long is good'. In fact, having attempted to write in an unvarnished manner, I must say that the first two holes are caricatures of a recurring bad dream. They are overly long, boring, artificial and totally misplaced. But on most holes and for separate reasons, Waterville excels — the setting alone ensures this. Be warned though, there are no let-up holes and for sheer toughness, it can be grouped with Carnoustie, the European Club, Royal St George's and maybe Royal County Down.

As a spectacle, your round takes flight on the third tee. Another gruelling par four, it is rescued by architectural merit and scenery — the River Inny down the right-hand side and a stunning dog-leg aspect that culminates in a plateauing green.

The fourth hole which is elevated and among dunes country is simply a classic — one of the finest par threes in the British Isles. In a strong right-to-left wind, aiming the ball right out over the dunes is mandatory and fills the player with pleasure, self-doubt and much challenge. As for length, its medium length is perfectly suited to accomplish these ends.

Waterville's 10th hole, Bottleneck, is one of Ireland's hardest and longest par fours. Named Bottleneck for good reason, the green's entrance is perilously narrow for all but the most accurate, although in reality most approach this par four with a short iron for their third shot.

The 11th is known as Tranquillity and aptly named. A shade under 500 yards, it is hardly a long par five, but all the ingredients to ingrain a golf hole in your mind are present — strategic excellence, dunes, twists and turns, lay-up potential, green light attempts for the big-hitters and superb natural undulations. Birdies are not uncommon here, but like all strong holes, poor driving will signal a bogey or worse.

The 12th hole is appropriately named Mass. In the days when being Catholic was a dangerous thing and celebrating it even more dangerous, locals would huddle together at the sheltered bottom of this hole, where the green now lies, to partake of their religious ceremonies.[83] It is an especially difficult 200-yard par three (all carry) with no shortage of marvellous links land to admire. Many keen judges suggest Mass is Waterville's signature hole and it may well be.

The 16th hole pays tribute to professional Liam Higgins, famed for his prodigious hitting. Known as Liam's Ace, he actually holed in one on this severe dog-leg by paying scant regard to convention. It is estimated that Higgins bludgeoned the ball around 340 yards in carry.[84] This fine hole has plenty of interest value — as an aside, many comment upon the peculiar and ugly plants that act as coastal fortification between beach and fairway.

The 17th hole, known as Mulcahy's Peak, is a colossal par three of nearly 200 yards from a high

PREVIOUS PAGE: The tumultuous
15th hole at Carne. Rarely will
golfers encounter dunes of this
magnitude

RIGHT: The 14th hole at Carne is
an enjoyable and visually
appealing par three

A downhill drive is an enthralling way to commence the inward nine holes at Carne. Note the open entrance to Hackett's green and a grassy hollow in the foreground

ABOVE: Most golfers struggle with the trouble-strewn par four 7th hole, The European Club

RIGHT: The 10th fairway and green at Pat Ruddy's links, The European Club

OPPOSITE: The round at Carnegie Club, Skibo, concludes with this magnificent sweeping par five. A hook at any stage will result in a lost ball

ABOVE: A great tradition on your arrival at Turnberry Hotel is to be greeted by a piper. For comfort and opulence, only Gleneagles and Skibo Castle can compare

RIGHT: Elie Golf Club in the Kingdom of Fife, Scotland, can boast a highly attractive and individual clubhouse

Four examples of the highly
distinctive bunkering at Royal
County Down, Newcastle,
Northern Ireland

The putting green at the West
Lancashire Golf Club, Lancashire,
England. In the distance, the 9th
green can be distinguished. The
tall white post is designed to
assist players from the 9th tee,
which calls for a blind drive.
Penalising rough is stationed on
either side of the fairway

A tee-to-green view from Mulcahy's Peak

elevation. Like the 12th hole, it will take your breath away on first sighting. Your tee-shot must clear a haze of trouble, and a favourable wind will allow you to appreciate its grandeur. Named after Waterville's owner, it was said he often used to visit the peak and contemplate in his mind's eye what future treasure would one day lay before him.[85] Tom Watson's assessment was accurate — the par threes at Waterville take a lot of beating.

Being semi-enclosed, driving from the 18th tee is quite an adventure; what with out of bounds and Ballinskellig's Bay on the right, and penalising rough down the left. And as always, natural elevation only enhances the view. From the tee, the golfer faces one of those drives which psychologically appears frightfully narrow, and driving out from a shute can easily leave that impression. In reality though, it's plenty wide enough. Unfortunately, both the second and third shots are less heroic, which is mainly due to the unflattering topography. Being anti-climactic, the round sadly concludes in the same uninspiring manner it began.

Waterville will not be tackled by the idle golfer. Players of this type rarely consider travelling to such outposts, merely for golf, although the fishing is first rate should you tire of the golf. Waterville, due to its wild and woolly desolation is for the links desperado, the type who would think little of driving from Edinburgh to Royal Dornoch for a game. From Cork, the distance is of little consequence but due to scenic distractions, allow three hours. Was it not Nick Faldo, who, after winning an Irish Open, said, 'In Ireland no-one dies of an ulcer'.

Golf addicts, Jan and Sean, enjoying the world-class scenery on the road from Cork to Waterville

You have to hand it to the Irish, they have an abiding love for the game and are fiercely protective of their great array of links — many of which are relatively new. Due to Scottish imposed restrictions, the majority of the new British links have been Irish creations — in particular by Eddie Hackett. This deeply religious man almost single-handedly carried on the great links tradition. Consider that in one stretch between 1971 and 1974, Ceann Sibeal, Waterville, Connemara, Donegal and Enniscrone sprang forth from this golfing legend — all on the west coast of Ireland. Of these, only Enniscrone was a redesign. As recently as 1995, Carne Golf Club in County Mayo was opened for play, and this links is detailed later in the chapter.

Tralee Golf Club

In 1984 Arnold Palmer and Ed Seay made their initial foray into designing links by creating Tralee. It, too, is on the west coast of Ireland. When I first played Tralee in 1989, I noted that it was rough and ready but stamped with great potential. By adhering to a programme of steady upgrading of links conditioning and club house facilities (of which there is good evidence), the links is now fully mature and a joy to play. The 1st hole, though no brain-teaser is a pleasant enough start, while the 2nd hole is outstanding and universally admired. This beguiling par five beckons you to drive as far to the right as you dare (cliff line), towards an elbow of land known as Cuilin Swink. But such a line is foolhardy. The best line is well left towards the wall, which looks frightfully close, but this is just depth perception playing tricks.

When assessing the relative merits of Tralee, some people maintain, 'The back-nine is Tralee'. To agree to this, is to snub your nose at several fine holes, especially when you consider the 2nd hole and the visually impressive 3rd — a par three to a tiny green perched out on Barrow point. From the back tees and into the breeze, this hole will raise even the most dormant pulse.

Granted, some of the inland holes are dreary by comparison to the dunal back nine holes, and the 6th in particular, offers little in the way of excitement. However, they all remain a reasonable challenge; easy golf is rare with the ever-present Dingle elements. Actually, the 4th hole, which is a dinky little par four along a stone wall, has much of the quirky links nature about it that I like. Others, as is their right, condemn it.

Safe passage away from the gaping cliff is a priority on the 8th tee — it juts into the fairway alarmingly more so than visitors first realise. I well remember the startled reaction to my words of concern by golfing partners, Jan, Ken and Sean, after they drove along seemingly safe lines. My ball, which appeared to be badly pushed well to the right, ended in the middle of the fairway. Two of their impressively struck drives became donations after falling victim to the vicissitudes of links land undulation. To validate the quality of this exciting hole, it features on Tralee's scorecard.

The 10th hole is a long downhill dog-legging left par four, where the natural lie of the land slews your drive towards the right hand rough — the type of tee-shot challenge made for Nick Faldo. From there, the second shot with a medium-to-long iron against an enthralling backdrop, sets the tone for the inward journey. But not quite yet. The 11th hole (Palmer's Peak) is a long, uphill and tedious par five. Why Palmer and Tralee Golf Club chose to honour his name with this hole is beyond me.

Beached on the marvellous 8th hole at Tralee. The elevated teeing ground is visible in the background

The 12th hole, known as 'Bracken' is a great links experience. Opinions vary enormously on its merit but most concur about the excitement factor. However, relatively few golfers can reach the green in regulation, regardless of the wind direction and some may not appreciate its charm as a result. Whereas Bottleneck (10th) at Waterville is massively long but flat, this is shorter but plays just as long due to the uphill second shot. Just beyond the dunal headland, a small elusive green awaits. Excellent shots will streak towards the green, only to be retarded by the steep incline of the hill. Depending on the time of year and degree of rough, your ball will stick into the hill or drop all the way down to the bottom, just as happens at Waterville's Mass hole. Despite the controversial nature of this hole, I like it for the unbridled challenge it presents and because it's different.

As for Tralee's par three 13th hole, some make comparisons with Royal Portrush's Calamity hole which features Locke's Hollow. This I feel, owes more to the rhyming nature of 'Brock's Hollow' than any architectural reality. The hole is much shorter but the sense of adventure is equally strong. To fully enjoy the challenge don't be short off the tee.

Many of the outstanding par fours in links golf belong to the medium and medium-long distance bracket. An exception is the 15th hole at Tralee, measuring only 279 metres long. From a secluded teeing ground, this dog-leg hole demands the golfer to find an island fairway; hitting the fairway is insufficient, for only balls directed towards the fairway's centre-right gain a view of the green protected by cut-out dunes on each side.

During one round at Tralee, I hit a career two iron and I'm glad it occurred on the par three, 16th hole. Off the back tees and into the wind, nothing less than your Sunday best will do. The elevated tee-shot scenery amid high ground is spectacular, and eases your mind from the task ahead. Coastal views along the right hand side of the hole, encapsulate the mood of links golf completely. The 16th hole is famous for another reason, namely, the amount of shipwrecks in the bay. The *Catherine Richards, Debbie, Wild Trader* and *Port Stanley* can all be observed from the tee, given a bright clear day.

The 12th hole at Tralee. Mercifully, a patch of grass has been mowed to assist your recovery in the advent of a failed approach shot, which by the way, is a near certainty. From 200 metres or so, the approach is all carry

The 17th hole is known as Ryan's Daughter. Though considerably less taxing than the 16th, this pretty golf hole derives much fame through its association with David Lean's film, *Ryan's Daughter*. A drive missed to the right hand side will ensure a bogey, while a well placed drive should guarantee a playable uphill approach through a textbook open entrance.

The finishing hole at Tralee is very long at 424 metres, but due to the prevailing wind, is tame when compared with the 12th hole. The area behind the 18th tee has significance — here, goats once huddled and took refuge from the elements. This area was known as Goat's Hole and when viewed from the beach below, they could be spotted peeping out from the cliff face.

An endearing feature of Tralee, is to reflect upon how Barrow was once laid out through fields. The 1st, 10th and 18th holes run through fields once known as Stoney, Parc na Vir and The Spade, respectively. The 4th hole was once known as The Aucaries (the small fields), while the adjacent 5th fairway utilised The Castle Fields. To the left of the 6th hole (second half) saw three separate fields: Sandy Gardens, The Randy Gardens and The Galleries. The uphill, par five 9th hole dissected The Pound and The Jib. Elsewhere, other named fields meandered over the links land.

The European Club

On the other side of Ireland at Brittas Bay, lies The European Club — bold in concept, high on octane ambition and among the upper echelon of links, notoriously difficult to produce a decent score on. It is also amid startling scenery. As a bonus for its members, the links is delightfully uncrowded and the pace is slow and easy; that's quite achievable when as few as 130 members bump into each other. Ambition that is clearly stated can never be misunderstood. Says owner, president and architect, Pat Ruddy:

The European Club is a private club with a friendly disposition towards visiting players. We hope that our guests will enjoy the experience of visiting one of the world's 160 golf links while observing the etiquette that is traditional and central to golf. In most cases, the great links took upwards of one hundred years to evolve into what they are today. So we feel no pain as we work at our own pace, which we describe simply as 'speeded-up evolution' as opposed to the 'dropped from the heaven' high finance approach common today. This allows us to think out our design features and keep our guest fees at popular levels.

At The European, we have encouraged gradual development and investment creates the situation where we can be true to our belief that manners, space and time, rather than money, should be the governors of access to our links. Our approach to golf is fundamentalist. Accordingly, you will not find fussy furniture on our links. You might take it to be spartan while we think it is akin to the way the game was in the beginning and should be now.

We believe that man-made fixtures should intrude as slightly as possible upon a landscape which has waited for centuries for the coming of man and, now that we are here, deserves our respect. Given respect, the place will retain its beauty to the benefit of man, beast and plant.

Into a strong breeze, few links holes are tougher than Tralee's 181-metre par three 16th hole

In essence, golf is a game of skill. So it is here. We make no apology for the fact that the thoughtless and inept player may suffer on our links. It was not created for such players. Yet, even the beginner will enjoy a game here subject to choosing the correct teeing-ground to play from and then playing within one's skill level. If you choose the wrong tees, please call it suicide rather than murder.

We love the game of golf. That is why we are not afraid to be different in our design approach. We see the game as a fun part of our lives and of those of our guests. For example, the links consists of two loops of ten holes instead of two loops of nine. This decimalised set-up is appropriate at The European Club. But the real reason for this situation is: If there are twenty fine golf holes out there, why stop at eighteen? We are here to golf.[86]

A delightful aspect of The European Club, is the manner in which each hole has been named in honour of a very famous golfer; the winning of at least one major being the main criterion, or having made a significant contribution to the game of golf. Tom Morris Snr and Bobby Jones have holes named to preserve their memory at St Andrews Old, so there was little need for further acknowledgement by The European Club. Recipients are the likes of Tom Watson, Gene Sarazen, Gary Player, Sir Henry Cotton, Sam Snead, Fred Daly to name several. Pat Ruddy held much affection for his friend, Harry Bradshaw, and the main putting green is named after him as a constant reminder of his prowess with the flat stick.

Golfers have always preferred variety in their greens and are easily repelled by non-stop sameness to each putting surface. Even good putters become robotic under these conditions and their stroke will eventually be reduced to mediocrity. Some architects fall for the trap of delivering 'dead elephants' too frequently, others elusive double and triple tiered greens; or just as bad, snooker table flatness. At The European Club, semi-plateau greens are present on holes 1, 3, 4, 8, 10 and 14, while holes 5, 6, 7, 9, 11, 12, 13, 16 and 17 provide great contrast with either semi-sunken or relatively flat greens. Variety of this order is a real feature of The European Club.

The European Club takes great pride in its twelfth green, which has been extended to measure 127 yards deep. By all accord, this may rank as the longest green in the world. Your thoughts will instantly stray to the stately double greens at St Andrews Old and ponder, surely there must be

something bigger there? Not quite. Ruddy's green is 9 yards longer than the widest at St Andrews. A green of this magnitude, according to Ruddy — 'Sets the scene for the restoration of the the art of the great three-putt as opposed to the disappointing version of the same'.

Alister MacKenzie credited a lot of his knowledge on the art of deception and camouflage to his stint as surgeon in the Boer War. The methods by which the Boers practised concealment and disguise of military positions impressed MacKenzie, and recognised as an expert in the field, he was later called on to establish the British School of Camouflage. His task was to assist the training of World War One soldiers in these disciplines. The astute battlefield principles he learned, were later superimposed upon his architectural philosophy to many wondrous layouts — most of which appear deceptively easier than they really are. Pat Ruddy is another to have benefited from knowledge on depth perception and lines:

> I have always admired the confusion that has been caused by optical illusions. I have been fortunate to have worked with a camera since boyhood and so have gathered an appreciation for and knowledge of matters like depth of field, perspective and composition. I am content that a number of the shots at The European Club look longer, shorter, wider or narrower than they really are; and every walk after each shot has been arranged so that the player is effectively and hopefully conscious some of the time of walking into a picture postcard with the vista constantly changing. At once, this will enchant him but also disorientate him, as his focus varies constantly and rapidly.[87]

While The European Club shows regard for most of the mainstream traditions of links golf, they are not afraid to castigate those they deem outdated or nonsensical — blind holes in particular. One that is very much retained though, is the time honoured tradition of open entrances to the greens. Rather than simply have each green entirely open, they have presented this feature by degrees. With the exception of the 2nd, 11th and 18th holes, all entrances vary from (reasonably) to (substantially) open, with swales and tilts to allow for aerial or terrestrial approaches.

Pat Ruddy has given much thought to the bunkering aspect at The European Club. He states:

> I have always liked bunkers. Especially links bunkers with the natural sand which cannot be raked into sissy conditions. Especially bunkers with depth. Also bunkers with sleepered faces. But I do not agree that there should be hundreds of bunkers to do the business. Rather, well placed bunkers that threaten and reward (I did a survey once that showed that there are over 300 bunkers at Royal Lytham and St Anne's and only 50 at Augusta National). We have 64 bunkers at The European Club and just half of these feature intimidating sleepered faces which accomplish a number of things at once:
>
> They allow us to show the bunkers from a distance as the sleeper emphasises the shadow effects which are often the only warnings of a bunker's existence on a links. I think it is fair to let the golfer see the test paper. Then, if he fails, he fails honestly.
>
> They allow us to bring the bunkers right in at greenside and into exciting banks. They prevent the sand banks from collapsing when we cut sheer faces. Gone are the days when the pitch-and-run game necessitated the placement of bunkers 50-60 yards short of the green so that a spoon or brassie shot could be sent over them and sent running that distance onto the green. I don't think Tiger Woods and his pals will find much business with bunkers that aren't crowding the target in a little bit more in the years ahead. And while we are not building exclusively for Tiger, it has to be felt that a links that wishes to be great, needs to be capable of being measured against the best players.

OPPOSITE: The 3rd hole at The European Club

They intimidate the hell out of fellows and that is part of being a man and golfer. They also introduce a nice element of ball bouncing to ensure that the game isn't always going to be an exact ball placing science. And they allow us to arrange tilts that allow for a golf shot, maybe not exactly the one you like, but a golf shot to be played out of them rather than finding a ball plugged under a sod-revetted face. They ease our maintenance programme which is the least consideration, but it helps us to keep the price of the game pitched right.

Also on bunkers, we have them centre, cross and sprinkled. MacKenzie, whom everyone quoted for the sissy thoughts about golf being a game that should be playable by the inept and lazy as well as the skilled (to misquote for effect) also wrote that 'A hazard no matter where it is placed cannot be said to be unfair because, once a golfer knows it is there, he knows that is not where he should place his ball'.

One silly American chap (who turned out to be a gent when golf educated) complained that we had too much sand in the bunkers. He obviously comes from a place where they build (and then fill) rather than just scrape out bunkers. 'How deep would you like it'? I asked. 'About 12 cm', he replied. 'Right, that will mean that most of our bunkers will be just about 35 metres deep because we are sitting on that amount of sand'.[88]

When the topic of length was raised, the same passion came to the fore – 'The European Club is long'. Ruddy further elaborated:

Length isn't everything, but you have to have some. So it is we measure 7,100 yards for eighteen holes and have two extra par threes measuring 165 and 210 yards. If we use the latter to replace a par three, we get up to 7,150 yards. And we have plenty of space to stretch the legs if that is ever needed. Changes must happen of course. If they have been changing the examination paper for hundreds of years elsewhere, we must keep mentally agile, too. So, this year alone our programme of work rivals Augusta – a new back tee at both the 3rd and 4th holes, killer new tee on the 7th making it a par four of 470 yards, a new par 3 called 12a, a new alignment for the tee-shot on the 13th which increases it from 540 to 610 yards, the huge extension to the green on the 12th, a new back tee and new green at the 15th. It will be less hectic in 1999 but we are still learning things about our links and striving to fine tune.[89]

As the fine-tuning continues, the influential *Golf Monthly* magazine in its May 1998 issue, listed The European Club as No. 27 among the top 100 courses of the British Isles. In their opinion, only Tom Weiskopf's inland gem at Loch Lomond rates higher for any new course built this century. Ruddy assessed this rating and offered the following comment:

To have people think us higher may take some time. Tradition has to be matched or overcome. We have to be enjoyed by a generation or two of golfers who may come to like us, as much as the present senior generations like the links on which they were suckled. Golf, and the affection for this playing field or that, is greatly a matter of perception and emotion, superimposed on facts (which must of course, be valid and good). I have tried hard to produce a links more perfect than anything that went before. No links has 18 perfect holes and so the gap exists to get ahead if one can see it clearly. [90]

Of his formative golfing years:

I was born to a golf-loving father who exposed me to a lot of good influences – including the essence of modest golf courses in the west of Ireland. Courses where there were no fancy add-ons beyond the sheer pleasure of being out in the field with nature and a set of clubs. No business deals. No social climbing. Just nature and friends and the joy of the challenge. And no matter how bad the greens were, it was all so lovely. The lovely golf to be found on links land where the shoes were clean and the ball was clean no matter what the weather; where the lark burst its heart in the skies above; where a young fellow having cycled twenty miles to play 54 holes, could lie exhausted in the long bent grasses chewing on a sandwich and gazing into the deep azure wondering if there were golfers out there, too.

The Golf Book. Before television, I was transported to Britain, America and even to Australia by the written word and I got to see these places in photographs. 'Old' Tom was my buddy, Harry Vardon an old mate, Ted Ray — as a pipe-smoker, I had to like him — just like my Scottish grandfather. Henry Cotton ... how was I to know we would be business partners one day, or that I would find this aged champion's soul to be as romantic and crazy as my own as we travelled through Britain and Ireland telling people in small villages to reserve a space for golf; a space for golf just like the 'village green' cricket field. Any golf would beat no golf and it needn't be fancy.

From an early age at school, I dreamt of golf and the possibility of owning a golf course. I never dreamt of the scale of course, just a course where I could hit millions of golf balls and become great at the game. Alas, I never dreamt of The European Club. But after years of this and that in golf, my day came and even as a somewhat informal soul in the matter of religion, I now walk the fairways looking over my shoulder and wondering who is the comic who delivered this ace.

I have had no choice but to play the shots and they seem to be working out. I strive to ensure that I do it more to give to others than to covet for myself. The essential motivation is to enjoy the game and to share that joy with as many other people as possible; both now and long after one has trudged off this coil.

In the years ahead, I will poke about and create little nooks here and there where a fellow can find half a golf hole in the gorse and dunes. There, he will be able to hit a few balls, lie on the grass and chew a sandwich like I did as a kid and dream how great it would have been to utilise this piece of ground in the main links — and how I must have missed it.[91]

Ballyliffin Golf Club

The rarity of quality links land is well accepted. Ballyliffin Golf Club, though, has the unusual distinction of laying out two links since the last Great War. The first of these was the Old Links in 1947, and more recently, Glashedy Links in 1995. Originally the Old was situated near the village amid terrain that inspired few. It was later relocated nearer the sea, first as a nine-hole links, and then the architectural firm of Cotton, Pennink, Lawrie & Partners, fashioned out a first-rate eighteen hole links ready for play in 1973. It would be remiss not to mention Eddie Hackett's role, for being attached to Bord Failte, he visited Ballyliffin and made worthwhile suggestions. While Carne is the most westerly links in Ireland, Ballyliffin can claim to be the most northerly situated.

In total, the club possesses nearly 400 acres of magnificent rolling land, and impressively, the two links retain their own identity, complete with separate charm and challenge. Glashedy Links has drawn comparisons with Ballybunion New, in reference to its mountainous dunes. The club calls it, 'That other World', as you retreat from the club house and head towards awe-inspiring countryside. The Old Links is old-fashioned in design, and renowned as a totally natural links. Both links are loaded with character, and one point of differentiation, is that less blind golf is required on the Old Links. By way of counterbalance, Glashedy Links confers more even stances.

In Ireland, competition runs high in the scenery stakes, and most regions have a legitimate claim upon tourists. The Donegal region, in particular, is famed for its circling mountains, valleys, quaint villages and beautiful coastal scenery. Ballyliffin Golf Club is truly fortunate to lie among these surrounds. Indeed, as one official put it ... 'This is where you go to leave chaos behind and be blissfully out of touch with the world and its problems'. Despite this, Ballyliffin is only thirty minutes from Derry Airport, and approximately two hours by car from Belfast.

Club spirit has always been very high at Ballyliffin. In the early days on the Old Links, members brought along their lawn mowers, and lent assistance, plus a good deal of respite to the resident sheep.

Scenery highlights on the Old are commonplace, but the highlight above all else occurs as you head towards the elevated and severely sloping 2nd green. At this point, the full majesty of ocean, hills, Glashedy Rock (Ballyliffin's answer to Turnberry's Ailsa Craig), and twisting links land reveals itself. Another highlight is the par five 4th hole, and its brilliant fairway contours. Played at dusk on a fine summer's evening, has prompted the romantic reference from locals, 'the fairway of a thousand shadows'.

There are many fine holes on the Old Links, but none more famous, or infamous as the case may be, than the par three 5th hole. The green lies perched precariously on high ground between two sand hills. It is known as the Tank hole, and only the most precise golf shots will be accepted.

The Club is justly proud of its par five 18th hole at the Old Links, and many members rate it their finest. In keeping with the rest of the links, the fairway twists and turns, but by then, the golfer is well used to the rapid eye-line adjustments. The final green nestles under the watchful eye of the club house.

Lying perilously close to the sea, the Old Links has been at great risk of coastal erosion. In hindsight, a great test case (of what not to do) took place. It involved the widespread removal of thousands of tonnes of natural gravel from the seaward boundary of the links. Horrified members and environmentalists made their feelings known to the Donegal County Council. Once, during a period when opinions were being aired, a large tract of land was lost. Slowly but surely, the folly of removing seashore material was agreed upon, and subsequently the activity was prohibited by Council. Thankfully, natural gravel barriers have reformed. Nevertheless, the Club knows only too well, that any complacency in regard to Nature's potential is unwise.

PUBLICITY CAN MAKE OR BREAK ANY GOLF CLUB, and here, Ballyliffin is well placed. It has greatly benefited by a visit from Nick Faldo in 1993, as part of his preparation to defend the Open Championship. He was also defending his Irish Open at Mt Juliet the following week. Completely bowled over by the Old Links, he claimed it was the finest natural links he had ever played, and in response to the tumbling links land, begged the question, 'Do you play bump and run here, or just run and bump?'

Although young in years, the Glashedy Links has quickly forged a reputation for its large, undulating greens. Many putting surfaces incorporate subtle breaks, and some greens are classically presented as two-tiered.

The bunkering is severe, and much to the chagrin of the poor bunker player, often sod-revetted. Architects, Pat Ruddy and Tom Craddock have signaled their intention of punishing the wayward. Sandy hazards are generally confronting, and those which protect the entrances of the 2nd and 3rd greens are simply gaping. Already, one conversational piece is the quintet of threatening bunkers that fortify and circle the short 5th green.

Glashedy is no pushover when it comes to length. The first three holes communicate straight away that a battle has begun. At 426, 432 and 428 yards respectively from the black tees, it is wise to have limbered up. In total, Glashedy measures 7135 from the black, 6884 from the gold, and 6466 yards from the white tees.

Having survived the steep walk leading from the 6th green to the elevated 7th tee, you are confronted by one of the most startling views in links golf. On display, is the Old Links with its stylishly demarcated ribbon-like fairways, Glashedy Rock (which positively dominates the whole scene), and the sea. All this occurs on a hole named Loch na nDeor, a challenging par three with a 33 m (36 yd) drop to the green. Any slightly pushed tee-shot on this short hole is destined to find the water hazard.

Commonly, golfers refer to the stretch between the 12th hole and 15th as standout quality golf. It contains a ferociously dog-legging par four, a par five of epic proportions, a delightful par three, and the 15th which is Glashedy's longest and sternest par four. Negotiate this collection in par figures and you are playing better than you know how.

Pleasingly, Glashedy concludes with a memorable hole. Your mettle is tested as you attempt to thread your drive between a narrow corridor of dunes, and then fire your approach between flanking revetted bunkers. An elusive green awaits.

It will be fascinating to observe how the Glashedy Links progresses from here; already the golf world marvels at the progress attained. The Club has come a long way, especially when you consider that as recently as 1992, the Committee met with Pat Ruddy and Tom Craddock to discuss the possibility of laying out an additional nine to reduce stress on the Old Links. The architects would have none of this, the terrain was simply too good not to insist upon an eighteen hole links. After much debate and discussion with members, including a reasonable amount of opposition, the all-clear was given and construction begun on 7 May 1993. No time was wasted and the opening day took place on 3 August 1995.

A real impetus to Glashedy Links was their successful staging of the Ladies Irish Open in 1998 won by Sophie Gufstaffson. The professionals were highly taken with the experience, and a return in the near future is in the planning.

Following the establishment of Glashedy Links, a positive flow-on effect has been duly noted. Tourism to the Inishowen Peninsula has sparked an upturn in the building industry. The golf club, itself, is delighted to be able to increase and utilise local employment.

Carne Golf Links

Concluding this chapter with Eddie Hackett's final contribution to links golf is fitting — and more than a few rate Carne as his finest work. Hackett himself was pleased with the outcome and predicted that in time, Carne may reveal itself as the best of all links in Ireland, and possibly anywhere. The club enjoys the distinction of being the most westerly links in Europe. Eamonn Mangan, a director of Carne Management, says of Eddie Hackett:

An exceptional gentleman. It was never a question of money with Eddie Hackett, it was a question of of good results and getting the best out of what we had. He was almost eighty years old, but he walked the course for three days, making drawings each night in his bed and breakfast. And he was enthusiastic from the very word go. He told me, 'If ever the Lord intended land for a golf course, Carne has it'.

Eddie wanted to disturb as little as possible of the natural territory but there were places we went into where there were just massive sand dunes, and we had to create fairways somehow. A few fairways cost us twenty or thirty thousand pounds and others cost us nothing.[92]

The Carne Golf Links (Galf Chursa Chairn) is the product of much local pride and enthusiasm. In 1984, while attempting to bolster tourism to the Erris region of County Mayo, a local group formed a company known as Erris Tourism Ltd. The activities planned to encourage tourism were varied but their major focus was the formation of a new golf club. This initiative is proving to be successful judging by the increasing yearly income generated from green fees. To reward your long journey, Carne is among the cheapest of all championship quality links to play.

The golf club and its impressive elevated club house was built on 260 acres of tumbling commonage, being part of the Carne banks land form. This land was purchased in 1985 and with a steady as it goes policy, the outward nine opened for play in 1992, the inward half in 1993 and the club house became fully functional in 1995.

Carne is the home of the Belmullet Club, which played on a nine-hole course at Cross until 1992. The club was founded in 1925 and they're a proud member of West Coast Links: Enniscrone, County Sligo, Connemara, Donegal and Ballyliffin. Being so remote, collegiality of this type is most helpful to each golf club.

One of the attractions of Carne is the marvellous variety of the terrain and views. On the front nine, in particular, it changes repeatedly. At various stages of your round, you will experience tremendous valleys and swales, low lying terrain, views of farm land and bog land, vistas that incorporate Blacksod Bay and the Atlantic — all the while, amid dunes that are staggering to the human eye.

By comparison to Hackett's other links, there is a reasonable amount of blind golf at Carne, but it is not excessive. Uppermost in mind was to keep a traditional look and being the beneficiary of such mountainous dunes, a degree of blindness was inevitable. The aim was to present an acceptable level; one in keeping with links such as Lahinch and Royal County Down.

One of the real talking points of Carne continues to be the deepest imaginable valley in front of the 18th green. Nature fashioned the Valley of Sin at St Andrews Old and it will not surprise if Valley of Carne becomes a links byword. Right up until his death, it concerned Hackett that at some point in the future this valley may be tampered with.

The links is not particularly long, but on good links, excessive length is not obligatory to challenge ability. Carne continues to gain favour with golfers of varying handicaps and ambition level; it is no exception to most other links, in that it demands accurate driving and crisply struck irons. These are aimed towards beautifully natural green sites — many of which lie in spectacular amphitheatres.

Carne enjoys one aspect that is unusual among championship links — not one par four is over 400 metres. From the medal tees, the par fours are 366, 376, 378, 363, 365, 327, 332, 300, 366 and 399 metres respectively — hardly meterage designed to slip a disc. This theme has been carried over to the par threes and again, most club golfers will be capable of hitting 133, 154, 162 and 183 metres. There are several outstanding holes at Carne: the secluded par three 2nd, the par five 10th through magnificent undulation, the par four 15th out to a distant valley, and the 17th with peaceful ocean views and a challenging drive to a plateau fairway set along a chasm edge. Notwithstanding, the main opinion is that the golf is uniformly good and consistent on both nines.

The routing is non-traditional, in the sense that it deviates from a straight line in and out design. This characteristic becomes apparent soon enough in your round and negates any chance of becoming too comfortable with a particular wind direction. For instance, the 1st hole runs in a northerly direction, the 2nd is due west, the 3rd due east, the 4th runs south-easterly, the 5th north-westerly, the 6th as the 4th, 7th due westerly, 8th northerly to north-westerly and the 9th meanders due south. On the entire layout, out of bounds is possible on eleven holes, though realistically, a menace only half of these times.

Golf clubs participate in the naming of holes in a fun and imaginative manner, but also acknowledge its serious side; for clever naming through association can ensure everlasting notoriety. At Carne, for instance, there is an abundance of wildflowers to go along with traditional links features and several types were utilised during the naming phase.

The 1st hole, Cnoc na Ros (Hill of the roses), becomes emblazoned with ivory coloured Burnet roses in summer. The 5th hole — Lus na mBrat, can be translated to Wild Thyme which is evident around the teeing ground. To the right of the Ladies 6th tee, primroses will be spotted, and as a result, the hole is known as Sraith na Sabhaircini (The Primrose Way). Another example is the 16th hole, where a wayward drive may easily see your ball land in Margalin (Wild Orchids), and so it is named.

There are other interesting non-floral connections: the 3rd hole is named An Traonach (Corncrake) in honour of the corncrake's distinctive call in nearby meadows. The next hole goes by the name of the Reservoir — not far from the 4th green is the reservoir that supplied Belmullet with water for many years. Well before Carne's land was converted into golfing territory, a racecourse occupied the area around the 7th hole, thus Ard na Gaoithe (Grandstand) is remembered. In a hollow to the right of the 18th tee, the lowly dead of Ar Iorrais are buried. The Daoine uaisle are buried on higher ground. Somewhat chillingly, the hole is named Log a Fola (The Bloody Hollow).

With each successive year the overall condition of the links continues to improve and impress both members and visitors alike. And now, professionals are singing its praises, as was noted recently during the club's first pro-am golf tournament. Eamonn Mangan was delighted with their collective response and told me 'the links is just about there'.

To arrive at the lovely destination of Carne, you drive pass the largest living, breathing and unspoilt bog land in Europe (the Blanket Bog). It is renowned for its plentiful flora, wildlife and eerie stillness. Nature lovers may be interested to know that many species of wildfowl take refuge at the bog while migrating from the Arctic, Canada and Greenland.

A view of the wilder expanse of
Killarney links land, Victoria,
Australia. This photo indicates its
suitability for routing a traditional
links — nine holes outward to a
distant point and returning inland
and adjacent for the 'inward' nine

CHAPTER THIRTEEN

Missing Links

Where climate, geography and evolutionary processes allow links land lies suitable for conversion into golfing country. The actualisation of any of the world's missing links is really a complex matter, but could be narrowed down to a four-part process. First, quality links land must be found and that is obvious. Second, a consortium of some kind must take steps to buy the land and overcome many obstacles along the way. Third, the holes need to be formally discovered by an architect (being already present), and lastly, after much fanfare, a golf club is instituted. But all too often, this process is blocked at the second hurdle. An explanation of this was detailed at the beginning of the previous chapter. However, this applied to links land in the United Kingdom. What about elsewhere?

One example of fruitless endeavour, is an area of prime links land, 350 km west of Melbourne, Australia. Due to strong ancestry ties with Ireland, it is known as the Belfast Coastal Reserve. The land in question meanders for twenty kilometres between Warrnambool and Port Fairy, and presents some of the highest quality links land imaginable. Not one, but five quality links could be routed — one after another. Many of the genuine links ingredients are present: robust grasses, sandhills to rival the best of Britain, along with impressive valleys, sheltered enclaves by the score and general intrigue. It also showcases a harmonious linking of land and sea. Granted, there is little in the way of gorse but this can mimic many British links. Why then won't this land be utilised and converted to a great modern links? Historical insight will help answer that question.

Aboriginal people lived on this coast for tens of thousands of years before the arrival of Europeans. The Aboriginals lived in small clans of several families, exploiting seasonally abundant

Killarney Beach, Australia. Should a future links come into being, nature has settled three matters promptly; a dog-leg hole to the right, a perfectly situated teeing ground and by its appearance, a medium-length par four

Killarney, Australia again.
An opportunity for a leftward
swinging dog-leg hole. A perfect
site exists for a bunker at the
dog-leg corner or left alone, it
would be troublesome enough.
There may be a touch of
blindness present and the overall
view reminds me of the 4th hole
at Lahinch

foods: fish, and eels in the nearby Moyne river; crayfish, kelp and shellfish from the rock pools and rock platforms; mammals, reptiles, fruits and berries from the coastal scrub and the bush. The places where Aborigines lived are often marked by accumulations of shells known as shell middens. These middens are scattered widely throughout the Killarney coastal area and considered precious.

MUCH OF THE INDIGENOUS VEGETATION of the area has been cleared or destroyed by European settlement. This has caused the sand dunes to move, exposing and damaging midden sites. The Conservation and Natural Resources Department have urged protection of these sites by insisting that people keep to walking tracks and roads. Gaining the authority to lay out a links in this region will not occur, nor probably should occur. But for links enthusiasts, it's impossible not to speculate on the possibilities.

While gazing at the photographs, it's easy to see how bulldozers can be viewed as excess baggage, where quality links land is concerned. They depict crude but inspiring images, the type that must have moved 'Old' Tom Morris upon first sighting Machrihanish, on the west coast of Scotland. Possibilities for hole configurations run rampant, but clearly, the dog-leg bias is dictated by nature's decree. Occupation for natural tee and green sites becomes obvious.

Given the close-out situation in Britain, it will be interesting to see if new links frontiers such as Australia's southern states, or New Zealand, with their suitable cooler climes, become targeted for links expansion. Will somebody 'do a Ruddy' and charter a helicopter for the purpose of extensive coastal research? And when land is found that resembles the topographical characteristics of links land, will the finished product actually play like a links? Unfortunately, the two do not automatically go together. Unless adherence to the basic fast-running game is maintained, golfers will most likely be exposed to an enjoyable but nevertheless links-like course.

Opportunity for a slight dog-leg hole at Killarney, Australia. Here, the teeing ground is pronounced. Played out between the dunes, golfers would aim to find the distant valley, and then combat an uneven stance when approaching.

Superintendent's mood or club policy on rough would dictate whether balls roll back off the dunes towards the fairway. In the distance, a depression would be utilised as a natural green site

Prior to the 1998 Open Championship at Royal Birkdale, Mark O'Meara teamed up with friends, Tiger Woods and the late Payne Stewart, to tune up and familiarise themselves with links golf. They headed for Ireland and chose to play at Waterville and Ballybunion. This photograph captures the innocence and awe that descends upon first time visitors to the Old Course Ballybunion — even seasoned golf professionals are not immune. Famed for his prowess with the long-irons, Stewart recorded a hole-in-one this day on the demanding 3rd hole, a 220-yard par three. One week later, O'Meara claimed golf's oldest championship by defeating Brian Watts in a four-hole play-off

Afterword

by Donald Steel

Shot-making, in the modern game, lacks the ingredients that used to be regarded as essential. It has turned its back on the need for imagination, ingenuity, improvisation and inventiveness. It has become so predictable and stereotyped that a computer print-out and yardage chart is now more valuable than a caddie.

Fairway irrigation, long carries and heavily bunkered greens have made it more important to hit the ball high than to keep it low. Some golf course architects have been guilty of giving players what they think they ought to have rather than what they want. However, links courses remain as the glorious exception. They signal the real world; golf as it was meant to be.

Tiger Woods is renowned for chopping courses down to size by means of astonishing suppleness of body and lightning speed of hand. After he won the 1997 US Masters, there was talk that only courses the size of the Sahara would hold him in check, but happily, Woods sees golf differently. At the Open at Royal Birkdale in July 1998, he soon made it clear that he would far rather play links golf than the stadium-type game in America 'where you just keep on using the lob wedge'. Warming to his subject of links, he went on, 'a player has the option of hitting any club in the bag. You have to be creative. You have to see the shots, feel them in your hands'. What music to the ears.

Two years earlier, Tom Lehman expressed his liking for links courses because you had to be imaginative in order to flourish. What a compliment and what an indictment of other types of course, if the converse is true, that they require you to be unimaginative. Other players express surprise — and delight — that, on links courses, the vast majority of greens are open in front.

Too many modern courses actively penalise the low or well flighted shot but, as the 1994 Open champion, Nick Price, remarked in speaking out in favour of skipping and running the ball on to greens. 'A lot of architects forget that a majority of golfers don't carry the ball through the air like professionals. You have to give them the opportunity to run the ball through to the greens. I have never felt you should penalise somebody for hitting the ball straight even if it is along the ground. If a golfer has hit the fairway, that is what the fairway is for'.

Today's professionals are spoilt to the point that some believe every shot that hits the fairway should give them a level stance and a perfect lie. Some believe it demeaning to have to squeeze a ball from a tight lie with left foot below right but, as Tom Watson observed, 'If a course needs to be in great condition to be played effectively, then the design strategy is flawed'.

That is not to say that links courses do not obtain good condition but simply that shots to open greens are possible from poor lies and that the true flavour of a links relies upon a high degree of bounce and run.

The opportunity to lend support to a rallying cry about links courses is more than a pleasure, it is a duty. By happy coincidence, my hero-worshipping days were those when Peter Thomson won the Open five times, showing a touch, skill and liking for links which nobody has ever exceeded.

Perhaps people have become blinkered in the belief that modern architecture should produce something new and revolutionary. They may be put off by the word traditional but one of its definitions means 'based on early style' and our early style courses form the basis of study for all golf course architects. It is the wise man who takes heed from what he learns. Too many forget.

The 14th hole, Camus, at
Glashedy Links, Ballyliffin is a
picture-perfect par three of
183 yards. In the background,
the entrancing Baluba Hills
contribute much to the golfer's
peace of mind

Glossary

AGRONOMY   Science of land/soil management and rural economics

ALKALINE   Pertaining to those electro-positive compounds that have a pH of more than 7. Unite with acid substances to form salts

APING   Imitating or directly copying another golfer's style

BENIGN   In a golfing sense, referring to calm weather conditions – a lack of influence by the elements

BENT GRASS   Any grass of the genus *Agrostis*

BLIND SHOT   The golfer is unable to view the target, be it the fairway or green. Golf shots can be either partially or totally blind

BLUFF   Steep cliff or headland, precipice, scarp

BRAE   Steep bank or hillside

BRASSIE   The early-days equivalent of the modern two wood

BUCKTHORN   Any thorny scrub of the genus *Rhamnus*, with berries

BURN   The term is derived from Old Teutonic – 'burna', 'burne', 'bournon' and later from the Old English words meaning a spring, fountain or river. More recently, it refers to a brook in the North of Britain

CADDIE   Carries clubs for golfer and may be called on to advise, confide in, assist with putting lines, choose clubs and identify distances. Some golfers employ a fore-caddie who is stationed in the distance to view the outcome of a drive

CUNNINGGIS   Old Scottish name for rabbits. No doubt, referring to their cunning nature

DELL   Hollow or valley – sometimes wooded but rarely wooded on a links. Also the name given to the famous par three 6th hole at Lahinch

DENE   A bare sandy tract, or low sand hill by the sea

DUNES   Mounds or ridges of loose sand formed primarily by the action of the wind. Generally found close by the sea or in the desert

ESCARPMENT   Abrupt face or cliff of a ridge or mountain range

ESTUARY   A wide, sometimes very wide, tidal mouth of a river

FEATHERY BALL   An early golf ball, made by stuffing leven geese feathers into leather casing. Featheries were in vogue until 1848, when replaced by gutta-percha balls

FESCUE Any grass of the genus *Festuca*. An important links grass, has several prominent varieties to be found on true links land

FIRTH Narrow inlet of sea, can be an estuary

FURZE Common gorse, known in some regions as furze. There is also a single branched variety known as dwarf furze

GOLF COURSE Strictly speaking, pertaining to (inland) courses. The term – 'links course' is an exercise in tautology ... 'course course'

GORSE Any spiny yellow-flowered shrub of the genus *Ulex*. Also known as furze

GREEN In earlier times, the 'green' was known as the entire links. In recent times, it has come to signify the area where golfers putt from, i.e. the putting green

GROYNE A timber framework or low broad wall built out from shore to check the erosion of a beach

GUTTA-PERCHA GOLF BALL Replaced the feathery golf ball around 1848. It was more durable than its predecessor and would fly longer distances. Importantly, made golf much cheaper for the masses. Gutta-percha was made from a sap-like, gummy substance which could be extracted from indigenous Malayan trees. Brilliantly conceived, the substance was malleable when boiled, but hardened upon cooling. The material had previously been used as insulation for underground cable

GUTTY Golfers affectionately referred to their gutta-percha ball as a 'gutty'

HAWTHORN Any thorny shrub of the genus *Crataegus*, especially *C. monogyn*a with white, red or pink blossom and small dark-red fruit or haws

HASKELL RUBBER CORE GOLF BALL Along with the advancement of steel shafts, possibly the greatest innovation ever introduced to golf? This is the modern ball with its predictable and durable rubber core. Introduced around 1900, it replaced the gutta-percha ball. An invention of an American, Coburn Haskell

HEATHER An evergreen shrub *Calluna vulgaris* with purple bell-shaped flowers. Also any of the genera *Erica* or *Daboecia*

HEATHLAND An area of flattish uncultivated land with low shrubs. Particularly common in Britain, where some of the finest heathland style courses are found, i.e. Sunningdale, Wentworth, The Berkshire, Woodhall Spa

HILLOCK Small hill or mound

HIMALAYA The name given to the par three 5th hole at Prestwick, Scotland. A blind golf hole measuring 206 yards, the tee-shot must carry a gigantic (himalayas like) hill to find the green

HONOURABLE COMPANY OF EDINBURGH GOLFERS   A golfing society formed in 1744. Originally its golfers played at Leith but eventually made Muirfield in the village of Gullane, Scotland their home

KEEPER OF THE GREEN   Early term for greenkeeper or superintendent. This person presided over all the important affairs of the links. They wielded more power and had greater responsibility than today's equivalent, chiefly because modern committees and sub-committees reduce the overall work load of greenkeepers

KIKUYU   An aggressive species of grass — *Pennisetum clandestinum* and is native to North East Africa and Kenya. Under close cutting, forms a thick mat and can keep out many weeds. Stands up to wear but never produces a fine turf. Generally not found on British links but is prevalent around the world on many seaside courses among warmer climates. Good golfers despise the grass because it encourages the faulty 'lifting' and 'scooping' action with the irons, particularly when chipping

KLONDYKE   One of the most famous of all blind holes — the par five 5th at Lahinch

KNOLL   Small hill or mound

MARRAM GRASS   A great 'binding' shore grass — *Ammophila arenaria* that has the ability to put out stems from its roots. It helps bind and protect sand dunes (through massive colonisation)

MYXOMATOSIS   An infectious, usually fatal viral disease in rabbits which causes swelling of the mucous membranes

OLD COURSE, ST ANDREWS   Architect unknown ... 'It simply grewed'. Remains the most famous and best loved of all golfing links and home of the Royal and Ancient Golf Club

'OLD' TOM   Tom Morris Snr — Influential Keeper of the Green at St Andrews Old and four times Open Champion. Designed many early links and acknowledged 'Father of Golf'. The world of golf, particularly links golf, remains in his debt

PLANTAIN   Any shrub of the genus *Plantago*, with broad flat leaves spread out close to the ground. Its seeds are used as food for birds. Nuisance value on a links

POA ANNUA   Also known as winter grass and has green foliage. *Poa annua* flowers over a long period and as its flowering heads lie so close to the soil, many escape the cutting power of the mower. Consequently, seeds are produced in abundance, and are a nuisance to links. Superintendents often refer to the constant menace of *Poa annua* and its unacceptably high levels. Although a grass, it has been relegated to weed status

POT-BUNKER   A tiny-sized bunker, often with very steep walls. Frequently, the golfer when playing the recovery shot will be forced to aim out sideways or backwards. Due to links land undulation, many pot-bunkers are blind to the golfer

PUNCHBOWL GREEN   A small, once fashionable green placed in a hollow, and invariably surrounded by banks. Golf balls played to the green will often end up pooled around the same area, due to the slopes. Ideally, will have evolved or been built upon sandy sub-soil; otherwise tends to have drainage problems

QUAIL HIGH   An Irish golfing saying, where golfers attempt to hit their ball very low and keep it relatively free from the influence of wind

ROTA   The collective term given to the eight links on which the Open Championship is played. The event returns to each of these on rotation

ROUTING   In this sense, a golfing architectural term that dictates how the golf course is laid out and flows (i.e. in which direction it runs, how holes are positioned within the overall layout). Routing of a links, usually attempts sympathetically to take into consideration the natural features of the land and the balance between the nines

SALINITY   Pertaining to salt, tasting of salt, impregnated with or containing salts

SCOTCH MIST   Misty, gloomy golfing conditions — appears to be drizzling light rain, but is really only condensation as in heavy, low cloud

SEA GABIONS   Rectangular baskets filled with rock and stone that are strategically placed along the shoreline to reduce effects of coastal erosion

SHINGLE   Small rounded pebbles, especially on seashore

SLEEPERS   Incorporated into links — either to fortify bunkers or to help support burns. They may be discarded railway sleepers or uniform lengths of timber. Visually, can be most intimidating to the golfer

SOD-REVETTING   Intricate (man-made) style of links bunkering. Done with many layers of turf, each layer laid back slightly from the previous layer, then filled and back-filled with sand. This design helps keep sand intact, rather than losing sand to the fury of the elements. Bunker walls in this style, are often quite vertical

SPECTACLES   A group of famous bunkers set on high ground at Carnoustie's 14th hole, Scotland. Visually, the bunkers look like a pair of spectacles

STRATH   A broad mountain valley

STYMIE   The stymie rule was discarded in 1951. It occurred when putting, if your ball was robbed of an unimpeded view of the hole by the opponent's ball. To overcome this problem, golfers commonly used pitching clubs to jump their ball over the obstructing ball

SWARD   An expanse of short grass — may or may not have velvety texture

SWILCAN BURN   The most famous burn in golf, it guards the first green at St Andrews Old

TARGET GOLF A term that is generally reserved for the inland style of golf, where the ball is launched high in the air to carry obstacles, such as water or bunkers fronting greens. Not uncommonly, the greens are watered to accommodate this approach to the game. Target golf is one of the distinguishing features of American style golf and considered alien to the tradition of links golf

TERRAIN Pertaining to the natural lie of the landscape

TORQUE The moment of any system of forces, tending to cause rotation (e.g. within a golf club). Today, clubmaking methods can ensure a minimum of rotation by incorporating anti-torque technology into golf shafts

TRACT A stretch or expanse of land – in this book, referring to a tract of links land

VALLEY OF SIN A revered territory of undulating terrain that fronts the 18th green at St Andrews Old. When approaching, your ball must either (carry) the Valley of Sin, or rely on the traditional Scottish run-up (through) the Valley itself. The manner in which this choice is negotiated has decided major championships

WHINS Another name for gorse or furze

Selected Bibliography

Aberdovey Golf Club — A Round of a Hundred Years, Aberdovey Golf Club, 1986.

A Century of Golf at Lahinch 1892-1992, Enda Glynn, 1991.

A Century of Opens, Geoffrey Cousins and Tom Scott, Shakespeare Head Press, 1971.

Advanced Golf, James Braid, Methuen, 1908.

A History of The Royal and Ancient Golf Club, St Andrews, H.S.C. Everard, W. Blackwood and Sons, 1907.

Arnold Palmer — The Man and the Legend, Mark McCormack, Cassell, 1967.

A Year at St Andrews — The Home of Golf, 1998.

Ballybunion Golf Club, an illustrated centenary history 1893-1993, John Redmond, Ballybunion Golf Club, 1993.

Bobby Locke on Golf, Bobby Locke, Country Life, 1953.

Carnegie Links at Skibo Castle — article, Bradley Klein, 1995.

Classic Golf Links of Great Britain and Ireland, Donald Steel, Chapman's, 1992, re-issued by Weidenfeld and Nicolson (The Orion Publishing Group) 1996.

Dooks 100 Years of Golf, privately printed by Dooks Golf Club.

Discovering Ayrshire, J. Strawhorn and K. Andrew, John Donald Publishers Ltd, 1988.

Early Irish Golf, William Gibson, Oakleaf Publications, 1988.

Golf In Scotland & Ireland — The Complete Guide to Courses, Clubs, Accommodation and Travel, by the editors of Golf World Magazine, Sackville Books, Golf World Magazine, 1987.

Golf On Gullane Hill, Archie Baird, Macdonald Lindsay Pindar, 1992.

Golfweek, July 22nd, 1995 — article 'Norman Skidoos to Carnegie's Skibo', James Achenbach.

Great Golf Courses of Ireland, J. Redmond, Gill and Macmillan Ltd, 1994.

History of Golf, Robert Browning, J.M. Dent and Sons, 1955.

History of Golf in Great Britain, B. Darwin and others, Cassell and Co, 1952.

Hunstanton Golf Club — One Hundred Years (1891-1991), Witley Press, 1991.

Inside The Tour Golf Magazine, Lawrence International, 1999.

Links of Heaven, Richard Phinney and Scott Whitley, Baltray Books, 1996.

100 Years of Golf at Machrihanish, D.J. McDiarmid, 1976.

Prestwick Golf Club — Birthplace of The Open, Prestwick Golf Club, 1989.

Royal County Down Golf Club — The First Century, H. McCaw and B. Henderson, The Royal County Down Golf Club, 1988.

Royal Liverpool Golf Club Publication – Hoylake 1998, extrapolation from article written about caddie, Alexander Campbell by club member, Leslie Edwards.

Royal Porthcawl Golf Club – 1891-1991, D. Brown and Sons, 1991.

Royal Portrush Golf Club – A History, Ian Bamford, Royal Portrush Golf Club, 1988.

Southerness Golf Club 1947-1997, Southerness Golf Club, The Forward Press, 1997.

St Andrews Home of Golf, J. Robertson, First published 1967 and revised in 1974 by J. and G. Innes, 2nd edition by F. Robertson and T. Jarrett, Macdonald Publishers.

The Confidential Guide to Golf Courses, Tom Doak, Sleeping Bear Press, 1996.

The Open – The British Open Golf Championship since the War, Peter Alliss with Michael Hobbs, William Collins, 1984.

The Rules of The Green, A History of the Rules of Golf, Kenneth Chapman, Virgin Books, 1997.

The Spirit of St Andrews by Alister MacKenzie, compiled by Raymund Haddock, Sleeping Bear Press, 1995.

The World Atlas of Golf – P. Ward-Thomas, H.W. Wind, C. Price & P. Thomson, Mitchell Beazley Ltd, 1976.

Turnberry Golf Club promotional article, 1995.

When Battle's Done, Mary O'Connor, The Kerryman, 1996.

Photographic Acknowledgements

The author and the publisher wish to thank all those who kindly gave permission to reproduce the images which appear in this book:

Aberdovey Golf Club

Alistaire Gilchrist

Ballyliffin Golf Club

Barry King

Brendan Landy, c/- Landy Photography, 17 Charles Street, Listowell, Ireland

Carne Golf Club

County Sligo Golf Club

David Kelly and Eric Hepworth, c/- Creative Services, 20 Tower Street, Brunswick Park, Liverpool, UK

Dooks Golf Club

Government of Ireland (1997) for depiction of Coastal Zone Management. Taken from 'A draft policy for Ireland discussion document'.

Great Yarmouth and Caister Golf Club

Hoylake Golf Club

Jan Kautsky

John Philp, Carnoustie, for donations from his private collection

Ken McNamara

Lundin Links

Machrie Golf Club

Mary O'Connor, c/- Tralee Golf Club

Michael Diggin, c/- Diggin Photography, 5 Castle Street, Tralee, Ireland

Northern Ireland Tourist Board

North Berwick Golf Club

Pat Ruddy

Prestwick Golf Club

Princes Golf Club

Sean Murray

Seapoint Golf Club

Stan Craig, Prestwick Golf Club

St Andrews University, Cowie collection

The Carnegie Club, Skibo

The European Golf Club

The West Lancashire Golf Club

Endnotes

1. *The Concise Oxford Dictionary*, 6th edition, 1976, (p. 632).

2. *History of Golf in Great Britain*, Darwin and others, Cassell and Co, 1952, (pp. 93-94).

3. *Golf on Gullane Hill*, Archie Baird, Macdonald Lindsay Pindar, 1992, (p. 7).

4. *When Battles Done*, Mary OConnor, by The Kerryman 1996, (p. 57).

5. *Spirit of St Andrews*, Alister MacKenzie, Sleeping Bear Press 1995, (p. 4).

6. *Arnold Palmer, The Man and The Legend*, Mark McCormack, Cassell, 1967, (p. 171).

7. *Advanced Golf*, James Braid, Methuen, 1908.

8. *Royal Porthcawl Golf Club – 1891-1991*, printed by D. Brown and Sons, 1991, (p. 107).

9. *Hunstanton Golf Club – 1891-1991*, Witley Press, 1991, (pp. 22-23).

10. Field evaluation report of Dooks Golf Club, by Donald Steel, 30 October 1996.

11. *The Spirit of St Andrews*, by Alister MacKenzie, compiled by Raymund Haddock, Sleeping Bear Press, 1995, (p. 6).

12. A year at St Andrews – The Home of Golf publication, 1998.

13. *Prestwick Golf Club – Birthplace of the Open*, Prestwick Golf Club, 1989, (p. 43).

14. Pat Ruddy, personal correspondence, 3 December 1998.

15. *The Spirit of St Andrews*, Alister MacKenzie, Sleeping Bear Press, 1995, (p. 54).

16. P. Ruddy, *op. cit.*

17. *Links of Heaven*, Richard Phinney and Scott Whitley, Baltray Books, 1996, (p. 61).

18. P. Ruddy, *op. cit.*

19. *Prestwick Golf Club – Birthplace of the Open*, Prestwick Golf Club, 1989, (p. 84).

20. *A Century of Golf at Lahinch 1892-1992*, Enda Glynn, 1991, (p. 35).

21. *Aberdovey Golf Club – A Round of a Hundred Years*, Aberdovey Golf Club, (pp. 23-32).

22. *History of Golf*, Robert Browning, J.M. Dent and Sons, 1955, (p. 65).

23. Browning, *ibid*, (p. 64).

24. Browning, *op. cit.*

25. Browning, *op. cit.*

26. Browning, *ibid*, (p. 67).

27. *A History of the Royal and Ancient Golf Club*, St Andrews, H.S.C. Everard, William Blackwood and Sons, 1907, (pp. 242-243).

28. St *Andrews – Home of Golf*, James Robertson 1967, J and G Innes, revised 1974 by Tom Jarrett, Macdonald Publishers, Edinburgh, (p. 43).

29. *100 Years of Golf at Machrihanish*, D.J. McDiarmid, 1976, (p. 9).

30. McDiarmid, *loc. cit*

31. *Hunstanton Golf Club – One Hundred Years (1891-1991)*, Witley Press, 1991, (p. 11).

32. *Royal Liverpool Golf Club – Hoylake 1998*, Leslie Edwards, 1998, (p. 17).

33. Edwards, *loc. cit.*

34. Edwards, *loc. cit.*

35. Edwards, *loc. cit.*

36.   Edwards, *loc. cit.*

37.   Edwards, *loc. cit.*

38.   Edwards, *loc. cit.*

39.   Edwards, *loc. cit.*

40.   Edwards, *loc. cit.*

41.   *Peter Alliss – The Open*, Peter Alliss, William Collins and Sons, 1984, (p.16).

42.   Turnberry Golf Club promotional article, 1995.

43.   *Prestwick Golf Club – Birthplace of The Open,* Prestwick Golf Club, 1989, (p. 89).

44.   *Early Irish Golf,* William Gibson, Oakleaf Publications, 1988, (p. 137).

45.   *ibid.,* (p. 193).

46.   *ibid.,* (p. 73).

47.   *Ballybunion Golf Club, an illustrated centenary history 1893-1993*, John Redmond, Ballybunion Golf Club, 1993, (p. 12).

48.   *Early Irish Golf,* William Gibson, Oakleaf Publications, 1988, (p. 68).

49.   *A History of The Royal and Ancient Golf Club*, St Andrews, H.S.C. Everard, William Blackwood and Sons, 1907, (p. 147).

50.   *Ballybunion Golf Club – an isllustrated centenary history 1893-1993*, John Redmond, Ballybunion Golf Club, 1993, (p. 40).

51.   *Royal County Down Golf Club – The First Century*, Harry McCaw and Brum Henderson, The Royal County Down Golf Club, 1988, (pp. 99-100).

52.   *Royal Portrush Golf Club – A History*, Ian Bamford, Royal Portrush Golf Club, 1988, (pp. 84-85).

53.   Bamford, *loc. cit.*

54.   *The Spirit of St Andrews*, Alister MacKenzie, compiled by Raymund Haddock, Sleeping Bear Press, 1995, (p.1).

55.   *Bobby Locke on Golf*, Bobby Locke, Country Life, 1953, (pp. 161-165).

56.   *Ballybunion Golf Club – an illustrated centenary history 1893-1993*, John Redmond, Ballybunion Golf Club, 1993, (p. 30).

57.   *Royal County Down Golf Club – The First Century*, Harry McCaw and Brum Henderson, The Royal County Down Golf Club, 1988, (p. 74).

58.   *Prestwick Golf Club – Birthplace Of The Open*, Prestwick Golf Club, 1989, (p. 49).

59.   *Inside The Tour* – article by Paul Trow on Sir Michael Bonallack, Lawrence International, 1999, (p. 122).

60.   *A Century of Opens*, Geoffrey Cousins and Tom Scott, Shakespeare Head Press, 1971, (Appendix 1).

61.   *ibid.,* (p. 13).

62.   *ibid.,* (p. 14).

63.   Cousins and Scott, *loc. cit*

64.   *ibid.,* (p. 27).

65.   *ibid.,* (p. 185).

66.   *The Open – The British Open Golf Championship since the War*, Peter Allis with Michael Hobbs, William Collins, 1984, (p. 101).

67.   *A Century of Opens*, Geoffrey Cousins and Tom Scott, Shakespeare Head Press, 1971, (Appendix I).

68.   *ibid.,* (p. 18).

69. *Southerness Golf Club 1947–1997*, Southerness Golf Club, The Forward Press, (pp. 8-13).

70. Carnegie Links at Skibo Castle – article by Bradley Klein, (pp. 1-4).

71. Golfweek, July 22nd, 1995, – article by Norman Skidoos to Carnegie's Skibo, by James Achenbach, (p. 27).

72. Achenbach, *loc. cit.*

73. *Classic Golf Links of Great Britain and Ireland*, Donald Steel, 1992, re-issued by Weidenfeld and Nicolson (The Orion Publishing Group) 1996, (p. 43).

74. Carnegie Links at Skibo Castle – article by Bradley Klein, (p. 1-4).

75. *Ballybunion Golf Club – an illustrated centenary history 1893-1993*, J. Redmond, Ballybunion Golf Club, 1993, (p. 42).

76. *The Confidential Guide to Golf Courses*, Tom Doak, Sleeping Bear Press, 1996, (pp.12-13).

77. Ballybunion – An illustrated Centenary History 1893-1993, J. Redmond, Ballybunion Golf Club, 1993, (p. 44).

78. Redmond, *loc. cit.*

79. *Classic Golf Links of Great Britain and Ireland*, Donald Steel, first published by Chapmans 1992, re-issued by Weidenfeld and Nicolson (The Orion Publishing Group) 1996, (p. 217).

80. *Great Golf Course of Ireland*, J. Redmond, Gill and Macmillan Ltd, 1994, (p. 130).

81. Redmond, *loc. cit.*

82. Redmond, *loc. cit.*

83. *Golf In Scotland and Ireland – The Complete Guide to Courses, Clubs, Accommodation and Travel*, by the editors of Golf World Magazine, Sackville Books, Published in association with Golf World Magazine, 1987, (p. 131).

84. *Classic Golf Links of Great Britain and Ireland*, Donald Steel, published by Chapmans 1992, re-issued by Weidenfeld and Nicolson (The Orion Publishing Group) 1996, (p. 211).

85. *Golf in Scotland and Ireland – The Complete Guide to Courses, Clubs, Accommodation and Travel*, by the editors of Golf World Magazine, Sackville Books. Published in association with Golf World Magazine, 1987, (p. 131).

86. Pat Ruddy, *op. cit.*

87. Pat Ruddy, *op. cit.*

88. Pat Ruddy, *op. cit.*

89. Pat Ruddy, *op. cit.*

90. Pat Ruddy, *op. cit.*

91. Pat Ruddy, *op. cit.*

92. *Links of Heaven*, R. Phinney and S. Whitely, Baltray Books, 1996, (p. 117).

The publishers wish to thank Sleeping Bear Press for the use of extracts in this book.
They can be contacted at:
121 South Main Street, PO Box 20, Chelsea, Michigan 48118
ph: (734) 475 4411 fax: (734) 475 0787
www.sleepingbearpress.com

THE TEENAGE WORRIER'S POCKET GUIDE TO ROMANCE

THE TEENAGE WORRIER'S

POCKET GUIDE TO

ROMANCE

Ros Asquith

as Letty Chubb

CORGI

THE TEENAGE WORRIER'S POCKET GUIDE TO ROMANCE
A CORGI BOOK : 0 552 146420

First publication in Great Britain

PRINTING HISTORY
Corgi edition published 1998

Set in 11½pt Linotype Garamond by
Phoenix Typesetting Ilkley, West Yorkshire

Corgi Books are published by Transworld Publishers Ltd,
61–63 Uxbridge Road, Ealing, London W5 5SA,
in Australia by Transworld Publishers (Australia) Pty. Ltd,
15–25 Helles Avenue, Moorebank, NSW 2170,
and in New Zealand by Transworld Publishers (NZ) Ltd,
3 William Pickering Drive, Albany, Auckland.

Made and printed in Great Britain by
Cox & Wyman Ltd, Reading, Berkshire.

CONTENTS

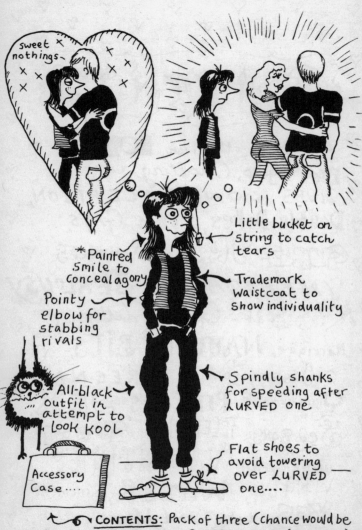

we have so much in common

Heart-shaped pillow
Waterbed
Luxury Suite
ROMANTIC Wayside Inn
Lurvers' Lane
Remotesville
Isle of View
Hotsex
KISS
1LUV U2

Dearest Teenage Worrier(s),

Is there a certain someone who makes your heart race
like drum'n'bass, your legs feel bendier than silly string,
your face feel as if each cheek had turned into a grilled
tomato? Do you weep deep into the night? Gaze for hours
at a time at blurry photo? Keep fragments of lurved one's
old chewing-gum under tear-stained duvet?

Here, at long last, is the handy Pocket Guide that
brings you all the secrets of True ROMANCE: how to
find the perfect partner; how to trap them in a willy
(sorry, wily) NET; how to KEEP them there by stunning
ruses such as, um, knowing how to stimulate their vital
zones (phew, hurl self into ice bucket) and how to be
V.V.V. Interesting while remaining elusively Kooool Etck.

I shall also be showing how to avoid all those tragic
ROMANTIC worries that plague the life of the average
spotty, greasy, pudding or beanpole-shaped Teenage

1

Worrier of the twenty-first century.

Such as: MUST I really go out with someone when I am V. Happy by myself? HAS everyone else on planet had sex except moi? WHEN that V.V. Attractive, dazzling, witty, intelligent person ignores me as though I were a mere ant, does it really mean they lurve me but are too kool to show it? OR is it they just don't care for the name 'Ant', arf arf, argh Etck. (NB Quick answers to the above questions are no, no and um (sorry), no.

It will tell you all about **Dates***: How to get one; How to avoid one; How to look; What to do . . . How Not to Care too much. How to say get lost, get found Etck.*

As my fan(s) will know, I haven't quite solved all of these myriad lurve-worries moiself just yet, but in the process of writing this advice-packed tome, I am sure I will advance to greater self-knowledge and enhance my ability to entrap any passing male that takes my fancy. I feel V.V. Highly qualified to talk of such matters now, as I have actually KISSED three whole boyz (well, akshully, only bits of their faces of course, ahem). I think this is a V. High number for someone of my humble age (although if you listened to some of the liars at my skule you wd think they had Done It with everyone in Universe) although I must admit that in each case I have only kissed them once, so I that I have still not, um, Gone the Whole Way, nor am I likely to until I am well over the age of consent, due to:

1) Lack of opportunity
2) Fear of breaking law

3) Fear of catching terminal illness
4) Fear of not knowing what bit to put where (will this buke help?)
5) Lack of interest (not mine, the boyz; they are always looking over my shoulder at my frend Hazel)

ROMANCE, anyway, is different to sex. It is about longing, dreaming, hoping, wanting, yearning, swooning, lusting, slavering, snogging (whoops, phew, ice bucket again).

So put away that box of tissues, close your ears to the screech of violins and the wail of banshees that make the life of a Teenage-Worrier-in-Lurve so tragic and learn how to, um, think positive (wish I could) and look on Bright Side (bright side of what?). In short, I will expose all the daft advice other bukes land you with and hope that by the time you've got from A to Z, you will either get happy in ROMANCE or throw this buke at the moron who doesn't care about you.

And go on to better boyz. Or gurlz.

—Lurve, as ever,

Letty Chubb

X X

An INTRO TO MOI . . .

A few werds about the ROMANCES of my life so far, full details of which you can find soulfully relayed in my three previous tomes . . .

Brian 'Brain' Bolt

Not exactly right for ROMANCE category, as although Brian faithfully cleaves to *moi*, I would really prefer to spend the day with my little brother's gerbil, Horace, who, come to think of it rather resembles Brian but lives much more exciting life. If a three-metre-high Valentine card arrives on Feb *13th* in order to embarrass the householder and give the recipient a day in which to return the favour, it will have Brian's exquisite copperplate hand upon it. But it is not his spots, or his fluffy teeth, that put me off Brian. It is more his obsessive, doggy devotion to *moi*. And, of course, that incident with the bicycle wheel and the flour . . .

Daniel Hope

The first true lurve of my LIFE, Daniel Hope still has hair the colour of wet sand at sunset (I tried to make *moi*self think it was more the colour of elastic bands when he left me but – sob – I just couldn't convince *moi*self) and eyes bluer than forget-me-nots. Nonetheless he has successfully forgotten-me-often and has raised my hopes only to cruelly dash them on the rocks of despair by abandoning me on *three* separate occasions, twice with two of my best friends. Tragickly, ROMANCE being what it is, I know that if I glimpse his manly form, or hear his sonorous tones, I am liable to swoon. On principle then, I only allow myself to pass his house (which involves, I admit, an elaborate detour from my school route) about four times a week. There is still something about being on the street where he lives . . .

Adam Stone

Daniel may be beautiful, but he has a wilful and negligent soul. Adam, whose hair is like little bunches of grapes, whose eyes are twin coals gleaming with mischief and smouldering with unleashed pashione, is as honest as the Day is Long. As noble as a knight of olde. As truthful as little Georgie Washington. And in Los Angeles. It is my tragedy that he escaped there because I was too foolish to believe his lurve for *moi* . . . Nightly I weep into my pillow (I wonder if I shld change pillowcases more often? Maybe this is why I sneeze so much) and beat my little fists against the walls in an agony of tribulation. Did he get my letter explaining All? Should I write again? I write nightly, but tear up my efforts. Oh, Adammmmmm, Adaaaaaam, is your soul like your surname? Will you never return?

With heavy pen, dear reader, I return to the task of this brief guide, hoping to inject a little hope, a little joy, into my life which is otherwise blighted by failed ROMANCE. Thank goodness I am comforted still by my only faithful lurve – my cat **Rover**. She may make me sneeze even more than my sodden pillow, but at least she is here . . .

NB If you buy loads of this book, maybe I can scrape up the fare to L.A. and see my darling Adam again, even if it is only once . . . even if it is to see him in the arms of Sharon Groan . . .

The BUTTERFLY
of ROMANCE
FLUTTERS BY

Adonis

Glorious Youth beloved of Venus, the goddess of
Lurve, and therefore a term used to describe V.
Fanciable blokes up to the present day. ie: that is,
Daniel and Adam (swoon). However, it is V. worth
bearing in mind that Brian Bolt may one day be
seen as an Adonis by someone or something,
possibly a relative of Benjy's gerbil. That day can't
come too fast for me. The Adonis is also a pleasant
species of butterfly — let no-one accuse me of failing
to educate you, dear reader(s).

Attraction

Is that magnetic force that impels you towards
someone, drawn by mysterious X-Files-type force
Etck. It is as mysterious — and invisible — as the
elemental force of gravity on all of earth's
inhabitants as discovered by Isaac Newton shortly
before going into coma when apple fell on head.
The great thing about attraction is, everyone has got
some of it. It is not about simple things like having
big bazoomz Etck, but about mysterious chemical
substances like pheromones, which we all give off
and which some people give off more of than others.
This partly explains universal oddities like: why is

person who looks like the back of a car ferry always pursued by fifty panting hunks? Or hunking pants. Why is V. Beautiful person sad and lonely? Etck.

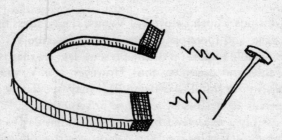

Magnets attract – but also repel. Ask yourself: do you really <u>WANT</u> that nail? No rude remarks about screws, <u>per-LEASE</u>).

However, not being attractive to the person you have set your heart on does not mean you have no pheromones, just that the right person for your particular brand hasn't turned up yet. Also, whether you attract people has as much to do with your own mood as how you look. And this in turn has to do with confidence. Confidence is what we Teenage Worriers need in bucketfuls but usually have only in tiny droplets . . .

But . . . dear fellow Worriers, remember that a ROMANTIC relationship cannot thrive on affection alone, nor must it ever try to survive on pity. It must contain ye elements of *sizzle*. So, however much you LIKE someone, don't bother if you don't fancy them too. It will only lead to heartache (theirs). If it's clear they don't fancy YOU, it will also only lead to heartache (yours). If you fancy them but don't much like them, also steer clear. This could lead to even bigger heartache (cue sound effects of squalling infants, tragick Teenage Worriers alone in endless docs' waiting-rooms Etck).

If only it were so easy...

BACHELORS

Unmarried males. These are what unmarried females are supposed to sniff out and lure into matrimonial web of cozy nest, nuclear family, Happy-Ever-After Etck. 'Nuclear' has always seemed to me a good word to apply to Family Life, due to loud bangs, flying objects, deadly fall-out Etck, but I think it's supposed to mean going round in circles, which is what life in *La Maison Chubb* feels like most of the time.

Beau

My dictionary says 'Fop, dandy, ladies' man', but maybe I shld get a more recent dictionary. Personally I like the term 'Beau', and think that reintroducing it wld enhance quality of ROMANCE. It seems to say yr LURVED one is all the things you want them to be, beautiful inside and out Etck, something to be proud of, and beautiful enough to be proud of you too Etck. That's enough on Beaux, phew, thunder of massed violins Etck.

Bezonian

The opposite. This means 'Rascal, beggarly fellow'. I also hope this isn't a description of Daniel. Wince. 'Ragamuffin' was a pretty old and confusing word to Teenage Worriers and that came back as a streetword, so why not Bezonian? 'Hey, y'all F***in' bezonians in here, shuh man!' That sort of thing . .

HEY, WOW, he's BEZONIAN INNIT?

BLIND DATES

Blind dates are obviously a great idea if you don't know how to meet someone any other way, and I imagine as long as you take V. good precautions, ie: don't give address to stranger Etck, meet in V. pubic (sorry, public) place and be sure to go home early on yr own Etck, that they might provide you with a few moments of fun.

There are several different ways of getting a Blind Date:

1) A dating agency where you pay through nose to feed yr details into a computer and get a 'perfect match' i.e: You say you are a size 25 when breathing in, with a low IQ and no prospects and they magically find you a heartbreakingly handsome, solvent companion looking for just such a one as you. El Chubb is unconvinced, but I have heard of one or two successes in groups of V. old people over 25.

2) Advertise. This enables you to weed out some (but not all) weirdos and usually gives you a chance to check out their appearances. If they do not include photo – hopefully, of their face – ask yourself: why? This method is also more common for old on-shelf (joke) group.

3) Best idea for Teenage Worriers is to get a frend of a frend to fix you up with someone they think you'll like.

As long as you are V. Careful (murderers, sadists Etck have been known to seek their victims through small ads), I think these methods wld be fun. After all, everyone is lonely some of the time and most of us are lonely most of the time, so there is NO SHAME.

Boyz

Must find my Boy Fancy dress

The fashionable idea that Boyz are aliens from another werld (or, if you are a boy, that gurlz are aliens from another planet) was first introduced to this country by *moi*, in my best-selling buke (puff, plug) *I Was a Teenage Worrier* (still available – my Mother has six copies). However, as I pointed out then and as I still believe, boyz are more like gurlz than:

a) they like to admit
b) gurlz like to admit
c) anything else around

If you don't believe (c) above, then ask yourself, if you are a gurl, the following question: am I more like a boy than say, an armadillo, or an elephant, or a piano stool?

If you are a boy, you may like to wonder: what is more like me? A gurl? Or a cardboard box?

Of course, having established the similarities, we must remind ourselves of the differences.

More gurlz (but not all) paint their nails pale green. More gurlz (but not all) wear V. silly flimsy leg covers that get torn by minute particles of grit so they have to buy another pair after ONE DAY.

More gurlz wear V. short skirts and shave their legs. Etck.

Boyz do silly things too. But one of the silliest things boyz do, in the opinion of many (though not all) gurlz, is to pay more attention to round things like footballs and wheels than to round things like us (or straight thingz with V. microscopic round bits like *moi*). In other werds, gurlz do all the nail-painting Etck to attract boys when all boyz really want to do is skulk around in sheds comparing their valve-gear.

True Equality of Ye Sexes can only come when they do stuff which pleases themselves in equal amounts. So, boyz shld get sillier about their appearances (why should a boy in make-up be assumed to be gay?) and gurlz shld get sillier about hobbies, sez L. Chubb. However, for those of you who are interested in dating boyz, here are a handful of types to watch out for:

1) Hamlet
V. Indecisive prince who lurved his Father more than his gurlfriend and ended up killing his gurlfriend's poor old innocent father instead of his wicked uncle cos he couldn't make his mind up what to do. The poor old bloke he killed said 'To Thine own self be True' (note for illiterate Worriers: this means Be True to Yourself) which seems V. Good advice to me and more useful on ROMANCE's merry-go-round than Hamlet's 'To Be or Not to Be'. Gnash, Worry.

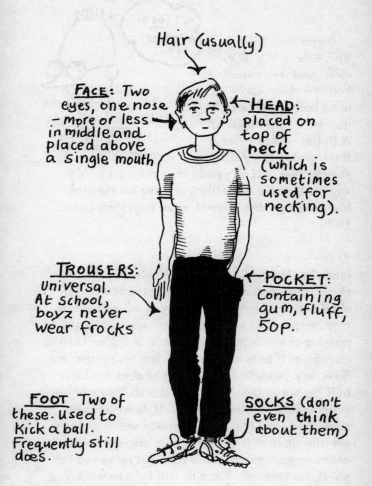

Hair (usually)

FACE: Two eyes, one nose — more or less — in middle and placed above a single mouth

HEAD: placed on top of neck (which is sometimes used for necking).

TROUSERS: Universal. At school, boyz never wear frocks

POCKET: Containing gum, fluff, 50p.

FOOT Two of these. Used to kick a ball. Frequently still does.

SOCKS (don't even think about them)

Points of a <u>BOY</u> – illustrating L. Chubb's thesis that BOYZ are more like GIRLZ than anything else on Planet Earth... (so end sexist krap now) sez Chubb.

2) *Boffin*

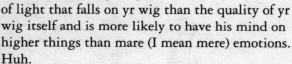

This type is V.V.V.V. clever and wears specs. A boffin without specs is not a boffin, although he may be V. interllekshual. A Boffin will be more interested in the quality of light that falls on yr wig than the quality of yr wig itself and is more likely to have his mind on higher things than mare (I mean mere) emotions. Huh.

3) *Shy*

Gurlz are V. often attracted to V. shy boyz as they think they are deep. This is often true but is also often not. If a boy seems too shy to ask you out, it may be that he is too bored to ask you out, or the number of words necessary to do it is higher than he can count. If he is too shy to declare his everlasting lurve, ask yourself: is it possible he does not lurve me? Do not assume that shyness is the cause of his extreme lack of interest in you. If, however, you really like a shy boy, it is definitely worth trying to get him interested by asking him out, say half-a-dozen times. I would think this is as far as you can go. If this succeeds, you will still have to work V. hard to get a shy boy interested in you. Since no-one has ever shown any interest in them before, they will take a long time to believe you.

16

4) Sexist Pig

This is a sub-category of Yob, and though Yob behaviour almost always involves Sexist Piggery ('You've 'ad the rest, now try the best, darlin' Etck), some Sexist Pigs are cunningly disguised as non-Yobs and seem V. Interesting and Nice until you realize they expect you to always be at their beck and call, wear what they want, shut up when they're talking Etck.

Avoid this type.

5) Perfecto

This is the one who Has it All and Can Do It All. No point in trying to compete. Basic adulation and flattery usually work, cos the one thing they tend not to be strong on is modesty. But how can you gain their interest? Try to find one thing they're NOT good at (Needlework? Canoeing? Making model cathedrals out of matchsticks?) and devote yourself to it. This will avoid the risk of comparison in other fields and they will hopefully be convinced that you are a committed Eccentric dedicated to Yr Art.

6) Self-Obsessed

They say: 'We've talked enough about me, let's talk about *you* . . . What do you think of my new haircut?'

They ask for one ticket at the box office, even though you paid last time. They walk down Lurvers' Lane running their fingers tenderly through their own hair.

Avoid this type.

7) Insecuresville

'Oh I could never do that' they say admiringly of your teeniest accomplishments, and you are V. charmed. But they really mean it. And they are V.

Sad that they cld never do it. And they go on about how V. Sad they are that they couldn't do it. And on and on and on. V. Exhausting. If you adore an Insecuresville, your patience may be rewarded by their other sterling qualities, although personally I wld prefer to find these without the insecurities (being a V. Insecure sort of person *moi*self, worry, moan, self-doubt, despondency).

8) Beardo
(Male, usually. If a gurl with a beard, you can get it removed by electrolysis, ask yr doc.)

Some Gurlz find beards, moustaches Etck V. Romantic and arty-looking teachers with beards, or V. Caring-looking ones with beards are often the Objects of Crushes. Big bushy beards are popular with Iron John types who thrash around in forests beating their chests, howling, crying, thinking about their Mothers and trying to find their True Selves. If they find them and then have a shave they are V. Welcome to look me up, but I do not fancy kissing a bird's nest. I know it's V. Unfair that men have to shave every day, and that I have a Campaign For Hairy Armpits, Legs Etck, but personal preference only goes as far, in my case, as a soft fuzz of Designer Stubble, though even this can look V. Posey, espesh with leather coat-collar turned up. Anyway, you get the picture. All of you in LURVE with hairy Boyz can relax because they're safe from *moi*.

9) Romeo

One who everyone fancies, but who has eyes only for yoooou. Exists, possibly, but only in your dreams.

Have censored this pic as each of us has own idea of Romeo (sigh).

Breaking up

There is an old song that says that breaking up is hard to do, and what it means is that it is hard to be left, which we all know, even if it hasn't happened to us yet. But it also means that it is hard to leave someone. Heed the advice of El Chubb: it is much better to be cruel to be kind and tell the truth *now*, rather than in two, three, or worse still thirty years' time. Never stay with someone out of pity, it just won't work. If they are trying to leave you, you have to let them do it too, instead of following first impulse, which is to plait yrself around their speeding limbs and emit long piercing howl. You definitely do not want to have six kids before he makes for the Exit, do not pass Go, do not collect gloom of spouse Etck.

TIPS FOR BREAKING UP
a) Be clear.
b) Be Kind.
c) Do not tell the person you are leaving that they are a bundle of old rubbidge. They will be feeling like that anyway.
d) Do not get back together under any circumstances for AT LEAST a year, even if you ARE lonely and tempted.
e) Remember, you broke up, so there was a REASON for it.

Hard as this is to do, always remember it is much, much worse for the person you are giving the old heave-ho to.

I often feel V. Guilty about my rejection of Brian, particularly since I inflamed his hopes Etck by going out with him again even after I'd told him it wouldn't work sharing gerbil stories with him Etck. This second episode made him miserable and, if it hadn't happened, I'd also still have a perfectly good bicycle . . .

If you are the one who is left, the best thing you can do is feel V.V.V.V. Sorry for yourself for a week. Cry constantly (preferably at a high, keening pitch), play lots of sad music and lock yourself in yr room Etck to Worry yr Mother (or other suitable caring adult) as much as possible, thereby ensuring maximum sympathy and making yourself V. Important to those around you. Over the next three weeks, emerge now and then with doleful expression to take light refreshment and allow yrself to be persuaded to sit in front of telly covered in blankets and weeping.

After one month, pick up relatively normal life. Tell yrself that Person-of-Yr-Dreams was, although perfect, Not Right For You. You cld never be happy with someone who didn't Love-you-as-you-loved-them. There is a worthier person (also better looking, funnier Etck) out there who you have yet to find. Life is worth living without a partner anyway and you are a special worthy person in yr own right Etck Etck.

Say these things to mirror every night. You will be surprised to find that within a few months you will be able to hear your lurved one's name without feeling as if you are going to die. Recovery has begun. It can only get better.

CHATTING UP

Er, sadly, the stumbling attempts of most Teen Worriers at Chatting Up will include the following touching, if naff, exchanges:

YOU: So where did you learn to do that?
HIM: What?
YOU: Hypnotize people with the back of your head. I just gazed at the back of your head for a second

and now I am hopelessly hypnotized and can think of nothing but you and will do whatever you say . . .

(NB Note bad mistake in this approach as it lays you open to total rejection. ie: he says, 'Get lost' and you have to.)

A better approach wld be:
YOU: So where did you learn to do that?
HIM: What?
YOU: Hypnotize people with the back of your head. I just gazed at the back of your head and now I feel that unless I can gaze at the front of it for the rest of my LIFE I will never be completely happy again. May I gaze at it for at least a few more minutes before you cast me into Oblivion?

(This wld take a V. hard-hearted person to refuse.)

I know it wld be V. Nice to be the recipient of such attempts to please, but you cld wait for eternity before a bloke wld summon up the courage to try these out on you, so it is better to practise yourself and not whinge if you are rejected.

CINEMA

Cinema tip: when Person-of-Yr-Dreams invites you to come to *Large Door*, do not take it at face value or as a rude remark about your size, as it will probably be the French movie *L'age D'Or* (Golden Age, to you illiterate monolingualists). This happened to me with Adam and I have since wondered whether I successfully disguised my mistake, or whether he realized at that moment that I was a true Moron.

Tip 2: do not assume that a PG, a 12 or even a U are for babies. The cinema classifications are so daft that a little bit of swearing (much less than you hear in the average household before breakfast) will shoot a film from U to 15 in milli-seconds, whereas violence quite unsuitable for one of my little brother Benjy's tender age will happily be classified PG. All you need to know before you go is: will it be so scary that I embarrass myself by hiding under seat (in the case of *moi*, this even applied to Walt Disney films until recently)? or will it be so violent I throw up into hot date's popcorn? Etck. Neither of these is advisable on a date, although a little tremor of fear can do wonders for canoodling possibilities as long as the slashing'n'burning on screen isn't too distracting.

24

CONTRACEPTION

This should be the Biggest Worry of all to Teenage
Worriers with the slightest hope – or fear – of ever
actually Doing It. But since many of you who
haven't even held hands yet will think it's light
years away, take El Chubb's advice: It can happen
before you know it and you should be prepared. The
number of single parents is rising and, arrrrg, over
70,000 are Teenagers!

25

Your questions answered by Auntie Letty:

I'm under 16. Can a doctor or nurse refuse to give me contraception?
They *can* but it's quite unlikely. They may suggest you talk to your parents, but they won't make you. If a doctor does refuse, go to a family planning centre. NB Remember to ask, though. They won't give you contraception if you just say you've got a sore throat and hang about looking hopeful.

But supposing they tell my family?
They won't. Doctors *have* to keep everything you tell them confidential.

Supposing my folks find out?
They'll be more likely to be happy to find a pack of
contraceptives than a little bundle of joy . . .
Anyway, they had to do stuff like this themselves
once, and were worried *their* folks might find out.
Try jogging their memories or even (gasp) talking
to them.

Won't it wreck the ROMANCE of Sex?
Not as much as a baby, or an STD (Sexually
Transmitted Disease) will . . .

*Isn't there ANY way I can get by without using
contraception?*
YES! Be a lesbian! (Gay boyz shld use condoms,
despite no fear of pregnancy). Or, stay a virgin! Or,
there's lots you can do without actually Doing It
and it is Auntie Letty's advice to experiment with
lots of fun before you actually have sex. But you
have to be careful; it's easy (so I'm told, ahem) to get
carried away, and possible, sadly, to get pregnant
without full intercourse.

So what's the best thing to use?
You've got to choose. Only two types – the female
condom and the male condom – actually protect you
against STDs (Sexually Transmitted Diseases) like
the HIV virus, which can lead to AIDS. The male
condom is a V. Effective protection and can also be
bought in supermarkets, chemists, Etck so it's worth

everyone having some of these. You also need to use them properly, which does not just mean to put them on willy rather than nose Etck, but remembering to read the leaflet thoroughly.

Other kinds include different kinds of pill (almost 100% effective in stopping pregnancy), diaphragm (sometimes called cap, but do not attempt to use on head unless being interviewed for fashion design course), implants, IUDs (devices inserted by a doctor into yr womb) and, V. recently, a male pill. Family planning centres give V. Good advice and leaflets on all of these (see details at end of buke). So, don't get drunk, have sex and THEN read a leaflet. Take Auntie Chubb's advice and BE PREPARED.

NB There is an *Emergency Contraception* you can take if you think you've slipped up. You have to take these pills within 72 hours at the latest, so ring Doc or go to clinic straight away.

DOUBLE DATING

Double dating is when four of you all go out together. It is a V. Good way of taking the heat, embarrassment, nerves, Worry, anxiety, stress, anguish, agitation (*that's enough adjectives — Ed.*) out of dating. F'rinstance, if all you can think of to say is 'what's your favourite colour?' you can just keep quiet and let three other people do the talking. Sadly, the only double date I've been on was with Hazel. This didn't work for the following reasons:

a) Both boyz spent whole evening drooling after her and ignoring *moi*.

b) She told them she was V. Sorry, but she only fancied gurlz and had only come on the date to cheer me up.

Hazel & moi: on
blind double date...
(if boy had been
blind, I might have
done better)

I wished she hadn't revealed her true nachure to them at this point as it made me feel even more plain, thick, ugly, dumb Etck. Bear this in mind if you are going on a double date and choose someone who is not most beautiful, desirable gurl in werld as your partner.

Delilah

'Temptress, seductive and wily woman.' Sounds just like *moi* or how *moi* would be if only I had curves, bazooms Etck. But Delilah got revenge on Samson by cutting off all his wig and I would never betray Adam that way. I might feed him up a bit on V. Fattening, Pluke-Generating foods, though, so he would be less attractive to any other Delilahs he might meet. But suppose I didn't like him any more after that? Gnash, confusion, which way to go Etck?

Eve

According to ye Holey Bible, Eve was the Mother of the Human Race. Clearly, the first woman didn't have to know much about ROMANCE, since if you were the only gurl in the werld and there was only one boy, you'd be almost bound to Do It together sooner or later especially since there were not yet any magazines to read instead (or football on the telly).

And I doubt Adam (that name again – swoooooon) had to think much about flowers and chocolates, or even nuts and beetles. Contraception might have been a more useful thing for Eve to know about, since one of her sons wound up killing the other, but obviously this was one bit of knowledge she didn't get when she bit that apple.

Fetishes

Seedy adults are prone to fetishes, which are
described as abnormal (whatever that means)
stimulants to sexual desire such as, I suppose,
only being able to get an erection if you are coated
in strawberry jam and beaten with rolled-up
copies of the *Parliamentary Times*. Frankly, I am still
young enough to think such things are V.V.
UnROMANTIC and hope they are many eons away
from *moi*, but then I used to get excited at just the
brush of Adam's sleeve against mine. Phew, cold
shower.

Firsts

In ROMANCE stakes, these can roughly be honed
down to:

First Impression
That laser-beam of sexual dynamism that crosses a
room and makes your eyes pop out on stalks like in
the cartoons. Sometimes, it's followed by *an
approach*. The approach usually passes on to yr best
friend, who he asks out. You get *his* best frend, who
closely resembles a vole. However, 'vole' is an

anagram of 'love' and if this were a story, you and the vole would walk off into sunset. In real life you spurn luckless pining vole to search for another love at-first-sight type. Same thing happens all over again.

(Feb 29)

First Date
This is the one you spend five years looking forward to, five weeks building up to, five days sorting out what to wear for, five hours getting ready for, five minutes taking everything off and putting on your usual clothes for (so that you look like you haven't bothered) and five seconds on the phone when he/she rings to say they can't make it. Other scenarios include waiting outside cinema, club, bus station Etck for three hours in hailstorm refusing to believe you have been jilted. What runs through your head at such moments is: 'He must have said an hour later, silly me'. 'He forgot to put the clock forward/back two weeks ago.' 'He's been knocked down.' (And he doesn't get up again, remaining horizontal in the arms of Tania Melt).

When you finally do get to go on a date, try to be yourself. This can be difficult, if you have no idea who that is. But if you spend the whole evening being someone else, your lurved one will wonder where you have gone. Remember, if he/she doesn't like the person you at least most resemble, he/she would not have asked you out. Remember to listen to your lurved one as well as attempting to captivate him/her with your dazzling wit Etck. Dazzling wit can lead to headaches. If you get that feeling that your twin souls have only been waiting for this moment to fly, tweeting and swooping, into each others' nests, this date will be likely to end with the . . .

First Kiss
Mine, as many readers will know, was with Brian Bolt, when I scratched my nose on his specs. Since then I have had a dazzling encounter with Daniel (argh! Betrayal! Revenge!) and something even better, including a fondle, from Adam. I was V. Worried about how to kiss, but I must tell you, dear reader, that although it was a disaster with Brian, it seemed to come naturally with the other two, especially – swoon, sob – with Adam. Teenage Worriers always put *How to Kiss* as a Big Worry, but, although I worried about little else for years, I was amazed how easy it was. See also KISSING.

Refusal to take the First Kiss any further (no contraceptives, do not know this person from Adam – sigh – told parents I'd be back two hours ago, V. Scared of Rising Feelings, Need Time to Think Etck) is bound to follow, as, some days later, will your . . .

First Tiff
Which, depending on how far relationship has progressed, leads to returning of letters, lurve tokens, storms of tears, recriminations Etck Etck. This is different from BREAKING UP, see earlier, as it is accompanied by much pashione: you vow never to have anything to do with each other ever again, and for two whole days you keep this promise. Since you still lurve each other, however, one of you is bound to crack, which leads to *First Reconciliation* and possibly, eventually, in far distant future when you have been canoodling for at least two years (this is a family buke) *First Actual Doing It*. Help, Worry, see SEX, CONTRACEPTION Etck.

FUDGE

No ROMANCE in the life of El Chubb is complete without juicy, subtle, crunchy, melting . . . fudge. No day is complete without fudge either, but if you wanted to woo *moi* then a bag of vanilla fudge would get you further than a bunch of roses. I mention this because

1) I hope my readers might send me any spare fudge they get, as long as not sampled first, and

2) Knowing what your lurved one really lurves is half the battle in the ROMANCE stakes. F'rinstance, why take Sharon Sharalike to an arty French movie when she'd prefer a ringside seat at the all-women mud wrestling championship?

GAYS

Are you gay? If so, you may feel alone but I promise you you are not. I've often pondered that no-one seems to be worried particularly if they fancy the opposite sex from themselves, but if they fancy the same sex they often feel rising panic, want to deny it, daren't tell their frendz, family, teachers Etck. In fact, it is just as normal to be gay as it is to be heterosexual, but less common. It is also slightly less common to have red or blond hair than brown hair but no-one thinks these things are abnormal.

The trouble with schools and other Teenage Worriers and the Big World Outside is that there is still a lot of prejudice out there and people still joke about gays and lesbians as though they couldn't possibly be one themselves. A lot of people are so scared of admitting they might be that they even get married and have kids before they do admit it,

Q: Which of these boyz is gay? (answer on page 68)

thus making four or five people V. Unhappy. Being Gay as a Teenage Worrier is therefore more difficult than being 'straight' (which is hard enough) and it's V. Important to be able to find other gay Teenage Worriers so you can have a good old Worry together.

Although I don't fancy gurlz myself, I sometimes have a sneaky feeling I might be happier that way, as we'd have so much more in common . . . but Hazel is still V. Shy about it and hasn't told her parents that she's a lesbian yet, which I think is a shame. As far as ROMANCE goes, the story is V. similar for gay Teenage Worriers – full of hope, lust, heartbreak Etck.

There are V. Few people who haven't ever felt a little bit ROMANTIC about someone of the same sex as themselves, so if you have these feelings just be open about them and wait and see what happens. You may fancy one, both or either sex as a Teenage Worrier and this will change as you get older, until you are sure which you prefer. Society will always push you one way, so heed El Chubb's advice and Listen to your Inner Voice. If you do what your inner voice tells you, you are much likelier to end up with Mr or Ms Right in the end.

One V. imp point is that if you have a frend who is Gay, it doesn't mean that they will fancy YOU. Lots of boyz and gurlz get worried about this, or think they may be thought gay themselves if they hang out with a Gay pal. It is very Sad to think someone cld lose frendz this way so don't let yrself be stoopid about it . . .

Paranoia can wreck yr life. Gay or straight,
don't make assumptions.

GRAPES

Always have a bunch handy, so you can lie back with Rose between teeth (as long as Rose doesn't object, arf arf, yeech) and snarl in husky, vamp-ish tones: 'Peel me a grape.'

GURLZ

If, to gurlz, boyz are aliens from another werld then it follows that if you are a boy, gurlz are similarly from another planet. However, as I pointed out in BOYZ, earlier, gurlz are actually far more like boyz than

    a) they like to admit

    b) boyz like to admit

    c) anything else around.

    Even the old idea that boyz like looking at dirty magazines Etck while gurlz just dream of ROMANCE (sigh) seems to be less true now we have unemployed gasfitters becoming strip artists Etck, and gurlz fearlessly paying to watch them show off their bits.

    There is a general feeling among Teenage Worriers that gurlz are more 'mature' than boyz. But I ask you, is reading *Smirk*, or giggling over *Weenybop* any more grown-up than getting excited over *Turbo-Anorak Weekly* or *Megatit*? Is plastering your walls with pix of Brad Pitpony significantly more mature than putting up Melinda Bazoom? Is painting each finger and toenail a different pattern of silver, purple, lime green Etck any cleverer than fart-lighting?

However, one important thing that still separates the gurlz from the boyz, is that gurlz can be mothers. Being a mother also stays a BIG WISH for lots of gurlz whereas it is rare to find a boy who is longing to be a dad . . . This may make gurlz more ROMANTIC and lead them to spend time thinking how they are going to get a family.

Resist it, dear gurlz, until you are well past being a Teenage Worrier. Get a contraception and an education. Cos that prince may not come and you will have to earn a living, even if he does too. You do not want to wind up selling spotty bod on streets or dressing your five-year-old up as a baby to tempt passers-by to chuck you a few pence . . .

Hay

AAAA ACHOO?

A Roll in the hay was what Rural lurvers did. Sounds V. prickly to *moi* but preferable, as long as not highly allergic, to bike shed, urban wasteground Etck.

41

HOLIDAY ROMANCES

You are walking on tropical beach, wearing just a
shimmer of polyester temptation, your hair blowing
lightly against your radiant tan. Suddenly, you feel a
soft burning down your back. Surely you put on
your factor 2000 lotion on top of your fake-tanning-
cream? You are a Worrier, after all, and do not want
skin cancer. But no, the burn you feel is the searing
glance of – Donatello Machismo. This dazzling
stranger, a symphony of sinews complete with natty
designer swimwear, mutters softly 'Are these yours?'
proferring an elegant pair of, wait for it, designer
sunglasses. 'N-no,' you stutter shyly, allowing your
fawn-like eyes to gleam softly beneath the fronds of
your newly washed, eloquently tousled mane. 'But I
wouldn't mind if they were,' you add, with a look
pregnant with meaning and so far little else, as he
slips his golden arm round your slender waist and
moves with you, as one, into the sparkling azure
foam that eternally breaks against the silver sand.
Ten days of bliss are followed by ten months of
wondering why you never heard from him again.
Surely, how could you? But surely? You gave him
the wrong address? He must even now be working
night and day to raise the air fare (funny, he said his
dad owned a fleet of aeroplanes). And so on. You
plot to return to the same place. If you are lucky

42

enough to get there, you will be tragically confronted, on your first day, by the sight of Donatello, approaching another sylph, proferring the pair of elegant designer sunglasses which he always carries especially for that purpose.

Even with this tragick ending, we all dream of a holiday ROMANCE like the one above. Better two weeks of passion, we think, than none at all. But if other Worriers are remotely like *moi*, then the nearest we will come will be a wet afternoon in Bognor with Kevin Snoad, who treated me to two games in the amusement arcade and half a bag of chips before trying to insist on a quickie behind the pier.

Britain is not a great place for holiday ROMANCE. And whatever the venue, the result is always the same: you write eight long letters and are lucky to get a postcard. If you do, it says: *Hope your OK. Im fine. Met a great new bird in magaluf. Kevin.*

INFATUATION

Is when you get obsessed with somebody, usually someone you have only just glimpsed and never talked to – and you just can't stop thinking about them. Ye film star Brad Pitpony has this effect on *moi*, or did have, as now I am fifteen I have thrown away such childish dreams in order to search for the True Meaning of ROMANCE. However, it is possible to be infatuated with the boy/gurl-next-door or whatever and it can be V. Painful when you linger about hoping to bump into them casually and they pass by as if you were but a flea. They don't do this to be mean but simply because, sadly, they have failed to notice your existence. If they *have* noticed you, because you have taken care to send them ill-disguised Valentines, lurve notes Etck or because you gaze at them with doggy affection whenever they appear, they will probably feel flattered. If you push it, though, they will feel cheesed off. If they are Nasty (sadly, objects of infatuation can be nasty) they may take advantage of you and then reject you. It is better to be infatuated from afar, as real ROMANCE can only happen when both people are involved and really no-one sensible wants to go out with someone who hangs on their every werd and drools as if they were a deity. If anyone did that to you, you'd think they were a few crumbs short of a slice of bread, wouldn't you?

JEALOUSY

The green-eyed monster. Why is it called that?
Why *green* with envy? Why not blue? Or red? El
Chubb's theory of colour cannot help but make her
wonder why the colour of grass, trees and natural
planties should be associated with the corkscrewing
sense of overpowering dume you feel when yr
beLurved walks off with someone much cleverer,
prettier, wittier, sportier Etck Etck than you.

However, it is a monster which attacks all of us from
time to time (*moi*, most of the time). You feel its
fiery tendrils when the object of your affection

objects to your affections and flings his arse (sorry, arms) around Tania Melt instead. The worst kind of jealousy though is not when you are wishing you could go out with someone and feeling dead jealous of the people who *are* going out with them — it is the jealousy you feel when you are with someone and think they might be seeing someone else. This is how I have felt on two occasions with Daniel and on one with Adam. I still lie awake nights just wondering who he lurves, now he is in Los Angeles (sigh).

The only ways you can deal with jealousy are:

a) Try not to feel it in the first place. This involves becoming a Buddhist and learning not to want.

3) Standing outside house of beLurved and howling like banshee. This involves unacceptable loss of dignity.

E) Locking self in room and sobbing until someone (probably yr poor old mum) comes to show they care.

F) BUT the most sensible (who ever said Teenage Worriers were sensible?) thing to do would be to realize that if your rival is preferred to you, then you can't be happy with this lurve object in the first place. If they are stupid enough just to like her because she sings like lark, has hair like angel, bazooms of sex goddess Etck then they are not classy enough to appreciate what's specially you, commune meaningfully with yr Soul Etck.

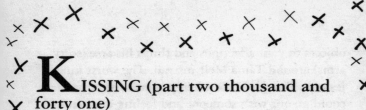

KISSING (part two thousand and forty one)

The reason many Teenage Worriers Worry so much about how to Kiss, is they are scared they will blow the Big Moment of the First Kiss, by producing

A) V. wet slobbery ones that make the recipient feel they have been leapt on by V. friendly, ancient dog

B) V. Dry rasping ones that sandpaper a few layers off beLurved's luscious lips; not opening mouth wide enough so teeth collide, doing untold damage that will mean centuries in the dentist's torture chamber, negotiating complicated co-production with bank, National Lottery Etck

C) Opening mouth too wide and finding it full of beLurved's nose and chin

D) Missing target altogether and ending up with mouthful of leather jacket

E) Being unable to breathe while kissing and therefore emitting noise like drowning rodent OR having to stop at high point in order to breathe in lungfuls of fresh mountain air (unlikely if venue is alley behind dustbins, or *Le Club Tarantulla*).

I've long argued that kissing shld be on National Curriculum. I spot a gap in the Market. If you can't get it on the school curriculum, why not go Private? If you know any V. sinuous sexperienced people, why not suggest they put an ad in their local paper offering sex tuition and kissing lessons to Teenage Worriers? Naturally I am not talking about seedy types who offer ads for demolishing temporary erections, or offering large white chests with no drawers for sale. I am talking about V. Kind people who would TEACH, but not take advantage. Am I an innocent abroad?

But kissing does come naturally with someone you like – it does, *really*, as I have discovered with Adam (moan gnash, tragic demeanour, will I ever feel like that again, Etck). However much I say this, though, you don't believe *moi*, so here, at last, are El

Chubb's definitive kissing tips. **Please read once, then never again**, otherwise you will keep thinking: Have I missed out Stage One? What comes next? Etck. Then the whole point of kissing will be lost . . .

ESSENTIAL KISSING TIPS

<u>KISSING TIP</u> (No.468): Do <u>NOT</u> arrange mouth in kissing position until in close proximity to Lurve object, for fear of dissuading same.

1. Make sure you are warm. A cold nose in the eye and chapped lips do little for passion.
2. Relax. Think hot maple syrup.
3. Trace shape of beLurved's lips with finger.
4. Murmur sweet nothing.
5. Rub your cheek against beLurved's cheek. (Make sure you use face.)

6. If yr beLurved has a wisp of hair floating across face, take it gently between yr lips and move it to side (this was a V.Seductive trick of Adam's and I writhe to think he might be doing this with Another as I write). But naturally harder with partner who has Afro or crew cut.

7. Move lips slowly towards beLurved's. Hover.

8. Draw back a moment to whisper another sweet nothing.

9. Place lips (closed) on beLurved's.

10. Purse lips and move them about. Open them V. Slightly.

11. Phew. Kiss then continues in variety of ways, the best of which is that beLurved moves tip of tongue into yr mouth and your tongue then connects with your beLurved's. I hope BOYZ are reading this cos they cld do with a few tips from Daniel Hope. After which whole business gets hungry, steamy Etck. I cannot prescribe future moves cos it takes a minimum of two people to make a good kiss and you can't be sure what each of them will do next. What I can say, is if you want to build up good head of steam, then keep it all V. SLOW.

Er, and DON'T do anything you don't want to do or are not prepared for. A boy f'rinstance who wants to take it further but has 'forgotten' his condoms is a boy Not Worth Bothering About. Here endeth first lesson in kissing. Now put self in ice bucket and forget about it until you are twenty-one.

51

LEAP YEAR

This is supposed to be the time when a gurl can propose marriage to a boy, but nowadays I hope liberated Teenage Worriers have no fear of proposing in any year (except normal fear of millstones round neck, life of domestic glume Etck).

LOVE LETTERS

These, like poems, are the most composed and least read of all Teenage Worriers' outpourings. Who among you has not lain awake imagining a letter they will send to their beLurved, only to realize, as the chill dawn stretches its clammy fingers Etck, that you simply don't have the courage. And what about the letters that you get? No-one can write one nearly as good as the one in your imagination . . .

V. sad point of Teenage Worriers' lives in 21st century may be final end of love letter flapping hopefully through letter-box as e.mail dot.com may overtake all handwritten stuff.

However, even if you are all wired up for e.mail, it is good to know how to write a love letter. A few well-chosen werds have V. Powerful effect.

1) Speling it more or less write is going two help. Yore trew luv may think yew stoopid if yew

Embarrassing envelope.

Unspeakably embarrassing envelope. Avoid at all costs.

cant spel. Thiss iz not nessessarilee trew, but a bak-
to-baysix noshiun that has cort onn, even amung
Teenage wurriers.

2) If you are serious, do not embarrass the
recipient by scrawling hearts all over envelope. Also,
do not write S.W.A.L.K. (sealed with a loving kiss)
or 'Hurry postman don't be slow, this is for my
Romeo' on the back. Your true lurve probably has a
younger sibling who will tease him or her
mercilessly at the sight of such stuff.

3) Say something about the time you last met,
that will feel special. Something original, like *I love
the way your mouth goes up at the corners even when you
aren't smiling*. Or *I never thought an anorak could look
OK with dreadlocks, but you've taught me different*, or
something.

Lust

Lust is strong fizzical attraction, often confused with
'fancying'. But fancying someone and lusting after
them are subtly different, as 'fancying' implies
actually liking them a bit whereas 'lust' is more,
ahem, rampant. It makes you feel: *cor, phew, sweat,
pant, don't-care-what-they're-really-like-just-got-to-have-
'em*. If boy approaches you in such a way, yell 'NO'
and run. Unless, of course, you feel the same.

Marriage

L. Chubb sez: Teenage Worriers should not get married. Course, if you want to tie knot when V. Old, like 25, then V. nice (wish own parents had got married, might have made me more secure, Etck. Sob).

L. Chubb
nose ring. → ⬭ Put it on yr
Lurved One's
Hooter and
LEAD them
around.

Monogamy

Although if you believed the newspapers you would think Teenage Worriers were at it like rabbits with every available passing person, most of us are V.V. ROMANTIC and, when you are ROMANTICally in love, you cannot imagine ever being with anyone else, so monogamy is an essential part of ROMANCE.

Even if I do have more than one love affair I am sure I will turn out to be at the very least a serial monogamist as I can't even talk to more than one boy at once.

Naughty Bits

Victorian times are past – when men swooned with fright when they discovered their wives didn't have willies, or did have pubic hair, or whatever it was – and now we all know better. But DO we? After years of giggling at the mention of bums, willies Etck and making rude noises to annoy grown-ups, deep embarrassment descends during the Teenage Worrier years at the thought of any Naughty Bit being mentioned in front of any adults. If you have reached this stage, you have probably started Worrying about your own Naughty Bits. These

Worries are usually concerned with shape, size, angle, or lack. The overwhelming question is: Are my naughty bits Normal?

The almost certain answer to this question is, yes.

Teenagers lie awake Worrying they might be different from everyone else and have no idea what size or shape their bits shld actually be. Well, kids, you're right. We are *all* different and no willy or vagina is exactly the same, so there. Sexual development also starts at very different times so there's no point in a thirteen-year-old gurl or boy even thinking about how small their willy or bazooms are until they are five years older. That's just the way it is. Not that it stops me Worrying about my miniscule bazooms, but at least it helps to know others are in the same *bâteau*.

The point, ahem, of Naughty Bits in ROMANTIC terms, is that they are Focal Points (that werd again) for seething pashiones Etck. This is why it is a V.Good idea to keep them under wraps if you are keen not to go too far. Don't ever make the mistake of thinking your bazooms are so small that no-one will like them. Or too big, either.

I would like to start a fashion for a new naughty bit. I would choose the earlobe, since earlobes are V. sensitive to nibbling Etck and could become just as naughty, with a little encouragement, as the bazoom. Also, they are freely available to both sexes. Ear lobe covers would be a must, in a variety of gorgeous fabrics and colourways – appliquéd, sequinned, whatever. Then, on hot summer days, we could all walk around naked except for our lobe covers. This would cheer up everyone who is Worried about their current naughty bits, cos no-one would pay any attention to willies or bazooms any more and all attention would be focused on the LOBE.

As all imaginative Teenage Worriers will have noted, those with tiny lobes, or lugs like taxi doors, would suffer.

No

V. Imp accessory for the ROMANTICally inclined, as a 'no' said early will prevent all kinds of future heartbreak.

A famous myth is that *'No doesn't always mean no.'* Oh, yes it does.

There will always be a few tragic boyz who think that, while a gurl knows what 'yes' and 'no' mean in everyday English, she means something completely different if she's talking about sex. If a gurl says no, and a boy forces her to have sex, this is rape. No-one ever ever *ever* has to have sex unless they want to. Don't *ever* feel guilty for saying no.

And, if someone says 'no' to you, just accept it. You can always try again later, to see if they've changed their mind.

El Chubb's TIP: practise chatting up boyz from age of twelve. Try it espesh on the V. handsome, world-weary ones who are bound to say *Non* and then you will not weep and moan and pull your hairs out one by one in anguish if Turned Down later when you really mean it, as you will be quite used to handling it.

NB Have plan ready if someone you don't like accepts and thinks this means they can have their wicked way with you. eg: 'I was only practising', 'I thought you were somebody else', 'I thought I was somebody else', Etck Etck.

ORGASM

Also known as 'coming' (and sadly, often a prelude to boy going), this is the big bit of overwhelming Feeling (surge, throb, choirs of birdies, clash of cymbals, raging waterfalls Etck) you get at the culmination of ye sexual act, or while doing things to your own Naughty Bits. Some V. Romantic people think you can get an orgasm just by looking at the one you feel V. ROMANTIC about, but even I, with all my seething pashiones, flowing juices Etck, find this hard to believe.

PHEROMONES

Obviously, these little chemical attractants have been working on the human race for centuries, without our even knowing it. They doubtless made the pharoahs moan, too, and perhaps that's how they got their name.

PORNOGRAPHY

Pheromones →
(or fleas?)

This is a word that sends parents running screaming. The idea that their offspring might have rude pictures of gurlz or boyz stuffed under their pillow is too much for them. BUT, although there is horrible pornography, there is also a lot of stuff that most boyz are bound to look at some time or another — and it seems to be catching on for gurlz too.

See Naughty Pix
on next Page →
(if you move FAST)

The main prob with these pix is they don't look like many real gurlz, ie: they have vast bazooms, curves where most of us have dents, and dents where most of us have big fat roly bits. The gurlz who pose for them often got their bits from a plastic sturgeon (sorry, surgeon) and I find it V. Tragick waste of human potential that this is all they can think to do with their life.

And then she RIPPED the flimsy covering to reveal, a LONG, FIRM, GLISTENING bar of fudge

Whatever turns you on...

One thing you can say about any kind of porn is that it's definitely not ROMANTIC.

62

PREGNANCY

The scene is a candlelit fast-food joint. A beautiful
Teenage Worrier is stirring her milkshake, with a
wistful, dreamy, faraway look in her soulful eyes.
There are no burgers because of the power cut. It is
freezing cold. But she is warmed by a secret
knowledge. She can't wait to tell Clint Cleft, the
Love-of-her-life, the marvellous news. The door
opens and an icy blast from the freezing mean streets
of the throbbing urban jungle blows in. And so does
Clint Cleft. They have known each other for six
whole months and now she knows that soon they
will be as ONE. Clint approaches, his boyish smile
decorating his manly chops, his long limbs
purposeful, blah blah . . .

Gurl: Darling, I've got some wonderful news.
Clint: Oh good. I'm glad you're happy, because there's something I want to tell you, too.
Gurl: Don't you want to know what it is?
Clint: No, that's fine, as long as you're pleased, because . . .
Gurl: There are no longer two of us in this relationship, sweetheart, there are three.
Clint: But I know. That's what I was going to tell you. I'm SO pleased you don't mind.
Gurl: How did you know? I've only just found out myself. And why should I mind?
Clint: Well, you know, I thought you'd be jealous.
Gurl: Jealous? Of our little baby?
Clint: Well, I wouldn't exactly call Gloria Scroggins a *baby* – I mean, she's got whopping . . .
Gurl: Gloria Scroggins! What's Gloria Scroggins got to do with it?
Clint: But you just said you *knew*. I've been seeing her for about a month . . .
Gurl: Boooo hoooo. Sob. Monster. Etck.

This tragic scenario is played up and down the country every day. So is another, involving the dreadful panic of late periods, over-the-counter pregnancy tests, huge relief, huger despair. Those ads that say a puppy is not just for Christmas, but for life, would be better applied to babies, since around 100,000 Teenagers a year become pregnant

64

ACCIDENTS CAUSE PEOPLE

and most of these are unplanned. It really is the most important thing of all to check out and use contraception before you get near sex, because by the time you are near, you may find yourself actually Doing It and then it will be Too Late. Arg, squirm, cling to virginity as to life-belt in raging ocean Etck.

PRUDERY

Is when people are V. Disapproving of sex and do not like to admit it is taking place. When the Victorians covered piano-legs in lace knickers, it was a sign of prudery. Although if they thought Men wld get excited and mount the piano, maybe they had a rather exaggerated view of the carnal instinct after all. Prudery usually leads to hypocrisy and people turning blind eyes, telling fibs Etck to keep harmony. Alternatively, it can just be a sign that sex is not your cup of tea and that your cup of tea is more likely to be – a cup of tea. Why not?

QUESTIONS

ROMANTIC QUESTIONS: EL CHUBB'S LIST
Write the numbers 1,2,3,4 in any order several times, on piece of paper. This is yr special personal chart. Choose a question and then close your eyes and wave your finger around before stabbing it down on chart. Then look up answer, ie: if you score a 2 for question B, you look up B2.
A)   Does the object of my desire lurve me?
B)   Does the one I am thinking of think of me as much as I think of them?
C)   Is the thing that I dread going to happen?

D) Has he/she done it as many times as they say?
E) Will I be a virgin for long?
F) Will my nose/bazooms/willy get any bigger?
Answers
a1) Yes a2) Much more than you think a3) More
than you love them a4) Why? Do you lurve them?
B1) Far more B2) Nearly B3) Depends what you
mean by 'think' B4) Ask them
C1) Never C2) Depends how good your
contraception was C3) Nothing as bad as you dread
will happen C4) No
D1) More D2)No, they haven't done it at all
D3) Not quite D4) Exactly
E1) As long as you choose E2) Ages E3) Six years,
ten months, one week, four days and two hours
E4) No
F1) No, smaller F2) Yes, much F3) So big you'll
need to get doors specially widened if you go in
sideways F4) Exactly the right size

Tips for analysing oracle
If you believe a single word of any of the above
replies, you are V. Gullible. How could *moi* possibly
know anything about you? F'rinstance, how could
the answers: E3) or F3) possibly be true? The same is
obviously true of all the other answers only, like
those daft quizzes in magazines like *Smirk* and *Yoo
Hoo*, they are more cleverly disguised and give the
appearance of TRUTH: beware quizzes, gentle
reader.

RED ROSES

Still best ROMANTIC gift. Cheapest, too, if you have any growing, since flowers from own garden or windowbox still most ROMANTIC of all. Do not, however, confuse geraniums with roses; geraniums do not pick well.

Answer to question on page 37

A: V, sorry, but can't remember whether ALL of the boyz are gay, or NONE of them. Never mind, eh?

SEASONS

Winter: What cld be more ROMANTIC than a
snowy stroll, mufflers entwined, throwing crumbs
to swans as they glide along icy lakeside? Even the
scarlet nose of yr companion, complete with frozen
drip, cannot detract from Winter's paradise . . .

Spring: is ye traditional season for ROMANCE.
What cld be more ROMANTIC than a Spring
stroll, patting the curly heads of bouncy lambs who
bleat their cheerful bleats as they Spring through
cowslips, primroses Etck? Even as you slip on cow-
pats, you may clutch the hand of your belurved...

Summer: nothing, surely, cld be more ROMANTIC
than a hot, hazy, stroll along a golden beach,
entwined in the strong arms of . . . Etck. (But see
HOLIDAY ROMANCES for, um, downside.)

Autumn: season of mists and mellow nostalgia much
belurved of teenage Worriers. What cld be more
ROMANTIC than wandering through crackling
leaves, the smell of bonfires in your hooter? So what
if you are wandering alone; the season itself will
instill you with all the same feeling you get with
ROMANCE: melancholy, longing, yearning,
shivering, unspeakable glume Etck, Etck.

☀The Romance☀

Ah! Ye Romance of WINTER: Season of Red roses,
I mean, noses.

Bless the Sexy SPRING, as it brings Hay Fever.

of the Seasons

The sultry SUMMER: season of SWEAT.

Turn over a new leaf and FALL for someone in Autumn.

SEX

When middle-aged Worriers think about their own dear little Teenage Worriers having sex, they tremble with trepidation. This is because middle-aged Worriers remember their own mis-spent yoof and although they wish they had mis-spent a bit more of it they are scared their own offspring will be Doing It all the time and fail their exams, have babies, get STDs (sexually transmitted diseases) Etck, Etck. What many of them have forgotten is how Worried they were about Sex themselves and how little of it they actually did. This is still true of Teenage Worriers today. Apparently the average age for first having sex is seventeen. Since people always lie about such things, this is quite likely to make the average age older. Also it could mean that even those who are Doing It at seventeen have only done it once. Even if all seventeen-year-olds did it several times a week (V.V. Unlikely, where would they go?), it still means that loads of other people have sex for the first time much later (and that doesn't count all the people who never have it at all . . .).

ROMANCE is V. Obvious prelude to SEX, but there doesn't have to be much sex at all in a ROMANCE, which can be a meeting of minds, or a brushing of fingertips, and still take up a bigger proportion of your heart, mind, head Etck than outrageous nooky with someone you're not that interested in as a person. There's lots of pressure to get off with people as a Teenage Worrier. You don't have to. Wait till you really like someone. In my case, sadly, the people I really like always get off with someone else, sob. But perhaps one day . . . yearn.

Kissing, cuddling and canoodling are all part of sex and you are having a sexual relationship if you are doing any of these – *and* it's much safer than full intercourse.

Meanwhile, here are El Chubb's answers to just some of the Sex Worries y'all have sent moi:

DON'T CONDOMS WRECK ROMANCE?

Opposite, obviously is true. STDs, pregnancies and endless Worry Etck wreck it, seriously. I have been carrying a pack of three condoms around ever since I can remember, but sadly I have never had the chance to offer them to my beLurved in moment of high pashione. (Must check their sell-by date.)

HE/SHE SEZ THEY WON'T GO OUT WITH ME UNLESS I DO IT. SO SHOULD I?

Pressure is not Romance. Your reply: get lost, sucker, plenty more fish in ocean Etck. (NB, although yr personal ocean may currently seem polluted and fish-free, you still have to think this way. Another bus *will* come along eventually.)

I'M SCARED IT MIGHT HURT AND THERE'LL BE LOADS OF BLOOD.
V.V.V.V. Unlikely. See also VIRGINITY.

WILL HE/SHE THINK LESS OF ME IF WE DO IT?
It has been known for a gurl to sleep with her dreamboat only to hear that dreaded werd *'slag'*. If such a boy is your dreamboat, could be you need a brain transplant. Check him OUT, then chuck him out.

IF WE HAVE SEX, WILL EVERYONE KNOW?
No. Having sex does not cause your Bits to glow in the dark, or change your fizzical appearance in any way. So unless you or your partner spray-paint the lavvies or tattoo your foreheads with the message 'We've dunnit', no-one will know. An element of mutual trust is obviously useful.

IF SOMEONE SEEMS TO HAVE DONE IT WITH LOTS OF PEOPLE, SURELY THAT MEANS THEY'LL DO IT WITH ME?
Arggg. Are any of you this stoopid? You know YOU wouldn't just do it with anyone, so why should someone else? And would you WANT to do it with someone who does it with everyone?

WORRY WORRY WORRY WORRY

I'M 22 AND I HAVEN'T DONE IT. DOES THIS MEAN I'M A WIMP?

This wd usually be a question asked by a boy, since gurlz who do it later are, unfairly, never called wimps, but put on pedestals Etck. Yawn. But boyz, as well as gurlz, should wait till they're ready to do it with someone they really like. Such a boy wld get more respeck from *moi*, I know that (gnash, moan, is Adam doing it with Another?).

Sofa

Yes! If you do not have a trew lurve with whom to be ROMANTIC, a sofa is a great replacement. Sofas are warm and cuddly, let you lie full length on them whenever you want without complaining and never disagree with a word you say. (Once you do get a ROMANCE going, introduce him or her to your sofa as soon as possible, har har leer.)

TELEPHONE

My Adored Father's inability to pay a telephone bill on time means that for about half the year our phone is cut off. This is a tragick disadvantage when it comes to ROMANCE. Just when I am longing to whisper melting sweet nothings into eager receiver Etck, there is nothing sweet but whirr and cackle of static. However, the fact that siblings, parents Etck are picking up telephone extensions to eavesdrop or blow raspberries means that most ROMANTIC telephone conversations are more likely to go like this:

Brrrrrrrr Brrrrrrrr
Teenage Worrier 1: Hi
Teenage Worrier 2: Hi
Teenage Worrier 1: It's me
Teenage Worrier 2: U-huh
Teenage Worrier 1: How you doing?
Teenage Worrier 2: Fine.
Teenage Worrier 1: Great.
Teenage Worrier 2: You OK?
Teenage Worrier 1: Fine.
Teenage Worrier 2: Great.
Teenage Worrier 1: yeh
Teenage Worrier 2: Well, uh, see you around
Teenage Worrier 1: yeh
Teenage Worrier 2: bye

Teenage Worrier 1: yeh

The above is a direct transcript of a Teenage Worrier's long-awaited phone call. What she went on to do immediately afterwards, was to phone three frendz in turn and discuss each element of above, ie: what did 'uh-huh' mean in the context of the conversation? How was she to interpret 'great'? The best bit, all the frendz agreed, was 'see you around' which gave great cause for hope. The fact that the BOY had phoned at all was also V. Exciting, everyone thought. Arg. Maybe it is better to have phone on blink than to be forced to endure such tortures.

TRUST

When you decide, in heat of pashione, to allow that lingering kiss to go a little further, only to find that your bra size is pinned on the school noticeboard the following day, you can bet your life your Trust has been Betrayed. Avoiding such humiliations means only snogging V. Nice trustworthy people who you like and who like you. Your intuition shld tell you who they are. NB When drunk, or under influence of other intoxicating substances, intuition is V.Blunt.

Underwear

As ROMANCE progresses (sigh), the chances are that underwear may become visible. You do not have to be at the stage of actually removing it to start Worrying about it. In fact, I have been Worrying about my own underwear since I was six years old and realized I had to display it to the whole class in PE lessons. Oh woe, those holes . . . those mortifying colour combinations. My little brother Benjy still suffers same indignity if my Only Mother forces him to wear pants with pictures of Timmy the tractor on . . .

Ye Boxer shorts are beating up Y-Fronts in battle
for boyz underbits.

However, if you're addicted to *Smirk*, you will be
bombarded by styles and materials. Arg. F'rinstance,
in a recent issue of *Yoo Hoo*, we could choose from
white lycra cotton vest and shorts, white lacey
v-neck T-shirt and shorts . . . silver satin vest and
brief set . . . white ribbed T-shirt with meshed
flowers (*what!*) or a blue velour T-shirt and white
heart knickers. Arg. The cheapest of these little
outfits is more than yours truly will ever see in a
month. Stay cheap and simple with . . . ***Letty
Chubb's Underwear Tips***:

Keep it clean.

Keep it neat.

Keep it snowy white or sooty black.

The tragedy of the pale grey knicker that should
have been dazzlingly white can be avoided by
buying black, but black too, can turn to fog. But

wait! Is this El Chubb enslaving herself and other
Teenage Worriers in the heartrending pit of
looksism? How can a plain grey knicker be a *tragedy*?
Get Real. Who cares if your knickers are beige or
grey? Up with mushroom panties! Down with white
panties! (whooops). Fact is, nice, neat, non-baggy
underwear is appealing on both sexes so, um, I think
I'll stick with convention on this one. No need for
fabu-bras (nothing to put in them in the sad case of
moi, anyway) or negligees in floaty wisps. Just clean
white bits to cover your bits. Same goes for boyz and
gurlz, OK? NB Boyz, no boxer shorts with naked
women on them (pictures, I mean), per-leeze.

VALENTINES

It is V. Cruel the way, year after year, Feb 14th
comes round just after Feb 13th (not that I believe
13 is unlucky, but Feb 13th does make you V.
Nervy and glumey) and yet it never EVER brings a
Valentine from the person you're hoping to hear
from. There may well be well-meaning Valentines
from your aunty or little brother or even one, in my
case, from Brian Bolt . . . but I know this year I will
look in vain for a Los Angeles postmark . . .

I have even got my reply card ready. On the front
it says: *What?? Be YOUR Valentine? You lousy
no-good two-timer!* And on the inside, it says: *Of
course* . . . But I feel it is destined to stay in my

bedside table along with the other Valentines I have bought over the years and never sent. Sob, self-pity Etck.

L. CHUBB'S TIP TO CHEER UP VALENTINES DAY

Lonely Hearts Party
Ask everyone who hasn't got a boy/gurlfrend to come. Put on V.V. sad music, or a tape of rain pattering into puddles, or sound effects of wailing violins or banshees. All stand in a circle and sob loudly. Who knows? Maybe a kindly tissue will be offered to you by an intriguing stranger . . . Think how V. ROMANTIC yr meeting will seem many years from now when you are old and grey.

NB When aroused by lust and indeed by ROMANCE, the human heart beats faster. I guess this is why it is used for valentines and all other symbols of lurve. But it doesn't change half as much as the male willy does when aroused (so I am told, ahem) so why not put Big Willies on Valentine's Cards Etck? Another thing that happens is you sweat more. How about lovely big fat drops of SWEAT?

CAMPAIGN for sweaty Valentines!

Vests

string vest (nice) →

L. Chubb Best vest gone west

Not most ROMANTIC of accessories (see
UNDERWEAR, earlier) but useful if you still can't
really fill a bra (sob, cringe) and don't want to reveal
whole bod during canoodling.

Virgins

Rather comforting to think that everyone has been
one of these and most Teenage Worriers, *moi*self
included, still are. I'm beginning to think it would
be nice just to Do It once, then not bother about it
again, as the Worry involved gives me sleepless
nights.

In ye olden daze it was V. Imp to be a virgin
when you married, if you were a gurl. This was so
the man wld be sure any offspring of the union were
his alone (though what stopped you from Doing It
with someone else in the afternoons I have no idea).
People were so keen to prove they were virgins that
they even had little fake bags of blood so they could
pretend their hymen (the wafer-thin covering across
the vagina) had broken on Day One of the
honeymoon. In fact, now as then, most gurlz'
hymens are broken long before they have sex, either
just by running about, or riding a bike, or anything,

and they don't even notice it. So the fear of agony, tearing and pouring bludde on your first sexshual encounter is one more Worry crossed off list (phew).

I am a grate believer, despite aforesaid worry about being a virgin, in having a ROMANTIC time the first time. It seems a bit glumey to think of a quickie behind the dustbins like poor old Rover, or a feverish snog while babysitting on a neighbour's sofa that goes too far – especially if the neighbours return in the middle and wonder why you are upside down with a hunk instead of glueing your ear to the baby alarm as you shld be . . .

For *moi*, it will be in a waterbed with Adam Stone – or Nothing (Pretty easy to guess which . . .). I s'pose I'll end up V. Proud of my virginity when I'm an old lady of thirty. In fact, I am determined to be V. Proud of it Now.

WATER

Ye ROMANCE of water! What cld be more ROMANTIC than a stroll by a moonlit lake? Or splashing in a cule pule on Californian mountainside? Or sitting by fountain (cor, spurt, Etck) in a sunny pizza, I mean piazza, listening to gentle strumming of stomach juices accompanied by gurgling of guitar?

There is an old psychology trick that asks you to think of some kind of water. Go on, do it now.

What did you think of?
Ocean means you are V. Sexy.
Sea, ditto but less.
Lake, calmly sensual.
Stream, working on it.

I always think of a dripping tap, which goes to prove such Deep Insights into Yuman condition are V. Unsound.

Let's hear it for WATER! Biggest ROMANTIC ingredient of all! (Also, if you drink same, less likely to end up in V. UnROMANTIC situation leading to regret, pining Etck.)

X CITEMENT

(OK, excitement, but I'm not doing XYLOPHONES in ROMANCE, and I've done KISSING, so there.)

What is ROMANCE without that fluttering of the heart, panting of the, er, pants, trembling of the nether regions (must check what a nether is before handing in buke) that accompanies a first date . . . or kiss. The excitement of seeing someone you really like the look of and (gulp) finding that they like the look of you too. Having checked it actually is you they're talking to (in the case of *moi*, it's usually Hazel, who is standing behind me, that has caused their eyes to light up and their willies, I mean spirits, to rise) you are now in a position to offer them your phone number. Excitement!

ROMANCE!

The next step is sitting by the phone. It rings! Excitement!

ROMANCE!

It is for your mum. It rings again. Excitement! ROMANCE!

It is for your dad! It rings again. Excitement! ROMANCE!

It is your beLurved. Double Excitement!

Double ROMANCE!

Then you get all that stuff about where to meet. Then there's the ten hours of getting ready, by which time the excitement is at such a fever pitch that no-one on earth could live up to your expectations. Never mind. Excitement is what ROMANCE is all about . . .

... which leads us to ...

YES

(OK, if you like, yeah, Yup, u-huh, mmm).

This may be the moment when you cast cares to the wind and decide to wallow in undiluted pashione. But it may equally be the time when you want to say Yes to a kiss, Yes to canoodling, but No to anything else. If ROMANCE is blossoming, this will not deter your lurve object (see SEX, earlier). And together you can waft on a sea of ROMANCE, saying Yes to all the things you both like, and even some of the things you're not crazy about but know your lurved one likes (by this, I mean consenting to watch mud-wrestling, not hanging upside down in frogman's flippers and beating yourself with a wet haddock).

However true my ROMANCE is, I will never however say Yes to fish and chips (can't stand fish).

ZITS

If a lonely zit is wandering the universe, searching for a home, it will zero in on Brian's sizeable conk even before my own. Yet even Adam has zits. And I lurve every last spot of them. So you see, although they plague the Teenage Worrier who has them, ROMANCE *can* shine through.

Endpiece

And now, dear reader, we end our brief stroll through the vineyards of ROMANCE. With sinking hearts, we bid farewell to the groves of grapes, eternal sunshine, sifting sands, twinkling fountains, scarlet blooms, golden summers Etck of our imagination and turn our sinking hearts once more to Sluggs Comprehensive, GCSEs, and our best chance of ROMANCE – a clash of teeth, or braces, with Syd Snogg round the corner.

And we ask ourselves: does ROMANCE really exist?

My answer, dearest reader, is yes, briefly, only to end in tears in the tragick case of moi . . . and yet, Hope does spring eternal, and even now, El Chubb is dusting herself off, writing one last heartfelt epistle to Adam Stone before brushing wig for first time in months and facing world with Spring in Step.

Who knows who might be waiting round next corner? What sweet nothings he might murmur? True ROMANCE can lie in smallest places, in cosiest corners, in a look, in a werd . . . and we all may find it someday . . .

Yrs truly, (amid sunshine, tears, glume mixed with sprinkling of JOY Etck.)

Letty Chubb

Help!

Useful telephone numbers

CONTRACEPTION

Brook Advisory Centres
0171 713 9000 (helpline, office hours)
0171 617 8000 (recorded information helpline)
Contraceptive and counselling service for the under 25s. Local clinics throughout the UK. Under 16s can obtain confidential help.

Family Planning Association
0171 837 5432 (confidential helpline)
Clinics throughout the UK. Can also send V. helpful leaflets.

GAY/LESBIAN

Lesbian and Gay Switchboard
0171 837 7324 (24 hours, Mon to Fri)
Advice and info service that also offers advice for friends and family. NB They are really hard to get through to, but don't give up.

North London Lesbian and Gay Project
0171 607 8346
Run the lesbian, gay and bisexual Youth Project for under 25s, and can provide advice, info and education resources.

PROBLEMS

Youth Access
0181 772 9900
Details of young people's counsellors throughout the country.

Childline
Freephone 0800 1111
For children only.